No part of this publication may be reproduced, stored in a retrieval system, or transmitted in any form by any means, electronic, mechanical, photocopying, or otherwise, without the prior written permission of the publisher, Triumph Books LLC, 814 North Franklin Street, Chicago, Illinois 60610.

Library of Congress Cataloging-in-Publication Data available upon request.

This book is available in quantity at special discounts for your group or organization. For further information, contact:

Triumph Books LLC
814 North Franklin Street
Chicago, Illinois 60610
(312) 337-0747
www.triumphbooks.com

Printed in the U.S.A.
ISBN: 978-1-63727-712-6
Design by Patricia Frey

All photos courtesy of the author except where otherwise noted.

WALKING WITH GREATNESS

My Caddie Life on the Tour with Fred, Fuzzy, Vijay, Tiger, and More

Cayce Kerr
with Andrew Both

TRIUMPH
BOOKS

In memory of John "Doc" Roman.
A gentle soul who made the world a better place.

Contents

Foreword

I**'ve lived and breathed golf** all my life and as much as I would love to have been a touring professional, I reckon being a professional tour caddie is the next best way to make a living.

We caddies have the best seat in the house to observe what really goes on inside the ropes, and few have seen and heard more great stories than Cayce Kerr in his career working for a who's who of major champions over no less than five decades.

I first met Cayce in the early 1990s while working for the late, great Seve Ballesteros, and we quickly struck up a friendship that has thrived and endured over the ensuing three-plus decades, so much so that we became regular housemates or roommates on tour.

Cayce and I have been fortunate enough to work for some of the greats of the sport, and we have spent countless evenings regaling each other with our best stories, invariably having a chuckle along the way.

As excellent as Cayce is at caddying, he perhaps is even better at storytelling, and boy does he have some great ones to tell from working more than 1,000 tournaments in the United States and around the world.

I can assure you from personal experience that few in the game possess such a treasure trove of fascinating yarns that lift the curtain on a sport that is far less button-downed than many assume.

Nobody in the professional game is better connected than Cayce. He is a raconteur of the highest order and I know that in the pages that follow you will be informed and amused, and always entertained.

His memoir is a fascinating read that will be appreciated not only by serious golf fans but by anyone with even a passing interest in the sport. Please enjoy the stories that follow.

—**Billy Foster** is one of the most
successful tour caddies of his generation.
He has worked for Seve Ballesteros
and Darren Clarke among many others.

Introduction

People often ask me how I became a caddie. My stock response is that I qualified because I was a complete failure at everything else in life.

My real name is David Anthony Kerr, but everyone calls me "Cayce." I have been a PGA Tour caddie since 1987, now in my fifth decade plying my trade, and have worked more than 1,000 professional tournaments in the United States and around the world, including 30 Masters.

I have caddied for 16 major champions, guys like Ernie Els, Vijay Singh, Fred Couples, Hubert Green, and, for the longest time, Fuzzy Zoeller.

Several were ranked No. 1 in the world at one time or another, and eight are in the World Golf Hall of Fame.

These days I spend more time running my various businesses than caddying, but I have not completely given up looping.

I have witnessed and heard a lot of interesting things, the best of which will unfold in the ensuing pages.

If some of the stories seem unbelievable, I can assure you that they are all true. Sometimes truth really is stranger than fiction.

At times serious but more often humorous, the book peels back the reality of life on tour with many never-before-told stories that offer a unique insight into what really happens in professional golf.

While it can certainly be read in order, the chapters can also be tackled in any order without significantly losing anything of note.

Now let's get the round started.

PART ONE

THE MASTERS

1

Fried Chicken

*How a poorly chosen sentence
will forever haunt Fuzzy*

Is Fuzzy Zoeller really a racist?

This is perhaps the most frequent question I've been asked over the years by people who know I caddied for Fuzzy when he made that infamous "fried chicken" comment about Tiger Woods at the 1997 Masters.

I can't speak for what is in Fuzzy's heart, but all I can say is that in more than a decade caddying for him, apart from those most unfortunate words he uttered at Augusta National, I never heard him say or do anything that could even remotely be construed as racist.

As for the first part of the question, there is no doubt it was a shocking thing to say and at the very least tone deaf.

But the context in which he spoke is important to remember. One thing that has been overlooked is that every player in the field was Tigered out by the end of the week, tired of having their asses kicked and tired of being asked relentlessly about the new kid on the block—or bully on the block to be more precise.

They would not admit as much publicly, but trust me, they whispered it in private. More on that in a bit.

Most of you probably know the story by now, but here is a recap.

As 21-year-old Woods was rewriting the history books en route to a 12-stroke victory at Augusta National, Fuzzy was playing a few groups ahead in the final round.

Journalists wanted reaction from other players about the performance of the young wunderkind, and a small group of reporters sought a few words from Fuzzy as he walked toward the clubhouse.

Under the circumstances, and with the benefit of hindsight, Fuzzy should have just kept his mouth shut, kept moving, and said absolutely nothing. That he stopped briefly is something he will regret for the rest of his life.

"He's doing quite well, pretty impressive," Zoeller said as the cameras rolled. "That little boy is driving it well and putting well. He's doing everything it takes to win. So you know what you guys do when he gets in here? Pat him on the back, say congratulations, enjoy it, and tell him not to serve fried chicken next year. Got it?"

Fuzzy then clicked his fingers, turned to head for the clubhouse, and before he was almost out of audio range added an inglorious kicker: "Or collard greens, or whatever the hell they serve."

It was a remark that might not have raised an eyebrow among regular golf journalists, because Fuzzy was well known as a jokester who was always good for a quip.

Still, there was certainly an edge to what he said.

You might not quite realize from watching the video how angry he was, because he maintained his jovial facade, but trust me, he was in a foul mood.

To clarify a couple of things, Fuzzy's remarks referred to the following year's champions dinner, a tradition where the reigning Masters champion selects the menu.

Fried chicken and collard greens are traditional Black American foods, so you can see that Zoeller's remarks were at the very least unnecessarily stereotypical.

The subsequent furor became one of the biggest news stories in the country, particularly since Tiger's performance had captured the attention of non-golf people who wouldn't know a double-eagle from an albatross, or, to be more specific, wouldn't know that there is no difference between a double-eagle and an albatross.

Fuzzy was accused of being everything but a card-carrying member of the Ku Klux Klan.

Before we go into how the furor affected him over the ensuing weeks, months, and years, it's worth going into the backstory that led up to the comments.

Fuzzy was 45 at the time and 18 years removed from his Masters victory, a bit long in the tooth to realistically expect a second Green Jacket.

Nonetheless, he had started Sunday in position to pick up a top-10 finish with a half-decent round. He was right there where every stroke was worth thousands of dollars.

We played with Tommy Tolles, who shot 67, a remarkable performance that was the equal best score of the day.

Tolles finished third. Fuzzy, meanwhile, did everything wrong, shot 78, and plunged all the way down into a tie for 34th. He played terribly. It was one of the few times in Fuzzy's career that he walked off the golf course absolutely filthy, beyond livid.

Fuzzy *rarely* got upset. Normally he took a poor round in his stride, but that day he completely lost the plot and was so angry he couldn't see straight.

ABSOLUT MISTAKE

The scorer's tent in those days used to be just behind the 18th green, and when he emerged from the tent his buddies were there with some plastic cups full of his favorite liquid refreshment. And it wasn't Kool-Aid.

He knocked back a few vodka tonics immediately and, trust me, he needed them, so by the time he got around to stopping under the famous oak tree in front of the clubhouse for that fateful interview, he'd had several quick shots.

I don't know exactly how many he had, but let's put it this way, he was feeling no pain. As the old saying that dates to World War II goes, loose lips sink ships.

If you look at that very brief interview—the 19-second clip is on YouTube—you will see he still had a plastic cup in his hand.

I was nearby and watched it, though I didn't hear what he said at the time and only found out afterward.

I don't interpret his poorly chosen words as proof that Fuzzy is racist. Rather, they were the result of a combination of an awful performance, being under the influence of alcohol, and having had a complete gutsful of Tiger questions.

As I wrote earlier, every other player was sick of talking about Tiger too. The difference was that Fuzzy was the only one to say anything.

People say things when they're angry and drinking that they would never normally say, and Fuzzy just cracked.

Had he played well that day, then the bitterness that came out in the post-round interview would not have been present and he most likely would never have made such an inflammatory remark.

Consider how demoralizing that week had been for everyone else in the field. Many had arrived with high hopes of leaving with a Green Jacket. Instead, their hopes quickly disappeared down the drain and they were reduced to being minor extras in a movie starring only one person.

It would not have mattered who the golfer had been, or his ethnicity. Fuzzy's reaction might have been the same had it been Sergio Garcia or Tommy Nakajima.

I can imagine him saying "tell him not to serve paella or gazpacho, or whatever the hell they serve" or "tell him not to serve sushi, or seaweed, or whatever the hell they serve."

JEALOUSY

Everyone was so envious of Tiger.

These were proud guys with big egos, alpha males who were used to being the center of attention. They really hated it when the first question after a round was not about their own performance, lame though it might have been, but rather, "What do you think of Tiger?"

It was a sobering reality check, made worse because it dawned on other players that a new era was at hand, and that the game had basically passed them by.

They were watching a young guy who could drive it 50 yards farther and had the complete physical and mental package to dominate the game for a couple of decades.

They were thinking: "Nobody's going to beat this guy if he plays at this level."

There was a change of the guard and the only player enjoying it was Tiger.

It began a whole new era of professional golf and the guys Tiger competed against weren't ready.

As Tom Kite said half-jokingly after finishing a distant second: "I won my golf tournament. Tiger won the other one."

Even I was jealous and tired of hearing about Tiger, to tell the truth, and I wasn't even playing. I just wanted the media to shut up for a few minutes.

Everything was about Tiger.

When the other players went back to their rental homes at night, all the people in their entourages were talking about Tiger.

Players got to the course and Tiger was the only subject: Where is he today? Is he at the course yet? What did he do on the first hole? Where's he taking a piss at? That sort of thing.

After players spoke with the press, there was a lot of quiet grumbling. They would walk away and you could hear them mumbling, "Jeez, could we give the Tiger questions a rest for a bit?"

Not that the media obsession with a new multi-ethnic superstar was unwarranted.

In fairness to Tiger and his career, as it turned out, he should have been the only storyline that week.

It wasn't his fault that his game was in a league of its own, or that he lapped the field against a bunch of guys who looked like they were playing a different game.

So while Fuzzy had had too much to drink, that wasn't the sole reason he said what he did. It was the culmination of the whole week.

ENOUGH OF TIGER

Everybody wanted to say they were sick of talking about Tiger, everybody thought it, but nobody said it, so by the end of the week Fuzzy's mind was slap-bang in the center of a perfect storm.

When you shoot 65 you have a lot of things to talk about that are positive. When you shoot 78 there's nothing to talk about that's any good.

He had endured enough Tiger questions and enough of the Masters. The golf course had beat him up, he'd frittered away a huge payday, and he'd had a few too many scoops of booze.

He figured nobody else had said anything, so he was going to say something, hence the caustic words.

Having not heard Fuzzy's comments, I left Augusta National thinking that it had been a very bad day in the office but nothing else, and I'd see him a week later at the Kmart Greater Greensboro Open, after he'd enjoyed a week off to hopefully put the Masters behind him.

Silly me.

The interesting thing is that not one of the handful of journalists who were there for Fuzzy's quick interview reported it at the time. Nor did any of the TV stations that had recorded it.

It seemed those who heard the comments deemed them lacking in news value.

Not until the following Sunday did the cable news network CNN air the brief interview. That's when all hell broke loose.

I received a phone call that day from journalist Tim Rosaforte, telling me that Fuzzy's comments had become a huge story, and I should be prepared for some choppy waters ahead.

I wondered whether I should phone Fuzzy but decided against it.

I figured there were enough people in his entourage who knew him better than me who could advise him how to handle the situation.

And had he not already heard about the blowback, I didn't want to be the one bringing him bad news. I like bringing people good news.

It turned out that my old boss Hubert Green had been the one to break the news to Fuzzy, *Sports Illustrated* reported.

The next day I arrived in North Carolina for the Greensboro PGA Tour event. Fuzzy was scheduled to play there at Forest Oaks, where he was the unofficial tournament ambassador.

The title sponsor Kmart was also his sponsor, but he arrived in town to find that the company had severed ties with him after a six-year relationship. It was reported at the time that the parting was a mutual decision, but nobody believed that, least of all me. Then, under pressure from PGA Tour commissioner

Tim Finchem, Fuzzy pulled out of the tournament two days before the first round.

That's when I fully realized the magnitude of the situation, which had become just about the biggest news story in the country.

I was told that Fuzzy was so distraught he had to be carried from the hotel bar to his bed. He thought his career was over.

"I started this, and I feel strongly that I have to make things right with Tiger first before anything else," he told the media in attendance on Tuesday, reading a statement and not taking questions. "I also regret the distraction this has caused the world of golf. What I said is distracting people at this tournament. And that's not fair to the other people on this course trying to play this tournament."

I believe the PGA Tour wrote the statement for Fuzzy.

Without a bag for the week, I left town, glad to get away from the circus.

Woods' response as this controversy was raging was to say exactly nothing for three days, until his management company put out a statement, which read:

"At first I was shocked to hear that Fuzzy Zoeller had made these unfortunate remarks. His attempt at humor was out of bounds, and I was disappointed by it.

"But having played golf with Fuzzy, I know he is a jokester; and I have concluded that no personal animosity toward me was intended. I respect Fuzzy as a golfer and as a person and for the many good things he has done for others."

I know that many in Fuzzy's orbit were upset that Tiger did not make a statement more quickly, which might have partly diffused the issue.

But my response is that why should he have? Tiger didn't make the comments. It wasn't his job to be the knight in shining armor riding to Fuzzy's rescue.

Tiger was eager to celebrate. Couldn't he just enjoy a 12-shot victory instead of having to put out the fire?

I would certainly want to enjoy my victory in those circumstances. I wouldn't want to have to be the judge and jury over some guy who was inebriated and had opened his mouth when he shouldn't have.

You can't blame Tiger. And who knew what endorsements were coming his way, and whether saying something without putting a lot of thought into every word might jeopardize some deals.

He was only 21. There was a lot to consider.

FALLOUT

So when Fuzzy suddenly withdrew from Greensboro, I figured it would be a while before he played again, and even wondered if perhaps he would be forced into premature retirement.

Fuzzy skipped the next three tournaments after Greensboro because he wanted to lie low for a while, and to ensure that his return to action coincided with a tournament Woods was playing.

They met over lunch pre-tournament at the Colonial in Fort Worth, Texas, and I was not there for the conversation, so I can't specifically address the details of what was said, but I observed in the aftermath that it did not improve the situation from Fuzzy's perspective.

He was a broken man, and the galleries made sure he could not put the matter behind him.

Not that he got much abuse from the fans. Let's remember that most spectators on tour were White back then, and still are for the most part. Almost without exception they still loved Fuzzy and for the most part did not seem bothered by his comment.

But their attempts to help him with lame humor backfired spectacularly.

People tried to make him feel good. If I had a dollar for every time someone told Fuzzy they liked fried chicken, I'd be a rich man. Everybody felt like they had to mention it, and it had a one-year cycle, because people only saw him once a year at various tour stops.

So the minute it went away, there was someone else in a different city saying something about it again. It was like a scab and they just kept picking at it.

This is how bad it got. I can't remember what the tournament was, but one time Fuzzy was standing over a putt when the silence was broken by two guys who started doing a chicken impression, "Bawk, bawk, bawk!"

These clowns thought they were being funny, but Fuzzy had to wait for them to finish before he putted.

It was a miserable time, trust me, because I was there every step of the way. Nobody witnessed it as close as me. His performances were also miserable, and I wasn't making any money. It was atrocious. Over the ensuing months, he was just going through the motions.

I worried that he was going to quit golf. His kids were threatened at school. He had issues that were terrible.

He was lost and sadly his dad was not alive and he really had no mentors to help him.

Fuzzy was all by himself. His manager couldn't help him, his friends couldn't help him, nobody could help him get to the other side and to realize that in time things would settle down.

He got so depressed he started drinking more and I thought for a while he was going to drink himself to death.

His wife, Diane, asked me to have a word with him about his drinking. I'd never been in that situation, and I didn't want to disappoint her, so I mentioned something to Fuzzy and he said, "Mind your own fucking business."

Lesson learned; I never broached the subject again.

DONALD TRUMP

He did get one piece of advice, though, from none other than an acquaintance by the name of Donald J. Trump, the man who would become president of the United States nearly two decades later.

It was at the PGA Championship at Winged Foot in August of 1997, four months after the Masters, that Trump walked onto the range as Fuzzy was hitting balls.

Trump approached Fuzzy and spoke thus: "Fuzzy, let me give you some advice. Don't ever apologize."

It was a philosophy Trump never abandoned, and Fuzzy did not reply to the remark. There was nothing he could say to help the situation. The comments about Tiger were still raw.

Had he said that he agreed, that might have opened a new can of worms. Had he disagreed, it might have provoked a needless debate.

So he just carried on hitting balls.

MASTERS RETURN

Twelve long months later, we returned to the Masters. It seemed like an eternity.

Fuzzy and Tiger had barely spoken since, but the golfing gods had a trick up their sleeve.

Due to weather delays, officials decided to rip up the second-round pairings and redo them as threesomes in a quest to make up for lost time.

Fuzzy and Tiger ended up by pure coincidence in the same threesome, with Colin Montgomerie. Fuzzy and Tiger did not say a word to each other for the first five holes. It was a weird atmosphere, and I was literally in the middle of it.

I was not in that spot by accident.

There was a long backup on the tee of the par-five hole, with the preceding group still waiting to tee off, and when Tiger and Fuzzy sat down, I thought I'd better nestle my fat, little ass between these guys in case a referee was needed. Thoughts of the great boxing referee Richard Steele came to my mind.

Tiger and Fuzzy did not say a word to each other during those few minutes on the bench, not that you would have expected it. Tiger, after he was done exchanging pleasantries on the first tee, was not usually one for idle chit-chat on the course.

But to his great credit, he did finally break the ice. At the par-three sixth, after everybody hit great tee shots close to the hole, we were leaving the tee and Tiger said, "Let's all walk off the greens with twos."

It was a classy comment that put everyone at ease, particularly Fuzzy. Even better, everyone did make birdie.

My respect for Tiger ramped up a hundred-fold that day. It wasn't class—it was world class.

LIFE SENTENCE

That does not mean that Tiger and Fuzzy will ever be close friends, but that is not important. They would never have been tight even if Fuzzy had never opened his mouth. Big age difference and not enough in common.

A lot of water has flowed under the bridge in the ensuing years, and Tiger has had more to worry about than an old Fuzzy comment.

I doubt he thinks of Fuzzy's ill-chosen words anymore, though I can't say whether he has totally forgiven Fuzzy.

And while I cannot prove this, I believe Fuzzy's comment prevented him from being inducted into the World Golf Hall of Fame, not that I think it matters to him one way or another.

Even though he won two majors, there will always be an asterisk next to his name.

He never was the same person after those Tiger remarks.

And though he never spoke with me about the incident, I know it just about destroyed him.

He got a life sentence for what I consider a misdemeanor crime.

2

The Six-Putt

The story behind the worst start
in Masters history

For all my great experiences at the Masters, the memory that is most seared into my brain is the first and only time I caddied there for Ernie Els and found myself slap-bang in the center of the highest first-hole score in the history of the great event.

Anyone who knows me can attest that I am rarely lost for words.

I can talk with the best of them, and pride myself on being quick on my feet and always ready for anything my player throws at me. Part of that comes from instinct, part from learned experience.

But I had trouble instantly coming up with the right words on that first hole at the 2016 Masters, and to this day wonder what might have turned out differently had my initial reaction to a code red alarm been different.

Ironically, the worst single-hole disaster I have ever been a part of gave way to what I would rate in many respects as my best performance at Augusta National.

It was only my second tournament with Ernie, and I was excited at the prospect of a good week, even though the South African was 46 at the time and his best days were behind him.

His previous caddie, amiable Irish caddie Colin Byrne, had tired of the verbal abuse and their relationship had come to an inevitably ugly end at the Arnold Palmer Invitational at Bay Hill in Florida, where Byrne, worn down by the constant negativity, dumped the bag mid-round and quit.

While this sort of thing is not an everyday occurrence on the PGA Tour, nor is it as rare as one might think. Sometimes the caddie just can't or won't take any more (see Caddies Dumping Players chapter). Ernie was at a low point and things would have ended in an ugly manner had Byrne not called it a day when he did.

People often ask if Ernie's nickname, "The Big Easy," reflects his true self, and sometimes I quietly chuckle and restrain myself from telling complete strangers that nothing could be further from the truth. Ernie is a fiery character who often struggles to keep his self-doubts from spiraling into a cascade of negativity.

But he could still play some damn good golf when the stars aligned and I had high hopes of helping to resurrect his confidence, especially during our honeymoon period. Also, veterans have a good record at Augusta National, a course where experience is priceless. There is a reason my erstwhile boss Fuzzy is the only player to win on debut since 1935.

Ernie and I arrived in town on Sunday night, and I thought everything was fine. He hit the ball quite well in practice rounds and seemed to be heading in the right direction. He was very excited to be there.

I didn't feel any tension other than normal major pressures and the grueling decision-making nature of Augusta National, which mentally takes more out of a player and a caddie than you might imagine. You don't realize until you get home at night that you're exhausted both physically and mentally.

The practice rounds gave me no pause to think it would be a bad week. There was no indication, no warning signs that Ernie was struggling with the putting yips. Many players are adept at disguising things, either because they are superstitious or their ego won't allow them to acknowledge their fragility.

And let's face it, putting in a practice round is totally different than when one is under the cosh, to use an old British term for pressure. In competition, that three-footer can look like six and the one-footer like three. In the words of Fuzzy, that's why we play them all.

A slight tweak of Ernie's putting stance in the lead-up to round one seemed to help his confidence. These guys are always searching for a magic bullet and he thought it might help him.

All seemed well as we played the first hole. The long par-four is a beast in the best of times, never mind when jangling first-tee nerves are added to the mix in what I consider the biggest tournament of all.

Augusta has been lengthened over the years, with the first tee moved back almost to the practice green, and the drive is fraught with danger.

On the right-hand side of the small dogleg lies a long, cavernous bunker that anyone not named Bryson DeChambeau cannot carry—absent a strong tailwind—while farther to the right sit pine trees that will likely block any chance of reaching the green with your second shot.

Unless you get lucky in there, all you can do is try to thread your recovery shot between the trees and back to the fairway. Left is even worse, with a row of pines and usually no viable angle to the green.

Ernie smoked his drive and wasted no time hitting a seven-iron approach shot that missed the green. Never mind, I thought, as he chipped up to three feet, facing little more than a gimme for an opening par.

But while I was standing at the back of the green, chatting with fellow competitor Matt Kuchar and preparing to walk to the second tee as soon as Ernie tapped in, he came over and said, "I can't feel the putter-head."

SNAKE

My mind immediately went into high alert and I replied, "What does it feel like?"

"It feels like a snake," he said.

My first thought was to get his mind to a different place. I told him to stand on his tippy toes 10 times and move the putter. It was the best I could think of at the time. I wanted to get his body moving again in a relaxed manner. He followed my advice and then said he felt worse.

I thought: "Shit, I'm out of suggestions. I'm dealing with a difficult case. I'm in trouble."

Trouble was an understatement. Ernie walked back out and six-putted for a bit of Masters history as I watched, aghast. It happened so quickly we weren't even sure how many putts he'd had, and neither was the scorer, nor it seemed, anyone else.

The Masters official website initially listed Ernie as having had a 10 at the hole, before later checking the video footage and determining that it was a quintuple-bogey nine, still the highest ever score by anyone at that hole.

The gruesome sideshow, which lasted less than a minute, was captured for posterity by TV cameras, and you can see me standing there helplessly as the carnage unfolds, a piece of footage that made all the sports highlights shows that night in the U.S. and around the golf world.

As he trudged off the green feeling humiliated, Ernie wanted to call it a day right then and there: "There's no sense going any further. I just feel like walking in," he said, embarrassed and shell-shocked as he stood at the back of the green looking back toward the clubhouse.

I urgently needed to buy time to give him a chance to mentally regroup. Yes, any hopes of a great tournament had been dashed in one fell swoop, but that was no excuse to quit. I had to stall him, so I dug deep into the Cayce Kerr bag of bullshit. I suggested we play the second hole and meet with the rules official assigned to that area of the course.

LIES, LIES, AND MORE LIES

I told Ernie we could get a ride back to the clubhouse in the official's golf cart. It was all a lie, but I had to come up with something on the spot. I ended up telling more lies on that day than any other day my entire life. And I've told a few lies in my life. He was not entirely convinced, but I'd at least talked him off the proverbial ledge for a few minutes.

On the second hole he hit a three-wood second shot at the downhill par-five to eight feet, leaving a lightning-fast downhill putt for eagle. I was worried he was going to knock it off the green, so I just gave a little bird in his ear and said, "Be careful, this is lightning fast."

He caressed it about a foot past the hole and then proceeded to miss the birdie putt, before tapping in for par. Even that third putt nearly missed, doing a 360-degree lap around the cup before finally falling. But at least by then the shock of the first hole had worn off and we didn't even talk to the nearby rules official, let alone ask for a ride back to the clubhouse. Ernie was ready to keep going.

Still, I knew I had my work cut out if we were to get through the day without any further train wrecks, so I went into high gear. A birdie at the fifth hole seemed to settle him down and I stayed in his ear the rest of the round, telling him how great he was.

I told him he was the greatest ever: "You're Ernie Els, remember who you are."

"You're not just an Open champion, you're an Open champion on two different continents. Pull yourself together."

I pumped him up relentlessly all day long to keep his head in the game. A caddie does not have the option of keeping his distance. There is nowhere to hide. That's what makes the job so exhilarating, because you are right next to your boss when he's feeling the heat and the pressure.

Somehow Ernie shot what under the circumstances was a pretty decent 80. That's eight over par, but only three over for the final 17 holes. Not bad, all things considered.

He went in and signed his card, came back out and that's when the press hit him. There were a bunch of journos wanting to talk to Ernie, and I think it's fair to guess they weren't interested in how he had birdied the fifth hole.

To his credit, Ernie didn't hide. He faced the music, spoke for several minutes and handled the situation as best he could. It was very noble of him, and he was very humble about his experience. He should be commended for that, especially given that he'd also missed a short putt on the last hole.

A lot of players would have blown off the media in those circumstances, but Ernie was all class.

"That's what happens when you have the heebie-jeebies," he said. "I can't explain it. I've played a lot of these things. I just couldn't pull the putter back on the first hole."

After that we went to the practice green and worked on his short putting, before I rode with Ernie and his wife, Liezl, back to their rental house. I knew the journey home was going to be difficult, and I didn't want to be a coward and say I'd get a lift with someone else, because that would look bad, so when we got in the car it was a little quiet as I sat in the back seat.

Finally, he said with what I thought was valor: "I've got to give credit where it's due, Cayce, I just want to thank you for the job you did today. You gave 100 percent."

I said, "And tomorrow I'm going to give 110 percent and so will you."

That prompted Liezl to gently hit his right arm while he was driving and chime in, "Yeah, so get ready for tomorrow, Ernie."

The wife and I tag-teamed him and mentally got him feeling good about himself. "I'm ready right now," he said.

It wasn't until later when I settled down at the rental house I shared with three other caddies that night that I realized what a big story the six-putt had become. My son Matthew called to tell me that I had been on *SportsCenter*, the nightly ESPN TV roundup of the day's sports news, and not in a good way.

As I went to bed that night, I couldn't help replaying that first-green scene over and over in my head, thinking about how I could have handled the situation differently. I had only one second to come up with a response, and under the circumstances I defy any caddie to say he could have had the perfect comeback. But here's what I decided I should have said:

"Just get it close. Just get it close."

I know it boggles the mind to think a four-time major champion and former world No. 1 would need to lag a three-footer, but Ernie had the yips. Had he just babied the first putt he probably would have made it, or at least left it within an inch or two. For three months afterward I was bothered by my response because I didn't have the right answer at the right time. That's not like me.

LEPERS

I slept fitfully and I'm guessing Ernie did too. We still had to play the second round, even though missing the cut was a fait accompli barring some sort of miracle. It was a peculiar feeling arriving at the course. Not one person said hello to us on the range pre-round. It was as though other players were afraid that we were lepers and that Ernie's putting was contagious. Nobody knows what to say and how to say it in a situation like that, so they figure they are better off not saying anything.

One thing about golf pros, everyone knows whose career has disappeared in one day. We all remember what happened to Ian Baker-Finch, a world top 10 player and a British Open champion whose career went up in smoke when he got the yips with his driver and couldn't find a fairway if his life depended on it.

Baker-Finch, known affectionately as "Finchy," is one of the nicest blokes you'll ever meet, but nobody wanted to be paired with him once his driving went south, and on that day at Augusta, nobody wanted to talk to us. Not a single soul said a word to me in the caddyshack. I mean, what are you going to say?

"Can you run me through that six-putt again?"

When everyone ignored Ernie on the range it disturbed him enough that he commented on it. "Everyone just walks past me," he said. I told him that for what it was worth, nobody had even acknowledged my presence in the caddyshack either.

The second round did not start well either, though a double-bogey at the opening hole was at least a three-shot improvement over the previous day.

The remainder of the day was relatively uneventful. Ernie shot a decent 73 and duly missed the cut, giving us the weekend off to regroup for the Heritage tournament on Hilton Head Island in South Carolina the following week.

And you might find this hard to believe, but he ranked No. 1 in putting that week at Harbour Town, where the greens are slower and the slopes less severe. He shot a closing round of 66 and finished equal 14th overall, which just shows how crazy golf is. He was in his comfort zone, and it was as though Augusta had never happened.

Something else happened that week that buoyed my spirits. Kuchar and Jason Day, the other members of our threesome at Augusta, both told me that it was one of the greatest caddie performances they had seen.

I might not have come up with exactly the right response on the first green at Augusta, but I could at least hold my head high at the way I helped Ernie to get his head back into the game to play the next 35 holes without quitting.

TURMOIL

Steve Williams, who caddied for Tiger Woods in 13 of the player's 15 major victories, once said that when a player is at his lowest, when his mind is in turmoil, that is when you find out what you're made of as a caddie.

When your player is throwing it at the flag every hole, hitting it inside the leather, all you need do is not fall off the horse. Which is why, under the circumstances, I reflect with pride on that first round at Augusta in 2016, because Ernie in turmoil is a monster, and he was in turmoil that day.

You do whatever it takes to help your player, and I guess I passed my audition with Ernie, because we ultimately worked together for three years, all the way up to when he turned 50 and started playing the Champions Tour.

A caddie's job is not always about winning the tournament. Sometimes it's about helping your man win an internal battle or at least fight it to a tie and get set up on the right track for future success.

Though I must note with regret that I did not get a chance to work for Ernie at Augusta again. At the time I was alternating with Ernie's previous longtime looper Ricci Roberts.

Ernie was superstitious (see Superstitions chapter), so it was fairly obvious why he used Roberts instead of me in 2017. He thought I had brought him bad luck in 2016 and my presence at Augusta again would only remind him of the experience.

In what turned out to be his final Masters appearance, Ernie made the cut, but struggled to an 83 in the third round and finished 53rd, last among those to play all four rounds.

I doubt many people recall that, but they do recall those damn six putts on the first green the previous year.

If only I had said, "Just get it close."

3

Augusta National

*Memories of Jack, Arnie, Sarazen,
and a wonderful homeowner*

It's hardly going out on a limb to assert that the Masters is the best tournament in the world by a country mile.

The club has worked so hard to maximize the quality of the experience, whether someone is visiting as a spectator—otherwise known as a "patron" in official Masters parlance—player, caddie, media representative, or marshal.

And the experience is further enhanced by a knowledgeable staff of workers who behave with a politeness and efficiency straight out of the *Leave It to Beaver* 1950s.

I made my Augusta National caddie debut for Hubert Green in 1988, the first of 29 consecutive appearances with nine different players, culminating with Ernie Els in 2016.

In between Green and Els, I worked for Fuzzy Zoeller, Sandy Lyle, Fulton Allem, Mike Hulbert, Fred Couples, and Vijay Singh.

After a two-year hiatus in 2017–18, I returned in 2019 with Ernie's nephew, Jovan Rebula.

It wasn't all fun and games, but I always felt a jolt of adrenaline when I walked through the gates or, on the rare occasion I got to drive down storied Magnolia Lane, a strip of pavement the length of a short par-four that separates garish and unappealing Washington Road from one of the most serene settings in golf.

Green tied for 19th in 1988, though I do not remember much about how he played to be honest.

What I do remember more clearly was how cramped the caddyshack was, as the photo in this book attests.

The photo is a who's who of caddies from yesteryear, including on the far right, wearing the number three overalls, Joe LaCava, the doyen of caddies after a career spent working mostly for Fred Couples, Dustin Johnson, and Tiger Woods.

The new caddyshack that opened in 2010 is nicer than the clubhouse at many upscale courses.

It has flat-screen TVs and a full buffet that I'm told offers the same food choices the players receive, in addition to a quality of service from the caddie master and staff that's second to none.

Any reasonable request is fulfilled at Mach speed.

But enough of the caddyshack. The real star of the show is the course: 365 acres of manicured grass, loblolly pines, dogwoods, azaleas, and the most famous creek in the game, Rae's.

Perhaps the only other linear body of water in golf with anything close to the same name recognition is the Swilcan Burn at St. Andrews.

I have worked more than 100 rounds at the Masters, including practice days, and know the course so well it is the only place where I would feel confident caddying without a yardage book.

It's a course where you need to be able to use every club in your bag to score well and if any area of your game is weak, you'll be exposed, because Augusta National requires length, touch, accuracy, courage, and sound judgment, everything that a golfer needs to win a tournament.

The first hole is seared so hard in my mind it almost hurts.

Fuzzy Zoeller birdied the hole my first year with him in 1995, and Vijay Singh pitched in there in our second round in 2015, but the hole was not always kind to me.

And, of course, there was also the small matter of a six-putt by Ernie Els in 2016, as detailed in the Six-Putt chapter.

FIRST WEEK

The Masters was my very first tournament working for Fuzzy, and he did not waste any time testing me.

It was a chilly morning for the first round, a little bit of a Scottish-like mist hanging over the course, and Fuzzy hit a good drive that settled in the fairway at the opening hole.

We were between clubs, and I gave him a yardage to a back-left hole location and he said, "What do you like?" and I thought, "Holy cow, first hole, our first week together, I'm at the Masters with Fuzzy, and he's asking me for a call right out of the gate."

As caddying goes, that was pressure. I suggested a six-iron rather than a seven, because it was cold, and he hit it to four feet, just past the hole.

So far, so good, but then he called me in to read the putt.

I thought to myself that I was like a pack mule working overtime, but fortunately he made the putt, and our long relationship together was off to a good start.

But Augusta was also the site of a bad experience with Fuzzy, the little matter of his "fried chicken" comment about Tiger Woods in 1997, a remark that made for a nervous return in 1998, when we coincidentally ended up in the same grouping as Tiger. (See Fried Chicken chapter.)

TOO MANY CLUBS

And in 2006 I made one of my worst mistakes, something that had never happened before and has not happened since.

The first day dawned cold and, unusually, I wasn't particularly excited to be there on this occasion. I was working for a 54-year-old who was playing terribly. I knew our over-under score that day was likely to be about 80.

So in my mind, Fuzzy had about an equal chance of shooting in the 80s as the 70s, which is why I was not as psyched up as usual. Though you try to be professional in all circumstances, sometimes one can get a little slack when the motivation is waning.

We had negotiated three holes and on the tee at the par-three fourth, Fuzzy asked me, "What do you like?" meaning what club.

I told him I liked a three-iron, and then looked in the bag and saw two three-irons. Talk about your heart sinking. I was responsible for the worst penalty of his career, simply because I had not done the basics and counted the clubs in his bag before teeing off.

It's something I nearly always did, but on this occasion I simply forgot. I had no choice but to sheepishly tell him that he had 15 clubs in the bag, one more than allowed, and I braced for the inevitable blowback.

We incurred four penalty strokes as per rule 4.1b—which imposes a penalty of two strokes for each hole played with more than 14 clubs, up to a maximum of four strokes. In other words, it would not have mattered if I had discovered the mistake on the third or the 13th tee. The penalty would have been the same. Had I realized it while playing the first hole, or before teeing off at the second, the penalty would have been only two strokes.

Enough of a rules lesson. Back to the story. When I nervously informed Fuzzy we had 15 clubs in the bag, he retorted with the biggest lie I ever heard him tell.

"The only reason I'm upset with you is that I really thought I had a chance this year," he said.

Twenty-seven years had passed since Fuzzy became the first since 1935 to win the Masters on debut, and his best days were very much in the rearview mirror.

I thought to myself, "Are you kidding me?" I wanted to say, "A chance of what?" but had to bite my tongue.

So how did he come to have 15 clubs in his bag?

At his previous tournament, the Toshiba Classic at Newport Beach, California, he played so poorly and was so frustrated that he had given away his clubs after the final round to a boy in the gallery.

The kid asked Fuzzy for his glove, which he handed over, nothing too unusual in that.

But then the cheeky youngster said: "Can I have your clubs?"

I've no idea if the boy was serious, but Fuzzy was so disgusted that he told me to hand them over. I took the bag off my shoulder, set it on the ground, removed the irons, and gave them to the equally surprised and delighted youngster.

I kept the driver and putter, however. I was pretty sure Fuzzy would soon regret it if I gave them away.

Consequently, he had to get refitted for new irons before the Masters, and so was tinkering on the range on practice days. We ended up with a couple of three-irons in the bag. My interest level wasn't very high and I did not count them. I did a poor job.

The weather was so bad that day that the round could not be completed on Thursday, so we returned on Friday morning. We were on the practice green preparing for the resumption and who else should be there but Jack Nicklaus. I was hoping the mistake was behind me, but no such luck.

The Golden Bear approached Fuzzy, looked into his bag and mischievously started counting, "One, two, three, four, five."

Fuzzy so badly wanted to crawl into a hole and strangle me at the same time.

I quietly asked Fuzzy's friend George Cataldo whether Fuzzy was going to fire me?

"No, but he's going to make your life hell for the next month," Cataldo replied.

And Fuzzy did, sort of.

He absolutely wore me out over the following couple of weeks, but he didn't sack me and thankfully started to ease up on me in less than a month, apparently having forgiven my sin.

He was just too kindhearted to stay angry forever.

Fuzzy shot 78, 81 at the Masters that year. The penalty made no difference in the big picture, but that did not make my blunder any less egregious.

KING AND BEAR

One of my favorite Augusta memories is from an occasion when Fuzzy played a practice round with Arnold Palmer and Jack Nicklaus in the mid-1990s.

Though their best golf was a long time behind them, Arnie and Jack were still rivals in at least one respect, exchanging verbal blows like Ali and Frazier.

It seemed like one of them had a story to boast of on every part of the course. And they had plenty to boast about too, given that they won 10 Green Jackets between them—six by Nicklaus and four by Palmer.

The pair owned Augusta National for a while, hogging the jacket for five straight years as one or the other won every time from 1962 to '66.

"This is where I made that putt to beat you in '63," Nicklaus said at one stage.

"This is where I made that putt to beat you in '64," Palmer retorted a few holes later, returning serve.

Palmer also told the story of a time from long ago when he disappeared into the woods to the left of the 11th fairway, a relatively secluded area of the course where spectators are not allowed. He had to make a quick pit stop to water the trees, but nothing that Arnie did went unnoticed in those days.

The following year he returned to Augusta to find the Masters committee had built a toilet adjacent to the 11th tee. There are no stinking port-o-lets at Augusta, only permanent structures that the staff clean throughout the day.

That practice round with two legends was the highlight of my week at Augusta, and the tournament itself was a bit of a letdown after that to be honest.

Fuzzy did not play very well and the other players in our threesome were instantly forgettable, so much so that I can't remember who they were.

GENE SARAZEN

I once met Gene Sarazen's daughter at the Masters, and she introduced me to the great man later that year at the Sarazen World Open outside Atlanta.

As many famous golfers and celebrities that I've met, it was still a thrill to talk to one of only five men to win the modern grand slam of all four majors.

I asked Mr. Sarazen to reminisce on the so-called "shot heard 'round the world"—the albatross he made with a four-wood at the par-five 15th at Augusta National en route to his victory in 1935, the second year of the tournament.

Sarazen said the legend of that shot had grown with time, and you might think that it was witnessed by thousands of people. But, in fact, there were only a couple dozen spectators gathered around the green. To listen to Sarazen, the shot was barely heard around Augusta National, let alone the world.

Still, that did not stop sportswriter Grantland Rice, in a massive piece of hyperbole, from coining the phrase, which stuck in what must be one of the greatest free promotion lines in the history of sports marketing.

As of 2024, there had been only four double-eagles at the Masters, one of each of the par-fives—the others recorded by

Louis Oosthuizen at the second hole in 2012, Bruce Devlin at the eighth hole in 1967 and Jeff Maggert at the 13th in 1994.

By pure chance, I witnessed Oosthuizen's feat from the adjacent eighth fairway. I was walking beside my boss that year, Couples, when we heard a roar from the gallery, only a few yards away next to the second green, which built to a crescendo.

My view of the cup was blocked by spectators but there was no doubt what had happened when they erupted in the sort of collective cheer that told every golf-savvy fan on the course that someone had just made either an albatross—otherwise known as a "double-eagle"—or a hole-in-one.

We could see Oosthuizen, high on the hill some 250 yards up the steeply downhill second fairway, raise his arms in celebration and high five his caddie.

TOUCHES OF CLASS

Many of the nice little touches that make the Masters unique are well known, such as a complete absence of corporate signage on the course, along with food and drink prices straight out of the 1970s.

The understated nature of the tournament counterintuitively enhances the experience.

At many PGA Tour events, the starter on the first tee sounds like a boxing announcer, bellowing out a player's bio, his voice building to a crescendo before he states the player's name.

The starter at the Masters simply says: "Four please, now driving, Scottie Scheffler" (or whoever the player is).

Some other touches are less well known. While cameras are banned on competition days (though not on practice days), every patron is entitled to a free photograph in front of the white Augusta National clubhouse, at what is known as Founders Circle.

The club employs professional photographers who ensure that it is a quality photo too. I've had dozens taken by those hardworking snappers.

The offer is not advertised. You can only find out about it through word of mouth or by happenstance if you stumble across it.

The waiting time can sometimes stretch up to an hour, but imagine how long it would be if everyone knew about it? The reward for the wait is a professional photograph.

The photographer allows you to quickly look at the picture for approval, before handing you a card that you can later use to retrieve it online.

SITTING ONLY

On the course, patrons can place chairs in designated "sitting only" areas to reserve the spot for the rest of the day, and then wander away for hours safe in the knowledge that the chair will still be there when they return. On the odd occasion when someone is using it, the interloper will politely vacate immediately to let the owner sit.

If you watch on TV, you will invariably see the coveted seating area behind the 12th tee at Amen Corner packed to the brim, but those chairs are mostly unoccupied for the early part of the day while the keen early-arriving patrons catch the action elsewhere.

There is also an unwritten protocol that small children are allowed to the front of the gallery in standing areas, and it's almost unheard of for anyone to object.

In my opinion, one of the most underrated parts of the course to view the action is behind the seventh green.

From there you can see not only the straight par-four seventh, but the elevation also affords a view of the second green, third tee, eighth tee, and part of the 17th fairway.

Another fun spot is the landing zone area between the adjacent 15th and 17th fairways. It's a great place to watch players hit recovery shots between the pines, and one can often get close enough to hear the conversation between player and caddie as they discuss their options.

NO PHONES

But perhaps the most unique aspect of the modern spectator experience is the absence of electronic devices. I know of no other contemporary sporting event that still bans them. And what a breath of fresh air it is to see fans actually watching the action with their eyes rather than through a smartphone camera lens.

Instead of taking unprofessional photos that nobody else will ever look at on their social media pages, spectators are forced to view the golf with their naked eyes. How shocking.

But fans are not completely cut off from the outside world. There are dozens of old-fashioned landlines scattered around the course, from which spectators can make free phone calls to anywhere in the world, courtesy of tournament sponsor AT&T.

Now I'm the first to acknowledge how much I use my phone, usually making and receiving dozens of calls every day, but at the Masters I learn to do without.

Whatever business I need to do I take care of either before I get to the course or after I depart.

"WELCOME BACK, BOYS"

Away from the course, the Masters is my favorite tournament too, because of where I have stayed most years.

I have only been in a hotel a handful of times at Augusta. Like almost all of the players, I quickly discovered the advantages of a private house, especially at the Masters, where roach motels that cost maybe $50 a night for 51 weeks jack up their rates to several hundred dollars a night for the Masters.

That's the law of supply and demand.

Houses within walking distance of the course are especially coveted, and one such house was very special to the caddies.

The owner was Joyce Culpepper, a nun and schoolteacher who struck up a friendship with virtually every caddie who crossed her front doorstep.

She rented her house to us caddies for 20 years, while staying in a small cottage in her backyard during tournament week.

Culpepper died at the age of 79 in 2010 and willed the house to her niece. But astonishingly she added a proviso that it be made available in perpetuity to caddies for Masters week. She wanted to make sure we always had a place to rest our weary heads.

The abode was a favorite for European caddies, and I stayed there several times in years gone by, while the outstanding English caddie Billy Foster still does. I write about Foster in several other places in this book.

Another English caddie, Pete Coleman, best known as Bernhard Langer's longtime sidekick, must be credited with finding the place. He used to stay in the cottage in the back, but when word got around about the main house, we asked Culpepper if she would rent that out to a group of us.

It was in mint condition, but without too many modern touches, so we chipped in to buy a new flatscreen TV, which we enjoyed during Masters week and Mrs. Culpepper hopefully enjoyed the rest of the year.

But one time I fell afoul of her for moving an antique chair onto the porch so that I could sit in it. She gently chided me and asked me to put it back.

The first time I stayed in the house, Foster, Kenny Comboy, and I invited Mrs. Culpepper to join us for dinner. Foster had whipped up a pretty good spaghetti Bolognese, and as we sat down for dinner, I asked Mrs. Culpepper if she would mind me saying grace.

Foster and Comboy, as befitting heathen Brits, rolled their eyes, but I was undeterred.

"In the name of the father, son, and holy ghost, bless us for this beautiful meal and how much we love Mrs. Culpepper and appreciate her hospitality in Augusta, Georgia, from all the way across the ocean," I said.

I laid it on thick and I think Mrs. Culpepper appreciated it.

Billy and Ken said later that they had almost exploded laughing because never had they heard such bullshit in all their life, but they were fully aware that I was the king of bullshit.

As befitted a teacher, Mrs. Culpepper left a message on a chalkboard in her kitchen when we returned each April.

"Welcome back, boys," it read.

The message was still there when we returned in 2011 for the first time since her death.

Mrs. Culpepper used to pray that one day one of her guests would caddie for a Masters champion.

J.P. Fitzgerald, a house guest in later years, looked set to do so in the first year after Mrs. Culpepper's passing when his man Rory McIlroy led by four strokes into the final round in 2011, only to collapse with a closing 80.

The quest was still ongoing as of the time of writing in the middle of 2024.

But even without any of us achieving the ultimate result, Augusta National remains the tournament my caddie friends and I most look forward to.

One thing about the Masters can be stated without equivocation. It overdelivers by leaps and bounds, no matter how high one's expectations.

The second greatest spectator experience in golf is attending the Masters the first time. The greatest is returning a second time, because by then you know the lay of the land and how best to maximize your experience.

It really is, to use the phrase coined by CBS host broadcaster Jim Nantz, and later copyrighted by Augusta National, "a tradition unlike any other."

PART TWO

THE PLAYERS

4

Fuzzy

*Stories from the mostly good old days
with the Indiana jokester*

I **caddied for Fuzzy Zoeller** from 1995 until 2009, both on
the regular tour and the senior circuit. Most of the time he
was great to work for and treated me with respect.

Working for Fuzzy was a dream compared with my first boss,
Hubert Green, because Fuzzy was far less intense. He was the
easiest player I ever worked for.

Not that every day was perfect. This isn't a fairytale story.

One of his bad days, sadly, was that fateful Sunday at the 1997
Masters. (See Fried Chicken chapter.) But that was the exception
to the rule.

People often ask whether Fuzzy is as nice off the course as
he appears to be inside the ropes. Over time, I have developed
a stock reply: "You know what, he's not."

To which people often fire back, "I thought so." His public
persona is surely too good to be true, they suspect.

And then I drop the punchline: "He's not as nice off the
course as on it; he's even nicer."

On the course, Fuzzy always made other players feel comfortable. Despite being a double major champion, he didn't act superior in any way.

He wanted to beat his fellow competitors, but to do so the old-fashioned way, by shooting a better score while acting with class and treating everyone with respect.

Fuzzy was also a mudder. He could play under any conditions—rain, wind, hot, cold, you name it. I reckon that was a result of his Midwest upbringing in Indiana. He was used to playing through cold winters and it hardened him for anything the weather gods threw his way.

He grew up playing on a nine-hole course, New Albany, where most of the holes dogleg left. That might explain why his stock shot was a draw. You can't play that course properly with a fade. As Hubert Green once joked, hookers make more money.

Below, in no particular order, are some of my favorite Fuzzy stories.

FOBBED OFF

If you caddie for long enough on tour you will encounter some really weird situations, those once-in-a-million occurrences that you could never imagine happening.

One such occasion unfolded when I was working for Fuzzy at a Champions Tour event in Houston.

Our tournament eve pro-am unfolded in much the usual way, with my boss getting on with his amateur partners like a house on fire, just par for the course for Fuzzy.

He told me after the round that he was adjourning to the clubhouse for lunch with his partners and instructed me to put his clubs in the trunk of his courtesy vehicle, then leave the keys on the passenger-side front tire. It was pretty common practice.

I had already retrieved Fuzzy's clubs from his vehicle that morning, so I remembered more or less where he was parked. I walked in that direction, hit the key fob button to open the trunk, placed the clubs down neatly, and followed Fuzzy's directions to leave the keys on his tire.

I swung by a local bar for a beer after that and had not been there long when my phone rang. It was Fuzzy, so naturally I answered.

"Where the hell are my clubs?" he said sternly. I knew instantly by the tone of his voice that he was agitated, and it sounded as though he had enjoyed a couple of cocktails to boot.

I told him I had left them exactly where he had asked.

"Well, they are not here," he said, adding that he had found his keys on the ground in front of his vehicle.

Bizarre, I thought.

I told him I would come straight over to iron out the issue.

There must be a simple explanation, I thought, though I could not figure out what it was. But I needed to do so, because losing your player's clubs is definitely grounds for dismissal.

I zipped back to the course, nervous as could be, and when he showed me where his keys had been, I realized I must have placed them on the tire of another courtesy vehicle—Wayne Levi's as it turned out. The two vehicles not only were identical Escalade SUV models, but exactly the same color. No wonder I hadn't noticed my mistake.

Levi's and Fuzzy's parking spots faced each other, and it seems that when I hit the trunk button on the key fob, Levi's vehicle must have gotten the signal first. While the odds of this happening are extremely low, it is possible when two vehicles of the same make are close together.

Levi's trunk had popped open, and I had placed Fuzzy's clubs inside, relocked it, and then put the keys on the passenger-side tire of the wrong SUV without giving the matter a second thought.

Levi had left by then, and when he drove off the keys must have been dislodged, which is why Fuzzy had found them on the ground.

We went to the tournament office, found out where Levi was staying, called him at his hotel, and asked if he would mind checking whether our missing clubs were in his vehicle.

He went outside and soon returned to confirm that they were indeed there. It turned out that he had left his clubs at the course, which is why he did not notice Fuzzy's clubs in his vehicle. He had not needed to open the trunk before departing.

Much relieved, I jumped back in my van and hightailed it to Levi's hotel to get Fuzzy's clubs and drop them at my boss' hotel, another fire extinguished, just another day in the life of a PGA Tour caddie.

SUPERMARKET SPLURGE

Fuzzy liked to stay privately in a rental house whenever convenient, and would sometimes share it with his pilots or, in the old days, Hubert Green.

Nearly every tour player these days has a sharing buddy. It was less common for players to rent houses in the not-so-distant past, before Airbnb and other similar sites, but Fuzzy more often than not found a place, and when room permitted often invited me to stay too.

One of the first ports of call upon arrival in town was a visit to a local supermarket to stock up the kitchen for the week. He loved that errand because it made him feel at home, and I loved a policy of his whenever I accompanied him.

I could throw anything I wanted into the cart and he would pay for it, no questions asked. That's just the way Fuzzy rolled.

I tried not to abuse the privilege, but it was still a beautiful feeling to walk around a store without ever having to look at an item's price.

Come to think of it, I didn't have many opportunities to abuse the privilege, even had I wanted, because he normally filled the cart to the brim himself.

He bought the best quality anyway, so I had no need to splurge. Fuzzy didn't miss too many meals, and it was always nice to eat at home, so to speak.

It was different in Fuzzy's era, but these days a lot of players have a personal chef, particularly for the majors, and I filled that role for one week for 2019 British Open champion Shane Lowry.

It was an occasion when I did not have a bag, but Lowry invited me to stay anyway because his caddie was a good friend of mine. If there is a more generous player out there than the Irishman, I'd like to meet him.

Shane, who had his parents over for the week, decided the menu each morning and I went out and bought the necessary ingredients, before spending the afternoon in the kitchen while keeping an eye on the golf telecast.

As you can probably tell by looking at Lowry, he loves his food. He's not a guy who asks a restaurant waiter to describe the soup and salad special.

"I'LL HAVE THE SAME"

Speaking of dining out, I had a rule whenever eating out with my boss. Whatever he ordered, I'd have the same thing.

Vijay Singh's trainer once asked why I didn't choose my own order, and I told him if it was good enough for Vijay, it was good enough for me. Money was never an issue when my bosses ordered, and I wanted to keep things as easy as possible for the waiter and the chef for what more often than not was a top-notch feast.

I remember once when Fuzzy and I dined with fellow pro John Jacobs in Savannah, Georgia. They were tipping the glass rather heavily and Jacobs ordered the red snapper, while Fuzzy decided on the New York strip steak. When it was my turn to order, John said he was paying for the meal, while Fuzzy joked that as he was my boss, I would obviously have the same as him.

Torn between the two, I ordered the snapper *and* the steak.

Fuzzy and Jacobs were hungry, so I shared some of my meals, and we all went home fat and happy, and not completely sober.

Jacobs told us later that when his wife perused his receipt, she suspiciously questioned who had been that fourth person at dinner, because he had told her there were only three of us.

Jacobs told the missus that they had been drinking a bit and that Cayce had been "forced" to order two meals.

She said, "Why does that not surprise me?"

LOWBROW HUMOR

Fuzzy had a great sense of humor, which helps one stay sane when your livelihood depends on how well you can hit a ball around hundreds of acres of terrain with a crooked stick.

He liked to enjoy a joke on the course, and in Greg Norman he found a kindred spirit. They often enjoyed a good bullshit session as though playing a $2 Nassau at home.

Norman did not seem to hold any grudge against Fuzzy over the latter's playoff victory at the 1984 U.S. Open.

I remember one particular piece of banter between the pair at the Arnold Palmer Invitational at the Bay Hill course in Orlando, Florida.

The ninth hole was a long par-four bordered by the driving range on the left where no spectators were allowed, which meant spectators were all confined to the right of the fairway.

Fuzzy's and Norman's drives stopped close to each other, far enough from the spectators that the players could speak softly without being overheard.

As Fuzzy stood over his ball preparing to hit his approach shot, Norman whispered to him, "Don't look now, but the girl of your dreams has been following you for the last two holes and she cannot take her eyes off you."

So Fuzzy, fancying himself a stud muffin, could not help but be flattered to hear this coming from Norman, a man with no shortage of female admirers. But Fuzzy did not want to appear too obvious, so, without raising his head to scan the gallery, he quietly asked Norman what the woman looked like.

Sharky replied, "She's got a black dress on; you can't miss her."

And he was right, you could not miss her. Let's just say that, at the risk of being politically incorrect, she was not what one might call slim. Quite the opposite in fact, as I discovered when I glanced over at the gallery with none of Fuzzy's subtlety.

But I didn't say anything to Fuzzy, who went through his regular pre-shot routine as per usual.

And then just before starting his backswing he peeked up expecting to feast his eyes on a beauty queen. Instead, he saw a very large woman in a black dress.

Fuzzy started laughing so hard he had to step away from his ball. He glanced at Norman and said, "You got me this time, you got me."

And there they were both cracking up with laughter in the middle of the fairway, while the gallery was completely oblivious to the conversation.

I know this is not exactly highbrow humor, but it rarely is in professional golf. And before you start complaining that I am a sexist fat-shamer, I'm just telling you the story.

And, yes, I know there are also plenty of overweight men who attend golf tournaments.

RARE ANGER

I can remember only one occasion when Fuzzy threw a club on the course.

We were at a Champions Tour event in Des Moines, Iowa, and Fuzzy had putted poorly the entire tournament.

Finally, on the final hole at the Arnold Palmer–designed Tournament Club of Iowa course, he snapped, took his putter and tomahawked it into a lake next to the 18th hole. That was the end of that club, I thought.

A few days later I was surprised to receive a phone call from the club pro. He told me that Fuzzy's putter had been fished out of the lake, and wondered if I would like it returned.

Not likely!

I politely thanked the pro for thinking of us but said that the putter had ended in the water for a reason. If I ever handed that putter back to Fuzzy, I'd be the next thing tossed into the lake, I explained. "That putter is never going back in Fuzzy's bag. You can do whatever you like with the putter, keep it as a souvenir, auction it, I don't care, but as far as I'm concerned, this phone call never happened."

I was reminded of that story when another player was telling me of the time that the quirky English player Mark James had endured a putting nightmare at a tournament in Europe. James evidently took the ferry home and waited until it was far out into the English Channel before taking the offending putter and hurling it to a watery grave.

Unlike Fuzzy's club, there was no chance of that putter ever being retrieved.

Speaking of water, Fuzzy used to host a TV fishing show.

I sometimes kidded him that there was little skill in fishing. You just threw the line in the water, snapped it back when you felt something, and reeled it in. I accompanied him along on a TV shoot in Minnesota one time and cast a line in one of the state's 10,000 or so lakes.

It did not take long before I had a nibble. My rod bent almost sideways under the strain, and I proudly started reeling in what I can only describe as a monster bass.

I almost had the fish in the boat and was just about to start boasting about my catch when the bass spit the bit and disappeared back into the lake.

Fuzzy was highly amused: "It doesn't count unless you get it onto the boat," he said with glee.

FLYING HIGH

Fuzzy was one of the first guys on tour to own his own plane. He had a Beechcraft King Air 300, a private jet that first hit the market in 1984.

Most players fly privately these days, but back then you were a whale if you did.

I usually drove my van between tournaments (see On the Road Again chapter) and he was always teasing me because I would go by road rather than hitch a ride with Fuzzy. He and his pilots would joke upon liftoff that I was stuck in traffic down below while they were cruising without a care high up above, though I did fly when it made sense and was cost effective.

Fuzzy and Robert Gamez were once scheduled to play a Monday pro-am together, and Fuzzy offered Gamez a ride there from the tournament they were at. Gamez did not feel comfortable enough to ask Fuzzy whether his caddie Brad Whittle could also ride, but I did, so I asked Fuzzy and he said that it would not be a problem.

I told Fuzzy that Gamez had been afraid to make the request, so Fuzzy decided to make Gamez act as the bartender for the flight. So Whittle and I settled back, smoked a cigar, and drank a scotch mixed by Gamez.

Whittle was determined to make the most of the trip, and had no hesitation ordering a second drink from Gamez. For once the boot was on the other foot, player fussing over the caddie rather than vice-versa.

"This is the only way to fly," Whittle said.

SMOKING AND DRINKING

Fuzzy smoked like a chimney on the course. I never paid attention to exactly how many, but I would say just under a pack per round. It was a different era back then. A lot of guys smoked—Ben Crenshaw, Nick Price, and, of course, John Daly, to name just three.

When players started hiring trainers and the fitness craze took over, that was pretty much the end of smoking on the course.

The tour did not like the image smoking presented either, so it would ask players to be discreet and try to keep the cigarettes out of sight of TV cameras, which was sometimes difficult to do for those on the leaderboard.

Fuzzy also drank enough to sink a battleship.

I was caddying once for Kenny Knox at a Champions Tour event in Hickory, North Carolina, and we were on the range when Kenny asked me who Fuzzy's coach was. Tom Kite was nearby, and he butted in and said, "Excuse me for overhearing the conversation, but I've known Fuzzy a long time and I didn't even know he had a coach."

I said, "Oh yeah, Tom, his coach is here every week. He has a coach when he plays good, a coach when he plays bad, and a coach when he plays average."

"What's his name?" a puzzled Kite asked.

"Absolut and tonic," I said, referring to Fuzzy's favorite vodka.

Tom and Kenny started cracking up laughing.

"You've got a good point there," Kite said.

INDIANA RED

Fuzzy's generosity was seemingly boundless.

He once had a Chevy Avalanche that was painted Indiana Red, for his beloved Hoosiers. He worried it was getting too old to be reliable, even though it had barely 20,000 miles on the clock, basically brand new in my eyes. I said I would be glad to take it off his hands, because it would be an ideal vehicle to tow my horses.

He said, "Bam" and handed me the keys right then and there, and from that day it was mine, no questions asked.

I had it detailed and repainted in an even brighter red and many years later it still looked brand spanking new. I keep it on my uncle's farm near San Antonio and use it whenever I go fishing on the coast in Corpus Christi.

SHIRTS

Fuzzy had an unusual litmus test to feel like he had made it as a player.

He wanted to be able to open a brand-new shirt every day. He had met that goal long before I started working for him, so I scooped up many of his once-worn shirts, literally hundreds of them over the years.

Fuzzy was an extra-large size, so they were too big for me, but all of my large friends were attired by Fuzzy, complimentary.

I'd give the shirts to people who put me up at tournaments, basically anyone who was good to me.

CHAMPION FINISH

I remember most vividly two final rounds I worked for Fuzzy on the Champions Tour in 2004.

One was in Tampa, where he birdied 12 of the first 14 holes and had a great chance to break 60 at the Outback Steakhouse Pro-Am. We arrived at the final hole still needing one more birdie to join the 59 club. That's a club even caddies want to get into.

Fuzzy hit a good drive which found the fairway, but unfortunately came to rest in a small depression near a drain and a sprinkler head.

He would have been granted a free drop without question had he called for a rules official, but Fuzzy loved playing quickly, so he played his approach shot from where his ball lay.

He was a momentum player and didn't want to wait for an official, so he just hit the shot, caught it a little heavy, missed the green barely, and did not get up-and-down.

The bogey left him to sign for a 61 and finish second. Notwithstanding the disappointing finish, it was the greatest round I'd ever witnessed Fuzzy play.

Exactly four weeks earlier at the MasterCard Championship on the Big Island of Hawaii, Fuzzy was very much in contention as he played the 14th hole of the final round.

However, his mood soured when he scorched a wedge from the rough and we both watched in dismay as the ball sailed over the green.

Fuzzy had caught a flier, but thought I'd given him the wrong yardage.

He rarely got mad at me, but had his moments, and this was one of them: "Goddamn it, Cayce, if you gave me the wrong yardage there, I'm going to kill you."

We had trouble even locating his ball, because it was nestled at the bottom of a thick clump of Bermuda rough, but fortunately it was just a touch off the back of the green.

He faced a short, if very delicate, chip shot, but judged and executed it exquisitely and, suitably buoyed, birdied the final four holes to shoot 64 and beat Dana Quigley by a shot.

Quigley provided me with a valuable lesson in not counting any chickens. He needed to get up-and-down from a bunker at the last to force a playoff and Fuzzy warned me not to underestimate the guy.

But in my mind, I thought it was as good as over, so when Quigley's sand shot hit the cup I almost had a heart attack. Fortunately for us it rimmed out.

"I told you not to count this guy out," Fuzzy said.

Not many players have birdied the last four holes to win a tournament. Charl Schwartzel at the 2011 Masters springs to mind, and though a Champions Tour event obviously doesn't carry the same importance, it was still a thrill for both of us to win in such a barnstorming manner.

A Champions Tour win might seem like small potatoes to most, but trust me it still gives even the best players an intense buzz. A lot of things go out of style, but winning is not one of them. That's what keeps these guys fueled. It's the adrenaline they get in the heat of the competition that drives them. It feels so good to get back in the mix.

And I maintain that I did not give Fuzzy the wrong yardage at the 14th hole. I'm happy to admit that I and every other caddie has made a mistake with the number now and then, but that was not one of those occasions.

LAST HOORAH

My final tournament with Fuzzy was the 2009 Senior Skins Game in Hawaii, an alternate-shot team event in which Fuzzy partnered for victory with "Gentle" Ben Crenshaw.

Gentle Ben was arguably the greatest putter ever, but in a strange twist it was Fuzzy who holed two big putts down the stretch.

As the Associated Press reported at the time: "Ben Crenshaw set them up and Fuzzy Zoeller knocked them down."

"The 57-year-old Zoeller, who won the Masters 30 years ago, made two birdie putts within five feet on [holes] 12 and 17 to win a half-million dollars in a span of six holes."

The unwritten story was even better.

Fuzzy was beginning to lose his vision at the time and could not see as well as he would have liked. He had little confidence in my ability to read putts, but fortunately it was a team event, so he could call upon his partner, and who better than Crenshaw?

I quietly told Ben before the event that Fuzzy could hole putts if he got the right read. Otherwise, there was no telling what might happen.

"If you don't read them, we won't have a chance, Ben," I said.

So Ben read Fuzzy's putts throughout the event and they beat three high-powered duos—Greg Norman and Jay Haas, Bernhard Langer and Gary Player, and Tom Watson and Jack Nicklaus.

Ben and I had a chuckle about it, because Ben had not let on to Fuzzy that he knew about his vision issues.

I said, "If you ever tell him, Ben, I'm going to deny our conversation."

I didn't want Fuzzy to think that before our final tournament together I had gone to his partner with a less-than-flattering observation. And as far as I know, Ben never did say anything to Fuzzy and I left Fuzzy on a high note. I never touched his bag again.

Everyone wants to go out on top, but so many try to milk the good times and end up getting fired amid acrimony and bitterness.

Thankfully it did not come to that with Fuzzy, and we remain in regular contact today.

5

Couplers

*Tales from two years
with golf's coolest cat*

Fred Couples is a certified superstar whose popularity is perhaps greater than any other winner of one major championship and 14 non-major PGA Tour events.

But anyone who has spent time around Fred understands why. Apart from his movie star good looks, which he still has in spades even in his sixties, he has a mystique that attracts fans in droves.

I did not work for Fred on the regular tour, but we had a couple of very successful years together on the Champions Tour.

In May of 2011, I was at the Tradition event at Shoal Creek in Birmingham, Alabama, to work for Steve Jones, who was then in his early fifties. While walking the course to finalize my notes before the first round, I bumped into Fred on the 14th tee while he was playing in the pro-am.

With his longtime caddie Joe LaCava standing right there, Fred asked if I wanted to come and work for him. I was taken by surprise and did not know what was going on between the pair.

But Fred quickly dispelled any potential awkwardness by telling me that Joe was leaving after more than two decades to start working for Dustin Johnson, at the time one of the biggest rising stars on the regular tour.

Absolutely I was interested in getting Fred's bag—are you kidding me?—but I wanted to be sure he wasn't yanking my giggle chain, so I walked the next couple of holes with him. At the 16th hole his ball ended up in a bunker and he was starting to get a bit annoyed that I had not answered his question.

"I'm not going to ask you again," he said firmly.

"I'm not sure you can afford me," I replied, tongue firmly in cheek.

"You let me worry about that," he said, and that was the end of the conversation. He had called my bluff, and I accepted.

GLUE

It was only later that I found out that Fred had kept me in mind for the job for 13 years for an act of goodwill I had displayed way back at the 1998 Masters, where I worked for Fuzzy Zoeller.

Fred was in contention there after 54 holes and before the final round I sought him out on the range to wish him luck. He told me he had sliced his thumb on a crab claw the previous night and could not get the cut closed. He was not even sure whether he could play.

I told him to wait a minute and I would try to help. Fuzzy always had a tube of crazy glue in his bag, because his thumb cracked in the middle with monotonous regularity. So I fished out the tube and glued Fred's thumb back together.

"Just hold it there for a few seconds," I said. "It will sting and it might hold all day. But I've got an extra tube in Fuzzy's bag, so you just keep this one and if the thumb breaks open again just reseal it, blow on it and let it dry and you'll be good to go."

Fred never played with a glove, but the glue held the thumb in place throughout the final round and he almost collected a second Green Jacket, losing by a shot to Mark O'Meara.

I did not know it at the time, but after I helped Fred that day, he told LaCava that if they ever split up, I would be his next caddie.

So the moral of the story is that it never hurts to help someone in need. Tour players can lead a lonely life traveling the country and the world, and they often don't know who to trust.

They really appreciate it when someone assists them without asking for anything in return. They remember that, because there are not many people out there who have their interest at heart. As with most anyone with a lot of money, it can be hard sometimes to know a true friend from someone who just wants something.

It was at the 2012 Senior British Open that I finally heard the story from Fred's lips. We had just won at majestic Turnberry and were dining in the clubhouse when the vice president of sponsor Rolex asked Fred how I had become his caddie.

Fred said, "I'm about to tell you a story that Cayce doesn't know," and proceeded to recite the cut thumb story from 14 years previously.

I had already heard it from someone in Fred's camp but didn't let on. I just pretended that it was the first time because I didn't want to put a damper on the conversation.

Fred was pleased with me that week, and not just because he won a senior major.

He is quite reserved and does not like being recognized off the course. Unfortunately, it is not something he has much control over, but I tried when I could to minimize his discomfort.

"COUSIN"

We had been in Dusseldorf, where Fred received treatment on his notoriously creaky back from a renowned specialist. He was there to try blood spinning—otherwise known as platelet-rich plasma therapy—which at the time was a fairly new, controversial, and unproven procedure.

After a couple of days in Germany we made the short flight to Edinburgh, where I had reserved a hire car, to use the British lingo, for a pretty good price, between $200–$300 for the week as I recall.

But when we arrived at the agency, it seemed everyone else had also found the same deal, because the line at this particular company's counter was longer than a Bryson DeChambeau drive. Fred was not impressed. A pro of his stature is not used to waiting for anything, and he certainly did not want to line up with the unwashed masses for a rental car.

So while I took my spot in the queue, he wandered off to enquire about prices at the other agencies, which had no lines to speak of.

He returned a few minutes later and said the cars were all about $800 for the week. I told him I was not going to pay triple just to get out of the airport a few minutes quicker and he, being even cheaper than me, did not argue.

I told him to chill out and wait, so he settled into a nearby seat, closed his eyes, and left me to continue standing in line.

Moments later I noticed a large group of American guys who, judging by their accompanying golf clubs, were making a pilgrimage to play Scottish links courses.

One guy who had seen me talking with Fred asked whether it was in fact the famous golfer. Oh, great. Now what was I to do? The last thing Fred wanted was to be bothered by autograph hunters or, even worse, selfie seekers.

I knew from bitter experience that once one person asks for an autograph, it opens the floodgates for everyone else, the domino theory if you like. I had seen it hundreds of times, so I prevented the first domino from falling.

Thinking quickly on my feet, I said that the napping gentleman was in fact my cousin. He just happened to resemble Couples. And for extra insurance to maximize the chances of Fred being left alone, I added that the guy who I was passing off as my cousin was going through a painful divorce and not in a good mood.

I said I could not assure them of a friendly reception if they approached the napping man. That did the trick and they left him alone.

When I finally got the keys to the car and we bolted out of the building at last, I told Fred he owed me big time.

"What do I owe you for now?" he said indignantly.

When I filled him in, he said, "Oh, you're a beauty."

It might be a coincidence that Fred won the championship the following Sunday, but getting the week off to a good start like that certainly did not hurt.

I also took care of a couple of other things after Fred won.

It's a tradition for the winning caddie to keep the 18th hole flag as a souvenir, and the Turnberry caddie master Willie McDines had been so good to me throughout the week that I gave it to him after having Fred autograph it.

"This flag belongs in Bonny Scotland," I told him.

Also, the tournament wanted a photo of Fred celebrating his victory by posing for the trophy while wearing a Rolex watch, but he had left his timepiece in his room.

I noticed that our playing companion Bernhard Langer wore a Rolex, so I explained the situation to Bernhard, and he was happy to lend his watch for the photo shoot.

As slow a player as he is—more on this later in the chapter—Bernhard is a first-class guy.

He had been the overnight leader, had shot a closing 75 to finish equal sixth, but was still willing to do us a favor.

The moral of the story is that a good caddie must look after his player both on and off the course. When you take care of a player in many ways, he can't help but like you and you are harder to replace.

A player might think something along the lines of, "He's an okay caddie, nothing special, but he does a lot of things for me off the course. I can play golf, I know how to pull a club, I don't need a lot of help on the course, so I might as well keep him working for me."

MAN OF MYSTERY

I had long known how popular Fred was, but working for him gave me an opportunity to see it firsthand day in and day out.

His good looks certainly did not hurt, and women often went weak at the knees in his presence. They still do from what I've heard. And people loved his silky swing that looked deceptively languid and almost effortless while at the same time generating considerable power. And it also helped that he never seemed arrogant and that his competitiveness was not an in-your-face kind. He preferred to let his clubs do the talking and win or lose with dignity, not unlike Jack Nicklaus in that regard.

It's often said that as well as being the best winner ever, as attested by a record 18 majors, Nicklaus was also the classiest loser. He had plenty of practice in that regard too, with 19 major runner-up finishes.

Not that Fred was easygoing inside the ropes. You might be surprised to learn that he could be quite a whiner when things were going badly. I recall while working for Fuzzy once that we were grouped with Fred and Colin Montgomerie.

"We couldn't get paired with two more miserable pricks if we tried," Fuzzy wryly noted.

There was always an element of mystery about Fred because no one on tour ever saw him hanging out in the locker room or player dining. Fred never went inside the clubhouse while I worked for him.

Most players would never give up the opportunity for an all-you-can buffet—and invariably pretty good food at that—but Fred did so every day. Privacy was more important to him.

Not that he was a recluse.

Fred just realized over the years that he wasn't getting any value out of hanging out in player dining.

Our daily routine went as follows: I would pick him up and drive him to the course and we would go straight from the players' parking lot to the range. Then, once our round was over, we would go somewhere off-site to each lunch or dinner.

He learned over the years that it was hard to just enjoy lunch in player dining, because other players were always pulling at him.

As I mentioned earlier, it can be lonely at the top and when guys get to the superstar level of Fred, they are always having to deal with people wanting something, and that includes fellow pros after a memento for an "auction" or whatever.

Fred just wanted to focus on his job. Whether he was in Los Angeles, Miami, or Boston, the purpose of his visit was to play golf. He wasn't there for the local chamber of commerce, and he wasn't there to make other people happy.

Not that he couldn't schmooze for a good cause, as the following example demonstrates.

In the spring of 2012, Fred rode in my van for a three-week stint traveling between tournaments rather than flying, and as far as I know he enjoyed the change of pace.

On the Monday after Jack Nicklaus' Memorial tournament in Ohio, we headed south for the Tradition Champions Tour event in Birmingham, where I had accepted the job with Fred the previous year. Kenny Perry had previously mentioned that we were welcome to drop by the course he owned near the Interstate 65 freeway in Franklin, Kentucky.

It was a Monday, so we had time up our sleeve, and when I mentioned to Fred that we were approaching Perry's course, he instructed me to pull in there.

Perry had a pro-am fundraiser that day, and as we drove past the first tee, we saw a guy take an almighty swing and miss the ball completely.

Fred told me to stop the van, jumped out, walked over to the tee, and gave the surprised amateur a couple of tips. It was like a scene from a golf commercial.

Fred stayed for the rest of the day, signed autographs, and hung out at the cookout that followed the golf. And all without charging a dime.

A guy like Fred charges up to $100,000 for a one-day corporate outing from what I've heard, so to do what he did for charity on the spur of the moment was quite the gesture.

When Perry arrived in Birmingham later that week, he gave Fred a big hug and thanked him profusely.

Perry was clearly moved that Fred had helped make the fundraiser such a success, and without even being officially asked.

"IS THAT FAST ENOUGH?"

Like every other pro, Fred was not completely impervious to frustration, and nothing frustrated him more than receiving a slow-play warning when he perceived it not to be his fault.

It is an occupational hazard that happens all the time, something along the following lines: A quick player is grouped with a tortoise, who, shot after shot after shot is so slow that the group falls too far behind the preceding group, getting "out of position" as they say.

So a tour rules official gives the out-of-position group a warning and starts paying close attention, timing how long each one takes over a shot.

And then the quicker player sometimes finds himself in a situation that requires an unusual amount of deliberation, such as a recovery shot from trees. He might not have been the one responsible for the group being timed, but now he's in trouble anyway for taking too long over one particularly tricky shot.

At a Champions Tour event in Calgary, Alberta, in 2013, Fred played with notorious slowpoke Langer, an occupational hazard if ever there was one.

You don't need a stopwatch to time Langer. A sundial will do!

Langer once complained on a green that another pro's shadow was in his putting line, to which the player groused, "It wasn't when it was your turn."

Okay, that's a joke, but back to the true story in Calgary. Fred was put "on the clock" and he went ballistic. I could not blame him, because it was 100 percent Langer's fault. I had never seen Fred so upset before, or since for that matter. He took it personally and was dropping enough f-bombs to make a construction worker blush.

He was so angry that he was determined to show the rules official that it was not his fault the group was out of position.

On the next hole he absolutely bombed a drive and had only 86 yards to the hole. I gave him the yardage, handed him a wedge, and he looked over at the official and screamed, "You want me to speed up? You want me to fucking speed up? I'll show you how to speed up."

And then without so much as a practice swing, he promptly jarred his approach shot for eagle. Talk about good timing. That's one way to speed up.

Of all the shots I've witnessed from my various players, that one ranked up there as one of the coolest and most memorable, because of the circumstances.

And how did Fred react? Suddenly he was as cool as a cucumber.

He just threw his wedge down, all cocky like, and didn't say anything. But I could almost hear him thinking, "Is that fast enough for you?"

MASTERS

The most exciting week of my stint with Couples was at the 2013 Masters, where Fred became the oldest man to play in the final third-round pairing at Augusta National.

He started with rounds of 68, 71, and was in the lead when we got done at Friday lunchtime. Fred was 53 at the time and by the end of the day was one shot behind halfway-leader Jason Day.

Fred and Jason were paired for the third round, and I remember feeling jacked up to the hilt that day, and so too it seemed was almost everyone who had my phone number.

I got 763 texts that week, easily the most I ever received. That's when it hit me that everyone who likes sport watches the Masters.

Fred's appearance on the leaderboard reminded me of the 1967 Masters, at which Ben Hogan at the age of 54 was only two shots from the 54-hole lead. Hogan, alas, had a poor final round of 77.

Fred similarly endured a bad third round in 2013. He also shot 77 and eventually tied for 13th.

I can honestly say I do not remember much specifically about that disappointing third round, other than that the proverbial wheels fell off and that Fred was not happy.

VIJAY BECKONS

I ended up leaving Fred later that year, after a chance meeting with another player that I can only describe as fate.

We had just finished a tournament at Kapolei Golf Club in Hawaii in September, and Fred was not in a good mood, despite finishing tied for sixth with, among others, Vijay Singh, who had chosen the Oahu event for his Champions Tour debut.

When we arrived at Honolulu airport, Couples asked me to let him and his girlfriend out at the curb before I returned the rental car. He was treating me like a junkyard dog, but I figured I'd do my duty as a valet, so I dropped off the car and took the shuttle back to the terminal.

And when I exited the bus, who should I run into at the curb but Singh. I asked if he needed some help with his clubs and luggage and while serving as his sherpa he asked me whether I would be free to caddie for him the following week on the regular tour. Talk about a job just falling into your lap.

"The guy I just had totally fucked me up," Vijay said, not mincing his words. "I'd have won today if you'd been on my bag."

That was an unprovable statement of course, but I was obviously flattered, and it made it an easy decision to work for him, because Fred was having the following week off anyway. So I changed my travel plans and joined Vijay at the Frys.com Open in central California, where he finished runner-up to Jimmy Walker.

It was Walker's first tour victory and boy did he have some luck. Vijay should have won, but that's another story. After that I was eager to keep working for Vijay.

He had turned 50 earlier that year and told me he was ready to play more on the Senior Tour. I thought it was perfect timing and that with his game he would be unbeatable on the 50-and-over circuit.

Vijay subsequently decided to stay focused on the main tour, and I could hardly blame him for that. He was just so competitive he wanted to keep battling the big boys rather than kicking proverbial sand in the faces of the old guys.

And besides, Fred was complaining about his bad back and saying he was ready to quit golf, so who knew how much longer I had with him?

But I didn't officially resign from working for Fred for another few weeks, until I was confident the Vijay job would not be a flash in the pan.

When you're leaving a player, you have to make sure you're strategically positioned with a secure job on the other end before you give up the position you hold. So I didn't quit Fred until Vijay had decided how he wanted to move forward.

These things are quite delicate, but as it turned out, Fred and I won our last tournament together, the Charles Schwab Cup in November of that year, 2013.

He never shared his feelings toward me on my choice, but I was told that he was disappointed because he thought we had a good thing going. And we had, but all good things come to an end sooner or later. He treated me as well as any caddie could expect. As a caddie, it's always better to leave a player when he's on top. It helps your reputation. When he's struggling, it adds salt to the wound.

6

Vijay

*In defense of an unloved
and unappreciated champion*

Vijay Singh is a surly, unpleasant character, right?

I'm sure anyone with even a passing interest in golf has heard the stories about his prickly character and reluctance to engage with the gallery or speak with members of the Fourth Estate.

And yes, Vijay is generally wary of the media, especially those he does not know and trust, a subject addressed later in the chapter. That wariness probably stems from the accusation that he altered a scorecard so that he would make the cut during an Asia Golf Circuit event in 1985, not long after he had turned pro.

Though he has always maintained his innocence, Vijay probably did cheat, but he was young, it was a long time ago, and I think he learned his lesson. And you can bet your bottom dollar he got sick of the press writing about it. He might not have read the stories, but I guarantee you someone in his orbit invariably did.

I certainly did not witness him do anything questionable during our time together, and I'm here to tell you that there is another side to Vijay that the public does not see.

And before you roll your eyes, thinking I'm just trying to protect someone I worked for, please hear me out.

Sure, he paid me well as a caddie, but his generosity did not stop there. In my two years working with Vijay, he took me out to dinner hundreds of times, and never, not once, did he allow me to pay. And we're not talking about a $70 bill at Applebee's either. Vijay is a red wine connoisseur, and he invariably ordered a $200-plus bottle for us to share as we chewed the fat, both literally and figuratively, at an upmarket steakhouse.

Say what you will about Vijay, but you can't deny the man's generosity, and not just in opening his wallet.

In January 2015, I broke my right ankle when I slipped on an icy curb while loading my van outside my hotel room in sub-freezing Chicago. I was getting ready to head to Chicago's O'Hare Airport and fly to Hawaii for the first tournament of the year on the Champions Tour.

I called Vijay and told him what had happened. "Man down, Big Daddy," I said (we both called each other Big Daddy).

"No worries," he replied, suggesting I fly out anyway and rest and recuperate at his house in Hawaii. So I drove to Des Moines, where a doctor friend named Ross Valone booked me in to have the ankle X-rayed, and where the fracture was confirmed, and my foot placed in a boot.

RUPTURED APPENDIX

I credit Valone for probably saving my life once before. I met him in a pro-am—where else?—and we quickly hit it off. A gynecologist, he has delivered thousands of babies.

A few years after befriending Valone, I was driving my van in Maryland when I started feeling extremely nauseous. I called Ross and told him of my symptoms, and he said it sounded like an appendix issue and that the organ was probably in danger of rupturing.

He urged me to drive straight to the nearest hospital, which I did. I was promptly admitted, and my appendix removed without any complications. I was told the organ might have exploded at any moment, so I was extremely relieved not to have dilly-dallied.

I repaid the doc by watching him hit balls whenever I was in town. He was always trying to improve his game and wanted swing tips, and I never had the heart to tell him he just wasn't very good. Though to be fair, most amateurs don't seem very good when you've become accustomed to working for the most elite pros.

HAWAII PARADISE

Returning to the broken-ankle saga, I eventually headed to Hawaii a day late and Vijay collected me at Hilo airport on the Big Island and took me to his little piece of tropical paradise. It was located on the quiet eastern part of the island, seemingly light-years away from the coastal Kona tourist strip and just about as close to heaven on earth as I can imagine.

He used to spend a month or so there at the start of each year preparing for the upcoming season. His 52-acre property was laid out in an L shape and included a driving range. Out front was a road lined with macadamia trees, maybe 400 or 500, which are harvested twice a year.

It was so peaceful. He had a couple of dogs and an employee who took care of the place.

I wasn't very mobile in my condition, and in a fair amount of discomfort, but I still enjoyed it, spending my days quietly contemplating life while Vijay pounded balls.

I was there for a couple of weeks and then we flew back to his main home in Ponte Vedra, Florida, where he put me up for a couple more months, right up until the Masters.

I stayed at his condo and worked every day on rehabilitating the joint, with the express goal of being fit for the Masters.

My therapist, whose clientele over the years had included Olympic champions, was impressed with my determination to do whatever it took to get back on my feet as soon as possible.

It was always going to be touch-and-go whether I would recover in time for the Masters, and on my first day there the ankle did not do well, but I spent hours every night in the warm, soothing waters of the Jacuzzi at the house where I stayed (See Augusta National chapter) and got through the week.

I am sure I could not have done it without Vijay's tender loving care. I can never thank him enough.

Not only did he feed and accommodate me, but more importantly provided the genuine hospitality that you can't put a value on. And all this for a mere caddie. It's not like he couldn't have found someone else for the Masters.

He wouldn't have gone out of his way to help me if he didn't have a kind heart, so I think the guy deserves a few accolades to counterbalance all the negative perceptions of him out there among the golf public.

Not that Vijay cares about perceptions. In fact, he doesn't like anyone to know he has a heart and that deep down he's a generous soul and a great person, because when you want to be the Big Daddy, and you want to beat everybody, you don't want anyone to think you're soft.

FORLORN FIJI SHACK

There have been more than two dozen world No. 1s since the ranking's inception in 1986, and of these there is absolutely no doubt that Vijay came from the humblest of beginnings.

I can personally attest to that after visiting the home in Nadi, Fiji, where he grew up, the son of an aircraft refueler at the island's international airport. We were there for the Fiji International tournament in 2018, where I was to work for Ernie Els.

Vijay took me to the Nadi Airport course he played with his dad as a young boy. Augusta National it was not. It was so rough we drove our car on the course. When you can do that on a course without inflicting further damage, you know it's in bad shape.

Vijay also took me to the house where his parents raised him and his two brothers and a sister. To call it a house is being generous. More like a forlorn basic shack. He used to share a bed with his siblings, sleeping with the head-to-toe method.

Then he took me to the school he attended. I know that growing up he had one overriding thought: "How do I get out of here?"

It's no wonder he earned a reputation throughout his career of beating more balls than anyone else, both at tournaments and during his rare weeks off. His work ethic was incredible and if you saw where he came from, you'd understand.

I arrived a couple of days before Vijay, who was booked as a guest speaker with Ernie at the pro-am dinner, but a flight delay after the Senior British Open prevented him from arriving on time.

Not to worry, I filled in for Vijay, sharing the stage with Ernie as we entertained some 350 of Fiji's movers and shakers, including the country's president as well as the president of the national golf body.

Australian pro Paul Gow, a former PGA Tour player, was the host, and after a few comments he introduced Ernie and me to an audience who were understandably disappointed by Vijay's absence. Ernie and I had never been on a stage together. Not to worry, we soon had the audience's rapt attention. I regaled the crowd with a few Vijay anecdotes, and they especially lapped it up when I told those gathered that it was their responsibility to find the next Vijay Singh from their great country, be it a man or a woman.

We got a standing ovation. If I may say so, I brought the house down, much to the surprise of Ernie and his wife, Liezl.

They said they had no idea I had those stories in me.

Ernie and I were playing a practice round the following day when Vijay belatedly showed up and wasted no time hitting the course to check it out.

When he caught up with us, he said, "I heard you had a lot of nice things to say about me."

I nonchalantly replied that I just told the truth.

He said he could not believe how many people had told him that my comments at the dinner had brought tears to their eyes. That's when I knew Vijay and I had bonded for life. Call it hokey if you like, but it's true.

MYSTERIOUS TEENAGER

Vijay was already Fiji's best golfer by the age of 17 and he turned pro in 1982 while still a teenager. An Australian friend of mine recalls seeing him play in the flesh at a tournament soon afterward at the Kooyonga course in Adelaide, where Gary Player won the 1958 Australian Open.

My friend had gone there to watch Jack Newton, the swashbuckling Australian who lost a playoff to Tom Watson at the 1975 British Open, and who five years later would also finish joint runner-up to Seve Ballesteros at the Masters.

Vijay already had a masterful short game, chipping in three times in the same round, prompting Newton to just shake his head at what he was seeing from this strapping young lad from a golfing backwater.

It wasn't long afterward that Singh was banned for life from the Asian Tour after it was determined that he had shaved two strokes from his score at the 1985 Indonesian Open.

From there he went into temporary exile as a teaching pro in Malaysia, and that could have been the end of his story if not for an incredible drive and determination that within five years led to a European Tour victory, and within a decade to PGA Tour membership.

BEST NON-AMERICAN

Thirty-four PGA Tour victories later, including three majors, Vijay is the most successful non-American player in tour history as judged by wins, with career earnings of more than $78 million.

Let that sink in for a moment. The most ever victories by a non-American player, and by a country mile to boot. Rory McIlroy, with 26 wins at the time of writing, may eventually pass Vijay, but it's no guarantee.

Vijay had just turned 50 and was past his prime by the time I worked for him for two years starting in late 2013, but he could still flat-out play.

When we arrived at the 2014 Masters, he said, "Big Daddy, have you ever played Augusta? No? Well, this year you're playing with me."

When I got to the course on Sunday, I found out we were playing with my old boss Fuzzy Zoeller and a friend of Fuzzy's, George Cataldo.

We played for $100. Fuzzy had one rule, that we had to play everything out, just as in a tournament. There were no gimmies. That was always Fuzzy's philosophy, because he knew that it was good practice to grind over the short putts.

I still cherish the picture I have, taken from behind, of Vijay, Fuzzy, and me walking down the 11th fairway, Vijay in the middle wearing a purple sweater.

At the par-five 13th I aimed well right to stay away from the trouble left, but pulled my drive, which worked out perfectly as the ball took a big first bounce and took off like a rocket down the fairway.

"Don't try and catch that or you'll pull a muscle," I quipped.

Vijay and I shot 97 and won the money from Fuzzy and Cataldo.

People sometimes ask me for my dream foursome, and my response is that it would be Tiger Woods and me playing Fuzzy and Fred Couples. If I could expand it to a fivesome, Vijay would get the final berth.

As if playing with Masters champions Vijay and Fuzzy that day wasn't enough, Vijay said, "We're going upstairs to the Champions locker room to have lunch and you're having it with me."

I was so overjoyed by the gesture that I bought a crystal decanter for $250 from the club gift shop, with all the Masters winners' names on it.

There's an art to giving a gift to a guy worth perhaps $100 million, that he won't re-gift, but I'd been to his house and saw he had a nice liquor tray. I thought the decanter would complement it. He absolutely loved it, so much so that he got me something as a note of thanks.

When we got to the first tee on Thursday, I was a little nervous, even though I knew he didn't have a chance. He said: "I got you a menu from the Champions dinner," the annual event held every Tuesday during Masters week.

In my own blunt terms, I said, "A menu? I don't fucking collect menus!"

He said, "You fucking idiot, it's got all the winners' autographs from the dinner."

Without missing a beat, I quipped, "I love the menu."

"BIG DADDY"

So why did we call each other Big Daddy?

It was a nickname I gave him because he was the Big Daddy on tour for several years, kicking ass well beyond what should have been his used-by date. When you win nine tournaments in one year at the age of 41, you *are* the Big Daddy.

There was a new sheriff in town, and the Big Daddy loved the nickname so much he started calling me Big Daddy too.

But though I have nothing but good things to say about Vijay, I must admit he was a demanding boss.

As you might imagine, he was a lone wolf who did not need an instructor. He was so self-sufficient that he did not see the need, so he was his own coach, which meant extra work for his caddie.

He would sometimes get me to videotape his swing, examine it, and decide if any adjustments were needed.

A conversation might go as follows: "Okay, see this? You watch my elbow every time and make sure I don't do it again. If you don't pay attention, you're fired. That's what I pay you for."

He was very regimented. Some players don't care if you pay close attention to their swing, but with Vijay you had to watch every shot closely, every single shot.

The long hours he spent on the range meant not only long hours for the caddie, but also long, focused hours. You couldn't just chat with someone walking past if Vijay was hitting balls.

One specific Vijay habit was that he never wanted to watch anyone else's swing on the range, the same as Phil Mickelson. Lefty Phil only goes to the side of the range where he faces away from other players.

As well as long hours on the range, Vijay and I would go to the gym twice a day, in the morning and again at night. I was in just about the best shape of my life during my time with Vijay. I was often surprised to see players in the gym that I would not have expected to be there. Jim Furyk, Patrick Reed, and Sergio Garcia spring to mind.

DEER ANTLER SPRAY

Vijay was a beast, and don't get me started on those who suspect that one of the reasons he played so brilliantly into his mid-forties was due to artificial help.

As far as I'm concerned, the reason he cut such an impressive figure in middle-age was because of the work he put in. Another reason for Vijay's longevity was that he avoided major injuries, in stark contrast to his chief antagonist, Tiger. The golfing injury gods certainly treated him well.

Anyone who says that golf is not an athletic activity has no idea what they are talking about. Try hitting 500 balls every day and see how you feel afterward. Tour players generate a clubhead speed of more than 110 mph on average, which creates tremendous torque, and tremendous stress on the entire body, particularly the spine.

Granted, good technique helps, but there is no getting around it, the game is hard on a pro's body. And while most players do not spend as much time on the sidelines as contact sport athletes, they are nearly always carrying some type of ache or pain that they do not talk about.

Sore backs are an occupational hazard, which is why many modern players have a massage therapist on the payroll.

While Vijay avoided serious injuries, he was no different from all other professional athletes looking for an edge. In his case, it came in the form of deer antler spray.

He was nearly 50 when he acknowledged to *Sports Illustrated* that he had used the spray, which at the time was on the tour's list of banned substances because it contained small amounts of IGF-1, a hormone that can promote muscle growth and help recovery.

Vijay's caddie at the time turned him on to the product.

Vijay was informed in 2013 that he would be suspended for three months, but the tour dropped the case shortly afterward, citing the World Anti-Doping Agency's decision to rescind the banning of the spray.

Vijay subsequently sued the tour for public humiliation and the two parties settled out of court for an undisclosed amount, which I am not privy to, but I guarantee you it was not chicken feed.

It was outrageous the way the tour treated Vijay, but he got the last laugh.

DRIVING MAT

People often ask whether Vijay spent more time on the range than anyone else. Before I answer that question, let me tell you a story from the 2015 PGA Tour event at the Robert Trent Jones course in Virginia.

Vijay was on the range beating balls and found something in his swing: "Big Daddy, I'm locked in. I've got it," he said, just as a sudden cloudburst prompted officials to blow the siren and close the course due to dangerous weather.

"Thank God," I'm thinking. "I don't have to watch him beat balls anymore."

So Vijay asked whether there was a Dick's Sporting Goods store nearby. I told him there was, so we jumped in his courtesy car and headed off for what I assumed was going to be a spot of shopping. No such luck.

We got there and he went straight to the mats and started hitting balls into the net. His dedication was relentless.

"I'm staying here until the storm has passed," he said, by which time I was hoping it would blow over quickly so that I could get out of the store. But the employees were happy having a famous pro on their premises. As far as they were concerned, the longer he stayed, the better.

When I started working for Vijay, it was a given that I'd be spending a lot of time on the range, but because of the money I anticipated making, I didn't care. It turned out that Vijay did not spend any longer practicing than my first regular boss, Hubert Green, in the late '80s and early '90s. (See Tour Beckons chapter.)

Hubert used to tell me that he and Tom Watson and Tom Kite in their day never left the range until they saw the other guys leave. They wanted to see who could last out there the longest.

There are basically two types of pros when it comes to practice.

One type never wants to step foot on the course outside of tournaments. They prefer instead to go to the range and beat balls. Hubert and Vijay belonged in that category.

When home in Florida, Vijay goes to the Sawgrass TPC but only to the range. He can play holes in his mind if he needs to.

Hubert practiced for as long as Vijay. People perhaps thought Vijay spent more time on the range than he did, but he never got to the course until 10:30 AM, whereas Hubert would be there by eight or nine o'clock.

Sure, Vijay did beat a lot of balls, but no more than a lot of the old-timers.

At the opposite end of the spectrum are pros who would rather play than practice.

Fuzzy Zoeller was in this category. He would rather have a round with his buddies. Players are hardwired differently.

DUVAL DIRT

Vijay's crowning glory was the 2000 Masters, the only major that year won by anyone whose initials weren't TW.

I learned a revealing tidbit from Vijay when I had dinner with him at Hilton Head the night following his Augusta victory, after giving his caddie Dave Renwick a ride for the two-hour-plus drive through rural South Carolina. Vijay even had a practice round at Harbour Town on Monday. His achievement the previous afternoon was no excuse for taking a day off, so his thinking went.

Renwick didn't want to eat with Vijay because he was around him all the time and couldn't stand the guy. Vijay didn't have any friends to celebrate with, so ended up dining with me.

He had played the final round at the Masters in the final pairing with David Duval, who had pulled within one shot of the lead after five holes. The pivotal moment, at least in Vijay's telling of it, came at the par-three sixth after Duval hit a superb tee shot in close, and in the process of using his club to flick his tee out of the ground flicked some dirt over Vijay's trousers.

It was no doubt careless rather than malicious on Duval's part, but it fired Vijay up.

"It was like 'Take that,'" Vijay told me.

"Let me tell you, Big Daddy was so mad, I got over the ball and I wasn't going to hit it until I knew it was going to scare the hole."

Vijay stuffed it in there eight feet beyond the hole, barely a couple of inches closer than his main rival.

Duval holed his birdie to momentarily tie it up, but Vijay immediately took the wind out of DD's sails by also sinking his birdie putt to regain the sole lead, and the rest was history.

"I knew I was taking the Green Jacket from then on," Vijay said.

TRUE TIGER RIVAL

Vijay's story taught me the valuable lesson of never giving another player any extra motivation, which is why I refrain from getting too animated when my man hits a great shot or holes or holes a big putt, or whatever. I prefer not to act in any way emotionally that could fuel another player to beat the player I'm caddying for, either today or down the track. I strive for a neutral persona, and I learned that from Vijay, the only player who in his prime managed to take down Tiger as often as vice-versa.

Think about it.

Jack Nicklaus in his heyday, from the early 1960s to the early '80s, had a lot of rivals who at least for a while gave as good as they got—Arnold Palmer, Gary Player, Billy Casper, Lee Trevino, Johnny Miller, Tom Weiskopf, Raymond Floyd, Watson, etc.

Who would qualify as a genuine rival to Tiger from 1997 to 2008?

Duval certainly for about 18 months from the autumn of 1997 until the spring of '99.

Phil Mickelson toward the end of Tiger's dominant period.

Els certainly went toe to toe with Tiger many times, but Tiger emerged victorious more often than not, much to Ernie's eternal disappointment.

And then there was Vijay.

Between June 1998 and October 2010, Tiger's reign as No. 1 was interrupted by only two players.

Duval occupied top spot for 15 weeks in 1999, while Vijay displaced Tiger for 26 weeks from September 2004 to March 2005, then three weeks later in March '05 and three more weeks in May '05. Vijay was No. 1 for 32 weeks all up, a record that is more impressive than it might seem at first glance, considering that it came while Tiger was at the peak of his powers.

Vijay's banner year was 2004, when he won nine times to Tiger's once.

He won a tour record 22 times after turning 40.

The Big Daddy not only had the game to push and often beat Tiger but had the mental package to thrive under the pressure.

Once he won the 2000 Masters and brought down Duval, Vijay had the confidence to take on anyone, and he relished battling Tiger.

He liked being pushed and was good enough to push back.

BAD PRESS

Vijay often refused to make himself available for media interviews, even when requested to do so by a PGA Tour official. We never spoke about it, but I sensed he did not believe he was accorded the respect his record deserved, and decided there was no value in being interviewed.

What would he gain?

I think he felt like the press did not talk to other players with similar records in the same way.

If it's not enjoyable and positive, why subject yourself to it. Some people say he had an obligation to talk, and I know the PGA Tour were displeased when he did not, but once you get on the bitter bus it's often hard to get off.

He figured the media needed him more than he needed them, and that they could kiss his ring. He wasn't going to suck up to anybody. He had a chip on his shoulder and didn't care who you were. The more he blew off the press, the worse press he got. And the more bad press he got, the less inclined he was to have anything to do with them. It was a vicious cycle.

Knowing him as well as I do, I am sure he thought, "Why am I going to grant you an interview for you to belittle me? I don't have to do that. I'm the Big Daddy."

So while Vijay in some respects contributed to his public image, I think it's a shame so many golf fans fail to truly appreciate how far he came from where he was born. It was truly an astonishing rags to riches story.

It would hardly be an exaggeration to say that he was disdained and whether he created that persona and brought it on himself I'm not sure, but I can tell you he did not give a damn.

He was going to be who he was, no matter what anyone said or thought.

He called me for my birthday recently, and while I appreciated the gesture, I had to have a bit of fun.

"Big Daddy," I said, "if people found out you're calling me for my birthday, your reputation would go downhill."

He started laughing. God forbid anyone should find out he was a real human being.

7

Taming a Beast

*And other stories of working for several
major champions (and a few that aren't)*

I've worked for some tough bosses over the years, but none
who came with a worse reputation for volatility than Darren
Clarke. Everybody outside the golf bubble thinks Clarke is the
nicest guy in the world, and he is—so long as you don't caddie
for him. But on the course, he is like an active volcano, ready
to erupt without warning.

Darren had not made a cut on either the PGA Tour or
European Tour in more than four months when I started a two-
week stint with him at Hartford in the summer of 2007.

His wife, Heather, had died of cancer the previous August
and his game had understandably gone into a tailspin as he tried
to pick up the pieces and carry on as a single father of two young
boys.

I knew from his reputation that he could be brutal to work
for at the best of times, an absolute beast on the course, and given
that he was mired in a slump with no end in sight, I knew he
would present a serious challenge to my player-management skills.

I'm not saying he meant to treat his caddies poorly, but he just let it out on his looper when he lost his temper, which happened with monotonous regularity when he was playing badly. If you were standing next to him, you just had to take it.

He had even made two of my caddie friends, J.P. Fitzgerald and Billy Foster, cry. They are both tough nuts, which gives you an idea of the invective they must have been subjected to.

I wanted to disarm Clarke right from the start and leave him with no chance of beating me down, so I immediately went on the offensive when we met in the parking lot at the TPC River Highlands.

"If you want to yell and scream and behave poorly, just knock yourself out, get it out of your system, and let it go," I said. "If you want to throw a club as far as you like, just let it go, I'll go and get it. I just want you to know up front that there's nothing you can say that is going to hurt my feelings. You can call me every name in the book and I'll tell you why, because, one, I don't have any feelings and, two, I have even less for you."

It was not your standard conversation with a new boss, and he clearly had never been spoken to like that before by a mere caddie.

In his thick Northern Irish brogue, he responded that he didn't really know how to take those comments.

"You can take them any way you like," I continued. "I don't give a shit."

I talked to him like a junkyard dog. It was all premeditated. He just needed some tough love.

Once they know they can't beat you, they just focus on playing golf, and he could certainly play. We have a saying that you want to work for a guy who can play and pay. Darren ticked both of those boxes.

Religious caddies add another verb to the saying. They want to work for someone who can play, pay, and pray.

I was never going to work full-time for Clarke, even if he had wanted it, because he was crazy. And besides, I was still with Fuzzy Zoeller at the time.

Clarke played well our first week together at Hartford but was mediocre on the greens and missed the cut, for which I must accept some responsibility.

There is a hole at that course, the par-five sixth, a dogleg right that always gave me trouble. At the time there were 15 bunkers, many of them strategically staggered to gobble up the second shot, and for the life of me I often struggled to come up with an ideal yardage when my man asked how far he needed to hit his layup. It was especially difficult because the yardages differed depending on what angle the player wanted to take.

I warned him in a practice round that I struggled to caddie that particular hole, and sure enough on Friday I gave him a bad yardage and laid him up right into the middle of a bunker. I just got it wrong, and provided a story that Darren subsequently relished telling at my expense, not that I blamed him.

Nevertheless, I remained in his employment for the following week's Buick Open at Warwick Hills in Michigan, where I whipped that donkey so hard he thought he was a thoroughbred.

We played the first two rounds with Justin Leonard, who tied for second that week, and Darren undoubtedly hit it as well as the 1997 British Open champion. But with three holes left we were in danger of missing another cut, needing to pick up two more shots to advance to the weekend.

At what was our 16th hole, the par-five seventh, Darren had a chance to get home in two, but his three-wood leaked into a greenside bunker.

He was absolutely steaming, even by his own standards, as he strode down the fairway, and I was looking up at the heavens trying to figure out something appropriate to say. At first, I had nothing, but within a few seconds it came to me. Fortunately, the long walk had given me time to think.

"Listen," I said, "I've seen you hole out bunker shots on TV before. Don't tell me you haven't. I've seen it. Get your head in the game here, pull yourself together."

Not that I had seen him hole any bunker shots on TV. I just made that part up. I figured that in all his years as a pro he must have done so a few times in front of the cameras.

We got a small piece of good news when we arrived at the bunker. The ball was sitting up perfectly, and it was slightly downhill from the top of the bunker to the hole. It was the sort of shot that, if struck perfectly, would trickle right down to the hole. Not that such a shot is ever easy, but it was the sort that a pro could picture and with the right execution imagine pulling off.

And he certainly pulled it off. He holed the bunker shot for an eagle and, suitably buoyed, parred his final two holes to make the cut with nothing to spare.

Clarke had a solid weekend and tied for 49th. Okay, it was not exactly headline-grabbing stuff, but under the circumstances it was just what the doctor ordered. It was the best tournament he'd had in eight months, and he cleared a hurdle that helped restore his confidence.

It took a while, but he won again the following April at the European Tour's Asian Open, and in 2011 of course had his crowning glory by winning the British Open at Royal St. George's.

MARK O'MEARA

Most of the players I worked for over the years were pretty normal guys, but there were an assorted handful of strange ones, and I'm not talking about Curtis.

Rather, Mark O'Meara was one of the most peculiar fellows I've ever met, which might surprise a few people, because he always came across as extremely normal during TV interviews.

I'm not saying he was a bad guy, but it didn't take me long to realize how insecure he was. When I started caddying for him in 2016, he immediately told me every tournament he'd won since he was a young boy, or a wee laddie, as the Scots would say.

Talk about a need to impress. It was as though I had never followed golf.

I knew most of the tournaments he had won, not that I cared. You would hope a double major champion—1998 Masters and British Open—wouldn't feel the need to tell you how good he was.

I'd never had a guy run down his list of victories. I thought to myself, "Does this guy really think I care about his whole life? Is he that insecure?"

The answer was yes.

When I told Fred Couples that story, Fred was not surprised. He did not particularly like O'Meara. O'Meara thought he should be in the Hall of Fame before Fred. If you think that, fair enough, keep it to yourself. But Mark told the whole world.

Early on while working for O'Meara I engaged in some small talk by asking him how many TVs he had in his man cave at home.

He responded by asking me to guess.

I wanted to say, "I don't give a fuck. What kind of a wanker asks that question?" I guessed 10. He said 27.

I was tempted to tell him he should go open an appliance store.

I had never met a guy who said "I" more than Lanny Wadkins—until I met O'Meara.

I worked for Mark for only a couple of weeks and left him the week before the Masters to work for Ernie Els. Mark was a little bitter at the time, though he has always been pleasant whenever we have crossed paths since.

STEVE ELKINGTON

Steve Elkington was another odd duck with whom I had a short stint. He was good to me, but a crazy guy.

Like Clarke and O'Meara, Elkington is a major champion—he beat Colin Montgomerie at the first extra hole at the 1995 PGA Championship at storied Riviera Country Club in Los Angeles.

I still remember Elkington doing something really smart. Instead of waiting for a golf cart to ferry him back to the 18th tee for the start of the playoff, Elkington and his caddie Dave Renwick strolled slowly back down the fairway, while Montgomerie was on the practice putting green.

That gave the Houston-based Aussie a few minutes to calm his nerves. By the time Montgomerie jumped in a cart for the 400-yard ride, Elkington was three-quarters of the way back to the tee, looking as loose as a goose.

He even walked slowly in the playoff in an effort to remain calm, and subsequently made a 20-foot birdie at the first extra hole to lift the Wanamaker Trophy.

I'm not saying he would not have won had he gotten a lift back to the tee as Monty did, but it was a great example of Elkington's golf smarts.

He was as hard as nails, one of the mentally toughest players I've ever encountered, possessing immense powers of focus and concentration.

Elk was all business. He put himself in the zone all the time and stayed in the zone. That's not easy to do, but he was rewarded with two Players Championship victories as well as a PGA Championship.

It didn't hurt that Elkington also had a silky smooth rhythmic swing that was regularly rated by his peers as one of the best on tour, if not the very best.

Among his idiosyncrasies, he did not have any head covers on his woods. He also liked you to stand by his right elbow and walk at his side. He never liked to walk by himself.

Elkington also made a habit of arriving very late for his rounds, not because he was running late, but by choice.

There were just too many distractions for his liking. He preferred to stay at his accommodation and go through every hole in his mind while he shadowboxed. He would then arrive on-site sometimes less than 30 minutes before his tee time, giving himself just enough time to hit a couple of drives, a couple of wedges, and a few putts. He was like a ghost.

Away from the course, nobody in the world could tell as many tall tales as Steve Elkington.

He never really got the level of respect that is usually afforded such a hell of a player. He was a regular winner and contender in big tournaments despite battling more injuries and illnesses than a dozen other random players put together.

But when he went to a bar it was not uncommon for nobody to know who he was.

When you're pals with Greg Norman and the Shark's getting all the attention, the ego's got to suffer a little bit.

Elkington once said he went fishing with Norman and caught a world-record marlin. And that while he was pulling it in, a shark jumped out of the water and ate it.

I worked for him for several months and he ended up firing me partly because I did not celebrate an ace enthusiastically enough for his liking.

It was the third hole at Sedgefield during the Wyndham Championship. When he questioned my reaction, I said, "You were aiming at it weren't you?"

His standards obviously weren't as high as mine! In all seriousness, I made it a policy to always remain equanimous on the course, which I felt helped keep my man on an even emotional keel.

As I detail in the Vijay chapter, I preferred my on-course reactions to be muted.

Still, that non-celebration was the straw that broke the camel's back. It was my last week with Elkington.

But I must say that he was generous. He liked to rent a house whenever possible on tour and would often let me stay with him for free.

With one proviso. I had to promise that I would take the money I saved in hotel accommodation and use it to buy Apple stock. He thought it was a company with a lot of growth potential. And he was right.

PAYNE STEWART

I also worked for the late Payne Stewart briefly, for two tournaments in the early 1990s, the Las Vegas Invitational in Nevada and the Disney World Classic in Florida.

This was long before cell phones became ubiquitous, and it was not always easy to track someone down back then.

When Payne wanted to hire me, he asked around on the range if anyone had my number, and one of the caddies must have passed along the home number of my Uncle Charlie. I am close to my uncle. He used to come out on tour regularly, and quickly got to know the other caddies. Once you drink with the caddies, you're in. He's a tax accountant who still handles the returns of a dozen or so caddies, which is why a lot of them knew his number.

So Stewart called Uncle Charlie's number in San Antonio, and his wife, Anna, answered the phone. Now it came to pass that Payne was her favorite golfer. She loved his knickers, NFL-themed outfits, good looks, charisma, everything about him.

Stewart had a six-year deal with the NFL in the first half of the 1990s to wear the colors of the NFL team closest to the tour event that he was playing. It certainly helped him stand out from his fellow pros who in those days were invariably decked out in drab, baggy khakis.

Anyway, my aunt picked up the phone and a voice at the other end said, "Hello, this is Payne Stewart; I'm looking for Cayce Kerr."

To which my skeptical aunt answered, "Yeah, right, you think you're going to pull that one on me," and promptly hung up the phone.

So I was being offered perhaps the job of a lifetime and my aunt cut him off abruptly.

Fortunately, Charlie had heard the conversation, and realized that it might have been Stewart and not a prank call.

A few seconds later the phone rang again, and my aunt picked it up, heard the same voice, and quickly put my uncle on the line. Charlie apologized for his wife having hung up the first time, and Payne proceeded to say that he was looking to get hold of me. He had parted company with his previous caddie, Mike Hicks, and planned to give me and another caddie, Scottie Steele, separate auditions, so to speak.

Stewart and Hicks had an on-again, off-again relationship, and Hicks was back on the bag by the time Stewart captured his 1999 U.S. Open victory at Pinehurst No. 2.

What made it tough auditioning for Payne was that he hired me for the Las Vegas and Disney tournaments, which were both played on three separate courses. They were all new to me, so despite trying to diligently do my homework as best I could, I did not know them as well as I would have liked.

You feel more comfortable and perhaps confident on tracks you have been around many times.

Unfortunately, I got passed up for the job in favor of Steele. I was disappointed of course, but Payne could not have been any nicer. What I remember most about Payne was how organized he was on the range.

He practiced diligently with every club, more than any golfer I've ever worked for.

A lot of players don't work on facets of the game that they're not good at—that is human nature, I guess—but Payne gave an equal amount of time to his driving, irons, short game, sand game, and putting.

There wasn't one box that he didn't check. He had his regimen down pat and he knew exactly what he wanted to work on when he came to the course. He had his routine and he did not deviate from it.

Stewart won three majors, most famously the 1999 U.S. Open, when he sank a 15-footer at the last to beat Phil Mickelson by a stroke.

His life was cut short in the most freakish of circumstances barely four months later when the private jet on which he was traveling lost cabin pressure, causing all six people on board, including the pilot and co-pilot, to pass out.

The plane, on autopilot, crashed when it ran out of fuel about four hours later into a South Dakota field on October 26. It was a Monday, and I was driving up Interstate freeway 55 heading north to Memphis when journalist Tim Rosaforte called and told me about the "ghost plane" carrying Stewart.

I burst into tears and had to pull over to the side of the road while I composed myself.

K.J. CHOI

K.J. Choi was the first Korean man to make it on the PGA Tour, a trailblazer who set the stage for what is now commonplace, a Korean player on the leaderboard.

Korean women were already highly successful on the LPGA Tour, but the men were a few years behind in taking their act on the road to the big time.

Choi landed at qualifying school in 1999 at Doral Resort in Miami and his management company IMG (International Management Group) rewarded me handsomely to caddie for him. They paid me like a slot machine, at least five grand from memory.

K.J. spoke very little English at the time, but he knew numbers, which was enough for us to communicate on a rudimentary level at least.

Choi duly earned his tour card, but only barely, on the number, as we say, without a shot to spare.

The top 35 players and ties qualified to play on tour in 2000, and Choi finished equal 35th. That fine margin changed his life, and he went on to win eight times on the PGA Tour.

Choi's wife, Hyunjung Kim, was so excited that her husband had punched his ticket to the PGA Tour that she said, "I love you"—not to K.J. but to me. That was the first time I had heard those words from a tour wife.

I also introduced K.J. to Jack Nicklaus that week. The Golden Bear was there to watch his son Gary, who was also at qualifying school, and who tied for 12th.

I worked for Choi for his first three months on tour. We started in Hawaii, where I taught him how to write a check. We went to a Korean barbeque restaurant every night that week in Honolulu. I picked him up in my van and drove him to and from the restaurant.

He was new to the United States, so I covered him like a blanket to make him comfortable in his new environment.

Choi was one of dozens of non-American players I worked for. I didn't care where they came from. I enjoyed caddying and adapting to the culture of the player I worked for, just little things like saying "g'day mate" to an Australian player.

As long as I could pull a couple of the words to help them feel at home, they did not feel so much like I was a foreigner. They realized you were making an effort when you did a little something extra to establish common ground.

GREG CHALMERS

Speaking of "g'day mate," I worked two tournaments for Greg Chalmers in 2002.

The left-handed Aussie tied for 38th at the Western Open in Chicago and then rode with me two hours up the road to Wisconsin for the Greater Milwaukee Open at Brown Deer Park, the course where Tiger Woods made his professional debut in 1996.

The moment I best remember from Milwaukee was a recovery shot Chalmers played from the woods at the ninth hole during the final round.

When we got to his ball, I saw no viable shot. I looked up, down, left, right, and I couldn't see anything.

He asked me what I liked, and for once I was completely lost for words. I could not give him an answer.

After a few seconds, I decided not to bullshit him. "I have absolutely no idea," I said.

That was the truth, and fortunately he chuckled.

Even better, he saw a sliver of an opening through the trees that he decided he could aim for, and proceeded to thread an astonishing eight-iron that somehow avoided every branch and found the green.

He got out of jail and eventually finished fifth, prompting his wife, Nicole, to kiss me on the lips, another first from a tour wife in my long career.

There would be no more kisses for me from Nicole, because that was my swan song with Chalmers. Zoeller and I had already decided to pair back up after a little separation, and at the time

I thought Fuzzy was a better player for me in the long run. I did not like breaking the news to Chalmers, but he was all class, and said he understood.

I headed straight to the British Open to work for Steve Jones, who finished tied for 43rd, and then returned to the U.S. to get back to work for Fuzzy at the Boston Champions Tour event.

MAC O'GRADY

I'll end this chapter with a blast from the past, a guy that older readers will probably remember but who might be a name unfamiliar to younger ones. I'm talking about the famed eccentric Mac O'Grady, a two-time PGA Tour winner in the mid-1980s.

O'Grady, among other things, was well known for not shying away from controversy. Once, after being fined by PGA Tour commissioner Deane Beman for allegedly insulting a volunteer in New Orleans, O'Grady called Beman a "thief with a capital T," according to the *New York Times*.

In an appearance on *The Late Show with David Letterman*, O'Grady flatly denied the allegation that he had insulted the volunteer, and described Beman as a "vindictive, abrasive, and callous man." O'Grady also claimed most top players were on beta-blockers, which strikes me as an exaggeration, not that I am naive enough to think that everyone was and is completely clean.

I got a taste of O'Grady when I worked for him for two rounds at the 1988 Bay Hill Classic in Orlando.

The circumstances under which I was hired were bizarre to say the least. I worked the first two rounds with George Burns, whose nickname in the caddyshack was the rather unflattering "Crash and Burn."

Burns shot 77, 75, and was absolutely fuming as he checked his card in the scoring tent. He was officially listed as a withdrawal, though he would have missed the cut anyway.

As chance would have it, we had played with O'Grady, who unlike Burns did make the cut. Hard though it is to believe, O'Grady had already used three caddies that week, and the tournament was only half over. Talk about hard to please.

Even before Burns had signed his card, O'Grady asked whether he could use me for the final two rounds, seeing as George was having the weekend off. That request did not sit well with Burns, who was already in a foul mood. In the Crash and Burn way, because he was crazy too, Burns barked, "I'm not Cayce's fucking agent."

I was happy to work the weekend, but O'Grady had a closing 78 to finish equal 43rd. Still, he owed me about a couple hundred bucks.

It amounted to little more than loose change for him, but Mac had a reputation of being funny with the money, so I asked him where he was staying at the next tournament, the Players Championship. He told me he would be at the Days Inn— you would be surprised at how many players back then stayed cheaply—which was convenient as I was booked at a nearby hotel.

So the following day I went to the Days Inn—this was before cell phones—and had the front desk clerk call his room. He answered the phone and I told him I was downstairs and ready to settle up. He said he was ready to leave for the course, and I got in the car with him, because I wanted my money sooner rather than later.

As we headed to the course, he had this new-age music playing that sounded like the wind. I already knew he was different, but that just confirmed it. Not that there was anything wrong with that, but it was not something that tour players typically did.

We arrived at the course, disembarked in the players' parking lot, and took a long walk all the way past the driving range to the TaylorMade trailer. After we entered, O'Grady pulled out a checkbook and wrote me a check with a fuchsia Sharpie. I mean, who writes a check with a fuchsia Sharpie?

He handed me the check and said, "Find your own ride back" to the hotel.

It was something like 5:00 PM, maybe later, and seeing as it was only Monday nearly everyone had already left the course, so I went over to the transportation trailer and told the volunteers who ran the operation that I was caddying for Hubert Green.

I told them what had happened and they kindly gave me a ride back to the Days Inn, where I had left my van.

I was thinking what a piece of work O'Grady was. Are you kidding me? The guy gave me a ride out to the course, wrote me a check, and then just left me to find my own way back. Not surprisingly, I never worked for him again. Two days was enough.

8

Tiger

*Why caddies have always loved
the incandescent superstar*

Hindsight bias might lead one to believe that Tiger Woods was always destined for greatness, but that was not universally obvious when he turned professional in 1996. I vividly recall the talk on the range at Tiger's first tournament as a pro, the Greater Milwaukee Open at Brown Deer Park in Wisconsin.

Nike had just announced with great fanfare that it had signed Woods to a five-year contract, which *Golf World* reported to be worth $40 million. Woods also had $20 million in other deals, including one with Titleist, according to Ron Sirak, then the Associated Press golf writer, so it was hardly surprising that Tiger was the talk of the town that week.

To reveal that the range was awash with petty jealousy would be an understatement. Those poor little players had their egos bent out of shape. It seemed that half the pros in the field believed that with so much sponsorship money going to Tiger, there would be little left over for the rest. Some players were outraged. How dare Nike waste so much money on an unproven commodity who did not even have his PGA Tour card.

It was hilarious listening to the bleating.

Yes, this multi-ethnic teenager had won three straight U.S. Amateur Championships, but that was like playing in the minors. Now he was in the big leagues.

Skepticism abounded as to whether Tiger would be the real deal. Nobody knew at the time that he would be a world beater for years to come.

Players had gotten used to the media crowning top amateurs as the next Jack Nicklaus, be it Bobby Clampett or John Cook, so it was sort of understandable that they were not convinced Woods would be arguably the greatest ever.

They might have complained less had they known that Tiger was going to be such a megastar that he single-handedly would be responsible for an explosion of tour purses over the following decade, which trickled down to every player on tour.

While the pros were whining, think about how much pressure Tiger was under. Nike had just signed him for an unheard-of amount, and he did not even have his tour card.

He had to earn that the old-fashioned way, either by winning or earning enough money over the remaining nine events of the season to finish at least 125th on the money list.

Otherwise, he was going to go to qualifying school at the end of the year. There were no guarantees.

PROPHETIC WORDS

I stayed with a friend that week and we had a backyard barbie every night. Of course, Tiger was the main topic of conversation, and I couldn't help recalling a conversation I had had a couple of years previously with tour rules official Vaughan Moise. On top of his day job, Moise was an accomplished amateur, who was beaten by Tiger 2&1 in the first round of the 1994 U.S. Amateur Championship.

I used to transport the rules officials' radios between tournaments in my van, so I knew them all well, and I remember gently teasing Moise about losing to a kid.

His response?

"Let me tell you, this guy can play the game like nothing I've ever seen."

Prophetic words indeed.

Tiger was popular with the caddies right off the bat. For starters, we were delighted he employed a regular tour caddie as his bagman, rather than bringing out a friend.

Tiger lured Mike "Fluff" Cowan away from Peter Jacobsen. Fluff did not have any enemies, so he was a popular choice.

In an interview with Curtis Strange before the Milwaukee tournament, Tiger said that his goal was to win, that he had once told his dad that "second sucks and third's even worse."

The remark prompted Strange to push back and say to Tiger "you'll learn" not to make comments like that which come across as being brash.

While you could understand where Strange was coming from, you could also understand if Tiger thought the two-time U.S. Open champion was being patronizing.

Strange later acknowledged that he had not appreciated how great Woods would be. At the same time, Strange maintained that for most players, runner-up was not always a bad result.

And for most players he would be correct. After all, Nicklaus finished second in 19 majors, one more time than he won. Jack used the law of averages to become the most prolific major winner of all time, with three more than Tiger.

Tiger foreshadowed what would be a career of spectacular feats by making a hole-in-one in his pro debut in Milwaukee.

Talk about box office. He had barely turned pro and already he was dominating the media coverage.

Though he finished tied 60th, he settled into life as a pro ominously quickly, following it up with 11th place at the Canadian Open the following week.

After that it was on to Moline, Illinois, where he stole the spotlight from the fledgling Presidents Cup by taking the third-round lead, only to be outplayed in the final round by Ed Fiori, a short, plump journeyman who was nobody's idea of a superstar.

I once stopped by Fiori's house in Sugar Land, Texas, and learned that of his four PGA Tour victories, one tournament did not even send him the trophy that was promised. When you only win four times, you'd like to have all three trophies.

Not that Ed really cared too much. He had earned himself an eternal place in golf trivia history. He even named his boat *Tiger Killer*.

But after Tiger's Moline disappointment, he won two starts later in Las Vegas. The floodgates had opened for the first of a record-equaling 82 tour wins.

"KIND OF"

In a greenside interview moments after clinching his maiden pro win, Tiger was asked whether he ever dreamed he could accomplish the feat so quickly.

"Kind of," he said.

Seven months later he blew away the field to win the Masters by 12 strokes, a game-changing performance that was eventually overshadowed by Fuzzy Zoeller's infamous "fried chicken" comment.

I was Fuzzy's caddie at the time, and have devoted an entire chapter to that saga (See Fried Chicken chapter), including the anecdote on how much class Tiger showed to break the ice when he coincidentally was grouped with Fuzzy the following year.

It was at the 1997 Masters that the penny finally dropped—for those still in need of convincing—that the game had a talent like nothing we had ever seen.

He threw out the oldest cliche at Augusta, that it doesn't start until the back nine on Sunday. That year it was well and truly over by the start of the back nine on Sunday.

There was a changing of the guard and Tiger just plowed through the pressure like General Grant went through Richmond during the Civil War. He embarrassed Augusta and annihilated that course to the extent that they had to redo it and make it Tiger-proof. Talk about one man changing the face of the game.

Tiger was here to stay, and if you wanted to beat him, you'd better up your game, get into the gym, start working out, have a different strategy, do whatever it took to get better. I think he lifted the performance of the other players, because everyone knew that if you were going to beat this guy, you'd better bring your A game.

Speaking of which, Woods rubbed a lot of players the wrong way the month after that Masters blowout by winning the Byron Nelson Classic with what he described as his "C-plus" game. Some pros thought that comment was patronizing, but I reckon it was just Woods being honest. He really was that good.

When he had his A game, such as at Augusta, he blew away the field, but he could still contend and sometimes win with his B or C game. He was just in a different class.

He was such a huge presence that whenever the groupings were released, word spread like wildfire who he was playing with.

It was always a big deal to caddie in his group. Just to be out with Tiger, and to have those memories of the experience was something that, to a man, we cherished. We weren't rooting for the guy, because we were working for players competing against him, but we definitely weren't rooting against him either.

And we were always dreaming that perhaps if we did a good job for our man he might notice, and that there might be a chance he might hire us one day.

As I mentioned above, Tiger was popular with the caddies from day one.

I would almost say he was beloved. He was polite, treated us with respect, and was responsible for purse increases, which meant we were making more money.

He knew most of our names and was so professional and cordial with all of us. He would shake our hands on the tee box, with that incandescent smile that was worth millions of dollars.

He was genuine and would say, "Hello, good luck, have a good round," or words to that effect. I remember being a little surprised the first time he did it. He was the ultimate gentleman.

However, once he got those niceties out of the way he was all business. He did not banter with us. Everyone handles the first tee differently, because we're getting ready to start battle. Some players don't want to be talked to, some don't want to be bothered, some don't want to be looked at. They've got to get in their own zone.

Tiger got rid of all that up front, and once he did that, he was ready to get into his next mode.

I realized Tiger's fame transcended golf as never before when I was in a Jiffy Lube auto shop in Michigan one day having my van's oil changed. The female manager had written "Go Tiger, Flint Michigan" on a big, yellow, fluorescent board inside the garage.

When I told her I was in town for the tournament, the now-defunct Buick Open, she begged me for tickets. The woman didn't know anything about golf but followed Tiger on TV all the time. I got her a couple of free passes and she was absolutely thrilled.

SEX SCANDAL

I cannot write about Tiger without addressing the 2009 sex scandal which led to the collapse of his marriage after he was caught in multiple affairs, including with adult film actresses, strippers, and party girls. People ask me whether I knew at the time that Tiger had been so busy with his extracurricular activities.

No, I did not. I was not part of his inner circle, and Tiger kept a pretty low profile. But was I surprised? Not in the least.

Everyone knew there were beautiful girls who came to golf and sometimes beautiful girls want to be with someone who's rich, good looking, and successful.

It comes with the territory of being No. 1 at anything.

As Tom Jones once sang, "It's not unusual to be loved by anyone."

When my old friend Billy Foster caddied for Seve Ballesteros, it was commonplace for women to give Billy their phone number to pass onto Seve. Billy would sometimes finish a round with a pocketful of numbers.

And think about Tiger's upbringing. His father had ingrained in him an ethic to work, work, work. But life is about balance. You need a bit of fun as well, and Tiger had so many opportunities.

Imagine you're a guy and there are 10 Playboy Bunnies every week offering themselves to you on a silver platter. Because you are married, at first you say, "No, no, no."

But most guys can only say no so many times before their resistance weakens. By the 10th occasion, it has been worn down. I mean, what heterosexual guy wouldn't want to be with these beautiful women? Can you imagine the temptation?

Eventually you're going to think to yourself, "What am I, a robot?" and you're going to say yes to one of the girls. Then she takes her clothes off, and you're thinking, "Holy cow, I'm human."

He probably got a taste of the fun and knew that being on tour he had ample opportunities to indulge. A player, or a caddie for that matter, might have one woman in New Orleans, another in Houston and another in Phoenix, for example. You see them once a year and they want to be with you and you're thinking, "How good is this?"

It's not as though Tiger was the only one on tour misbehaving. As we like to say, there is one thing a player's caddie always knows that the wife doesn't—the name of the player's girlfriend.

Trust me, there are caddies who have little sugar shacks around the country. So when I found out Tiger was doing it too I didn't think it made him a bad person. I thought it made him human.

I know women probably look at it very differently, but as far as men go, I think those who criticized Tiger were mainly jealous. Who isn't going to be jealous of guys who've got women throwing their bras and panties at them? They're not throwing them at me, that's for sure.

But I don't want to dwell on Tiger's sex scandal any longer. He paid his price in the form of an expensive divorce and the humiliation of issuing a public apology with a speech at a painfully awkward televised gathering, with his mother among the audience, sitting in the front row. I can't imagine how embarrassing that must have been.

Tiger has since become an elder statesman and the following generation of players to a man feel indebted to him for growing the pie.

The jealousy many of his peers felt in 1996 has been replaced by gratitude.

Knee and back injuries prevented him from having a good crack at matching or surpassing Nicklaus' major victory record—Tiger has 15 to Jack's 18—and the debate will go on for decades as to who was better.

Nicklaus certainly was superior when it came to consistency and longevity, but few would disagree that Tiger's best was the best that anyone has ever seen. A record-matching 82 PGA Tour victories is a dry if impressive statistic, but it hardly captures the verve, panache, and excitement he brought to the tour.

It was a blessing to work in the same era as an unsurpassed golf genius.

He was a rare case of someone who not only lived up to the hype, but over-delivered, and for that everyone who loves watching golf or makes a living on the PGA Tour should be grateful.

PART THREE

MY LIFE

9

Stumbling Around

From rags to riches to rags again

I was born in 1960, in San Antonio, Texas, where I spent my first five years on this little planet we call home. My grandparents on my mother's side were Mexican, on my father's side Irish, so I'm a second-generation American, and the second of three brothers.

My mother was a public servant for the federal government, working variously at the Department of Labor, Department of the Interior, and at the Equal Employment Opportunity Commission. My father was in the military, a maintenance worker on presidential aircraft in hangars five, six, and seven at Andrews Air Force Base in Maryland, just south of the capital of the United States, Washington D.C.

When we first moved to Maryland so that he could take up his new post at Andrews, we lived at the end of Poplar Hill Lane in Clinton, just outside the base, which had two excellent golf courses on the property. The head pro at the time was a guy named Fred King. Our house almost backed onto the course, and we were so close to the boundary that my brothers and I could crawl through a hole that had been cut in the base's wire fence, sneak onto the course, and steal balls. That was my first taste of a game I would come to love.

Someone reported the theft of golf balls and word got around that the authorities had been sniffing around our neighborhood seeking answers. We never snuck onto the base again.

A couple of years later our family moved a few miles south. Our address in Prince George's County was still in Clinton, which was also the childhood home long ago of Mary Surratt, the first woman to be hanged by the U.S. government.

My story turned out considerably better.

I would describe our upbringing as middle-class, perhaps bordering on lower middle-class. We were not poor, but money was tight. Our family did not have a lot of discretionary income.

I learned quickly that if I wanted money, I had to earn it myself.

At least my father, unlike many in the armed forces, did not have to move again after he began working at Andrews, so I was able to plant roots and stay in the same place for much of my upbringing.

Funny then that I have been perpetually on the move ever since.

I call San Antonio my home these days because that is where my mother now lives. She returned there after my parents divorced.

But on any given day you are more likely to find me in another part of the country, either caddying or, as is more often the case these days, working on one of my business projects.

I have also been overseas too often to count and have made it a policy throughout my career never to leave home without a passport, because when a last-minute offer pops up, you must be ready to go.

I was never particularly interested in school. I didn't really want to be there. My behavior was poor. I wish now that I had been a more diligent student.

My highest grades were three As and three Bs, but they were easy subjects, so I considered them fake numbers that didn't really count. One such subject was physical education.

From a young age I was more interested in making money than hitting the books.

If I wanted money, I had to get it myself.

My goal in life was to be a millionaire. I didn't know how I was going to achieve that, but I was determined to figure it out. Everybody's got to have a dream. My whole life I just wanted to be on the go, so as it turned out, caddying was the perfect job for me. You didn't have to stay in one place more than seven days, whether you behaved poorly or otherwise.

As for sports, I followed the path of most American boys in those days by playing baseball (first base) and football (linebacker) from a young age. I wasn't particularly good at either, but I loved sports and found I had a knack for boxing.

SUGAR RAY LEONARD

Boxing felt better than baseball and football because I got to indulge in the primal thrill of punching people in the face, and I won five national Golden Glove titles. I boxed in the same era and state as Sugar Ray Leonard, and we even fought on the same card occasionally at Prince George's Community College. Fortunately, I was in a different weight class, so never had the honor of having him punch my lights out.

It was common at the time for anyone in Sugar Ray's weight class to move up or down a class as quickly as possible. We boxers might have been mad, but we weren't stupid.

Sugar Ray was a man on a mission, and nobody from Maryland boxing circles was surprised that he became a world champion and all-time great.

I boxed for seven years, had a 102–5 career record, and knocked out a lot of guys, though not as many as Sugar Ray, before quitting at the age of 17, at the urging of my mother. She wanted me to keep my teeth and avoid having my face disfigured. I often think that maybe I could have made it to the top in boxing, but who knows? Sure, I have some regrets wondering what might have been, but I'm happy the way life has turned out. And at least my face is still in order.

PATTY BERG

My father introduced me to golf when I was 14 or 15. He had a set of MacGregor clubs and took me to a clinic at the Andrews Base where I watched a woman named Patty Berg.

I did not know Patty Berg from Patty Duke, but subsequently found out Berg was a pioneer for women's golf, a founder of the LPGA and a winner of 15 major championships, a women's record to this day.

Berg served in the Marine Reserves during World War II and continued to give of her time in later years with free clinics for military golfers and their families. I could not believe how good she was. Her accuracy was uncanny.

She had a guy stand out on the range and she hit balls at him, again and again with such precise ball flight and uncanny accuracy that he could catch them with a baseball glove while barely moving. She would instruct the catcher to move forward or backward, depending on what club she wanted to hit.

It was like watching a magic trick over and over. How could someone be that good, I wondered?

Golf wasn't particularly cool back in the '70s. It was still viewed as a game primarily for geeks. It certainly wasn't as sexy as being the high school football quarterback. You didn't get any girls throwing themselves at you because you played golf, but that visit to watch Berg fueled my interest in the game.

My dad belonged to a club called Robin Dale, which closed only a few years ago. Membership was $500 a year. There was nothing fancy about the place, but it was a good place for a kid to go.

I was self-taught and never took a lesson, started out shooting 100 or more, then gradually improved to the 90s, and then the 80s. I shot in the 70s a couple of times, but that was as far as it went.

I was an 85-shooter for the most part and never aspired to be a pro, because quite frankly I didn't have the talent. Golf, you could say, was my weakest sport. I played on the high school team only because it often got me out of class and we played for free.

Socially, I had one good friend growing up. He sometimes stayed overnight at my house, but we more often spent the night at his house, because his parents didn't have a curfew. My parents had a 12 o'clock curfew, which is about the time the party usually started.

Not that I was a big party animal. In truth, I was a bit of a loner. I was not picked on thankfully, but I didn't hang around the jocks, didn't hang around the dopers, didn't hang around the drinkers, didn't hang around any cliques. I liked being a clique of my own. I just wanted to work and make lots of money. I was a busy boy.

I quickly figured out that if I wanted money, I had to do honest (or mostly honest) labor, unless I wanted to rob a bank or something, which didn't seem like a good idea.

I was 10 years old when I started my first money-making endeavor. I made up some flyers with our home phone number printed on them, offering to do odd jobs around the house, mowing the lawn, painting, whatever.

I put them in everyone's mailbox in the neighborhood and sure enough the phone started ringing and I had my first source of income.

Soon afterward I started delivering newspapers—the *Washington Evening Star* every afternoon and the local publication, the *Prince George's Sentinel*, once a week.

Back then the paper boy had to collect his money from customers at the end of the month, a task that taught me at a young age the subtleties of getting paid on time. Collecting money is an art. I discovered the best line to use on someone who owed me money was "Can we settle up?"

It was not offensive, and it worked smoothly. Sometimes people would ask me to come back the following day.

In that case it was best to pin them down specifically.

"Tomorrow it is then. What time? Okay, three o'clock. I look forward to seeing you then."

I would leave customers an envelope to put the money in.

On the paper route we'd make extra money from some older people by placing the paper on their doorstep rather than just sticking it in the mailbox.

We saved them from having to walk to the mailbox and we'd get some tips for the extra service we provided.

It was a job that many kids from my era did back in the day and it was time well spent in learning some business basics, such as delivering your product on time, maintaining a friendly disposition, and keeping track of your financial ledger.

SELLING WEED

I sold cinnamon sticks, bubble gum, and other candy in junior high, but when I got to high school I stumbled into a more lucrative enterprise—selling marijuana.

I worked picking tobacco at a local farm during the summer, and that's where the source found me. He had a source that supplied him with lots of pot and he knew I knew everybody in high school. He asked me whether I smoked weed and I said, "Absolutely not, it makes you stupid."

But he was not deterred, stating accurately that teenagers loved the stuff, and tantalizingly dangled a fat profit margin in front of me.

"Let's do the math," he said.

He said he would sell me the weed for $350 a pound and that I could flog it in small batches and nearly double my money. I was convinced. He would throw the contraband in the back of my truck, and I'd hand him an envelope of cash.

There were only two strands in my area back then—Colombian and Acapulco gold.

Acapulco gold was a sexy name. It had a little bit of gold on the leaf. That's how you knew it was Acapulco gold. I could look at it, hold it with my hands, rub it with my fingers, put it to my nose, and tell you if it was good.

I couldn't keep up demand once I started selling it at school, because everyone knew I was the man.

I would sell half an ounce for $20, or $17.50 for friends. That was the going rate back then.

For a while I sold between one and three pounds a week, pocketing a tidy profit of at least $200 a pound. I thought I was a gangster and that it was the greatest job in the world. I did it for my final two years in high school.

HONEST LABOR

Back in the legitimate business world, my older brother took over a company that cleans furnaces and fireplace chimneys in the Washington metro area. The business was owned by the father of my brother's girlfriend at the time. The man was retiring, so my mother got an SBA loan of $25,000 to buy the company. That's how my brother got started. More than four decades later, he still runs the company, Johnson Chimney Service.

I worked there for a couple of years, cleaning chimneys and getting covered in soot.

The best skill I learned in that job was map reading. Back then before GPS made navigating easy, it could be tricky to find an address in the hilly Washington area.

But after a while I could interpret any map or street directory so well that there wasn't a place I couldn't find. That experience held me in good stead once I got on the road as a caddie.

My other brother graduated from Texas Christian University but wasn't very ambitious. He now works as an Uber driver in Raleigh, North Carolina. One thing he's never been in though, he's never been in a hurry.

One of the most profitable jobs I dabbled in as a teenager was buying firewood from the Amish in nearby St. Mary's country. One summer and fall a friend and I drove down to an Amish lumberyard and bought this slab wood, which was basically tree bark. But it was good wood, and the Amish would charge us $1.25 or $1.50 a truckload depending on the wood's quality. They didn't have any use for the excess wood, and by selling it to us they got it off their hands without having to worry about any labor costs.

We would fill the back of my pickup truck, drive home, chop it up, and sell it for about $60 in our local neighborhood. It was especially popular in autumn, when people were stocking up their wood for cozy winter fires. We would stack the wood for our customers. As soon as we were done selling one load, we would hightail back to the lumberyard for more. We would often make two or three trips a day.

I also worked at the commissary at Andrews Air Force Base, bagging groceries, and I'd take them out to the car on a cart and people would give me a tip, normally $1, but sometimes $2 for a big order, or maybe 50 cents for a small one. I'd average $100 a day doing that.

Then at night I worked loading trailers for United Parcel Service, better known as UPS. I've been hustling my whole life and have always had money in my pocket.

Another job was selling flowers on a street corner on Pennsylvania Avenue in the heart of D.C.

A friend's father owned a florist shop and a group of us would take several bunches each and sit there like poor White kids waiting for people to buy them. After a while of so-so business, I thought of a better idea, so I went to a local McDonald's and offloaded my flowers there, because there were always people at McDonald's.

That's when I learned to take business to wherever the best market was.

Perhaps the best paying job I had as a teenager was working for a concrete construction company which had a contract with the Army Corps of Engineers to build a dam on the Potomac River. I worked there for a couple of months and though it was hard work, it paid almost $20 an hour, which was a lot of money for a young man back in the 1970s. I thought I was rich.

I always felt there was nothing that I couldn't do but none of it amounted to anything long-term because I was still out there finding myself.

In my early twenties I moved to the Carolinas and sold time-shares in Myrtle Beach and in the storied Pinehurst area.

I was successful and the money soon rolled in. I had a girl-friend I was absolutely besotted with. Life was good, but then I got this awful disease called "love sickness." I was completely in love with this girl and then she dumped me.

Oh my god, I thought I would never recover from that.

I'd saved $400,000 and had frittered away every penny. How could I blow through that amount? By living the high life in the expectation that the money would never dry up, silly behavior by a young man who didn't know any better.

My girlfriend and I took a long trip to Europe, visiting London, Switzerland, France, and Italy. And we did it in luxury, no expenses spared. We certainly didn't do *Europe on $20 a Day* (the title of a famous tourist guide at the time). More like $320 a day.

DUMPED AND BROKE

Then we went to Florida for a month—and then she dumped me. I wasn't prepared for that. I was in my mid-twenties, broke, completely busted, and inconsolable.

I'd frittered away nearly every penny, was struggling both financially and emotionally, so that's when I returned home to Maryland and moved back in with my father and tried to figure out my next move in life.

Dad told me to take time to lick my wounds and regroup. I had been almost halfway to my goal of becoming a millionaire, without any formal education beyond high school, and now I had to start all over again.

Mentally I was a wreck and for several months I did nothing, but very slowly, almost unnoticeably at first, I found my mind incrementally getting to a better place.

I was ready to go back to work. At the time I did not really have a plan, but I knew I had to start at the bottom.

There was a famous liquor store on Naylor Road in D.C. called Bar 51 (since renamed 51 Liquor) and I started working there as the nighttime manager for $7.50 an hour, and everyone I knew thought I was nuts. The store was in a rough, predominantly Black neighborhood but I was very comfortable. I had once worked briefly at a friend's liquor store less than a mile away, so I was in my backyard so to speak.

We got robbed once by a drunk man with a rifle, but I grabbed it from him and used my famous left hook to knock him out. When the police arrived, I told them the man was inebriated.

"He'll be fine," I recall saying to the cops. "Just throw some water on him, he'll wake up."

That was the only time we got robbed during my time there. It was a popular place with good prices and good customers who loved to party and loved to drink.

We had three cash registers. I worked the middle register and on weekends the place was hopping, customers often lined up six deep.

I wouldn't say I was miserable there, but let's be honest, it wasn't a dream job. I was just doing the best I could in the moment, making ends meet while I struggled looking for direction.

I had been there three months, constantly ruminating on what path to take in life, when a customer came in, a young Black guy wearing a new Congressional Country Club cap.

Not to be disrespectful, but at the risk of sounding stereotypical, I didn't think he looked like a member. I wasn't in a neighborhood that breeds Congressional members, so I said, "Hey, brother, what do you know about that golf course?"

He replied, and I quote verbatim, "I'm a motherfucker caddie out there."

"How much bread do you make?" I inquired.

When he said he took home $1,000 a week, all cash, there was no need for further discussion. I asked him for the name of the caddie master and had a new plan in life.

It was the last night I ever worked at the liquor store.

10

Tour Beckons

*From Congressional club caddie
to major champion in four months*

The day after my chance liquor store encounter with that Congressional caddie, which is detailed in the previous chapter, I arrived at Congressional Country Club bright and early on a crisp March morning in 1987 and introduced myself to the caddie master.

I had never been in such salubrious golf surroundings. The property's 36 holes, situated in leafy Bethesda, Maryland, just outside Washington D.C.'s famous beltway, has been a favored locale of the capital's political and business elite since its founding just over a century ago. Long-ago presidents Coolidge, Taft, Hoover, Wilson, and Harding were lifetime members, but the club's history was hardly on my mind that day. Rather, I was thinking of money.

The caddie master's name was Bill Moran, and he told me I looked like a shady character, but he would give me a chance. That, I said, was all I sought. I went into my first ever caddyshack—I was the only White guy in there—and waited to be called for a bag.

All the caddies had nicknames—"Skunk," "Screwball," "Snake," "Popeye," and so on.

The caddies passed their time playing cards, usually either a game called Tunk or another named Coon Can. I was initially unfamiliar with either game, but they did not take long to learn.

I was last on the totem pole, so had to be patient for a bag. But when Mr. Moran finally summoned me, I got my loop and enjoyed it enough to come back the next day and do it all over again. I couldn't get enough of the place at first. The caddies at Congressional soon started to call me Mr. Turnaround because every time I finished 18 holes, I was ready to go another 18.

We were allowed to play on Monday when the course was closed to members, and the other caddies loved betting. I insisted we settle up in cash on the 18th green.

Not that I was particularly good, but I had enough game to take their money more often than not, so they started calling me "Pro."

It was time for me to come up with a real nickname, though. One that would stick. The club pro's name was Kent Casey, so I figured that was as good a name as any. The name stuck and I've been known as "Cayce" ever since, rather than my real name, David.

ONWARDS AND UPWARDS

Congressional members were very high end, owners of established companies, lawyers, doctors, politicians. They were hardly down on their luck. It's one of the poshest country clubs in the D.C. area. If you're a member at Congressional, people want to know you because they want to play there.

As for the membership fee, it goes something along the old line that if you have to ask how much, you probably can't afford it. *Forbes* magazine reported in 2018 that the initiation fee was $120,000, with a 10-year waiting list.

The members paid well. We made good money for those days, at least $100 a loop, sometimes up to $140. The caddie who had tipped me off at the liquor store was right. I was living at home, so my overheads were low, and in less than three months I had already saved $10,000. I only needed $990,000 more to become a millionaire and was already thinking beyond club caddying.

I knew that Congressional, a frequent site of major championships over the years, had also hosted the PGA Tour's Kemper Open the previous seven years—Greg Norman won in a playoff in 1986—but in 1987 it moved down the road to the new TPC Avenel, and I decided to check it out.

I was already getting tired of watching amateurs, because most of them were terrible and it quickly ceased to be enjoyable, so I staked out the parking lot at Avenel on tournament week to observe and listen.

Caddies always waited in the parking lot for their player to arrive and I wanted to extort information to find out how the system worked. From the way they dressed and talked, it didn't take long to figure out that 99 percent of the caddies were undesirable reprobates like me.

They talked about ways to cut costs—I discovered they often shared three to a hotel room—and discussed how to get to the next tournament. It was a struggle for most caddies back then because most purses in 1987 were only $600,000. A caddie's standard 5 percent cut of the prize money—10 percent for the win—along with a base wage of a few hundred dollars, did not go a long way.

A lot of caddies did not own a car and traveled from tournament to tournament by bus.

Lest I get accused of embellishment, I will acknowledge that there were a few financially comfortable caddies who worked for the top players, but they had a clique of their own. They didn't want anything to do with a new guy, because that guy might take your job down the road.

I hardly said a word the whole week, but eventually spoke with a few guys who told me I would have to buy a yardage book and learn how to read it.

FIRST TOUR JOB

After that week of observation at Avenel, I decided that surely with a bit of application I could learn to do the job as well as most of the caddies who already had bags. So that's when I decided to take my act on the road. A caddie at Avenel had told me that his player, Brad Greer, was playing so poorly that he was dumping him for someone better. I had never heard of Greer, but that was the only name I needed.

The next tournament was at Westchester Country Club in the wealthy county of the same name north of New York City, and I told my dad I was going to drive up the New Jersey Turnpike in my 1977 metallic blue Camaro and see if I could find a bag.

I slept in my car in a hotel parking lot, got up before dawn, and went inside to a bathroom where I washed up to make myself look vaguely presentable.

I drove past the multi-million-dollar mansions on the leafy side streets adjacent to the club. It was still dark and there was no security that early at the course entrance, so I drove in and parked in a discreet spot and began to stake out the players' parking lot.

I had done some homework to find out what Greer looked like.

Back then, just about the only place to get a job was the parking lot. There were no mobile phones, no texting, no social media, so the smart strategy was to wait in a judicious place and when you saw a golfer carrying his own bag, it generally indicated that he did not have a caddie.

You had to be on your toes, pay attention, and attack your prey as soon as he got out of the car. It did not pay to be shy. I have been accused of a lot of things, but shyness is not among them.

I nailed Greer as soon as he got out of his car. I sidled up and without any small talk said, "Do you need a caddie?" That's all I said, and it worked.

He said "Yes," told me how much he paid—$300 plus the usual prize-money percentage of 10 percent for a win and 5 percent for any other position—so I picked up the bag and went to work. I wasn't in a position to negotiate.

He missed the cut and fired me after that first week, for the rather bizarre reason that he did not like my tennis shoes. I didn't want to get sacked again for having crappy shoes, so I used part of my $300 to buy myself a new pair.

While it was not exactly a fairytale start to my professional caddying career, it was at least a start, and I've been going ever since.

After my PGA Tour debut at Westchester, I returned home for a week off while the big boys headed out west for the U.S. Open at Olympic Club in California. Scott Simpson was a surprise winner there, beating Tom Watson by a shot, and then the tour immediately headed back east for the Greater Hartford Open at TPC Connecticut in Cromwell, next to the Connecticut River.

The tournament back then attracted some of the biggest galleries on tour, and I had lined up a job with a Southern California journeyman named Ted Lehmann—not to be confused with 1996 British Open champion and former world No. 1 Tom Lehman.

Lehmann was a nice guy but not quite good enough to stay on the PGA Tour, as it turned out. He played in 29 tournaments in 1987 but made only five cuts, lost his card, and after that made only sporadic tour appearances in 1992, 1996, and 2000.

I worked for him at Hartford and the following week at the Canadian Open. He missed the cut both times and then told me he would be looking for a different looper at the next tournament, which, as coincidence would have it, was in Williamsburg, Virginia, not far from my hometown.

I arrived at the Anheuser-Busch Classic at Kingsmill without a job but found a bag for a Tuesday practice round with Canadian Ray Stewart.

But my performance that morning evidently was not enough to clinch the deal for the tournament proper.

Stewart left me hanging afterward, telling me he was going into the locker room to have lunch and would let me know afterward whether he wanted to engage my services.

Knowing the writing was on the wall, I decided to be proactive.

"DO YOU NEED A CADDIE?"

I saw this guy on the practice putting green named Hubert Green and didn't need to be told that he was a tour legend, with 19 PGA Tour titles under his belt, including two majors—the 1977 U.S. Open at Southern Hills in Oklahoma and the 1985 PGA Championship at Cherry Hills in Colorado. Hard as it was to believe, he didn't have a caddie. I was to find out later that his previous looper had just quit because Green was such a tough boss. He wasn't known as "the Doberman" for nothing, not that it would have bothered me had I been privy to the information. I approached Green and introduced myself.

I said, "I've been around golf all my life and I've already been 18 holes today. Do you need a caddie?"

He said, "Well I've been around golf all my life and are you saying you want to go 18 holes again?"

I told him, "Yes, sir, I'm ready," picked up the bag, and carried it for the next five years.

Green was past his prime by then and did not win again after the '85 PGA Championship, but he was only 40 at the time and I could not believe I had landed such a big name so quickly. I called my dad on the phone and excitedly told him the news and that Green was paying me $500 for the week.

Not only that, but Green had offered me the keys to his van and said I could use it if I took his clothes to the dry cleaner and collected them when they were ready. He even let me drive it between tournaments, so I didn't have to worry about arranging transportation. (See On the Road Again chapter.)

I remember my dad saying, "Son, don't screw this one up."

Well thanks for the vote of confidence, Pop!

Green tied for 32nd that week, earning $3,542, of which I collected $177 as my 5 percent cut. That was on top of my $500 base pay.

It wasn't much but I was learning my trade with one of the best.

I just followed the lead of the more experienced caddies early on. So when the other caddies put their bags down beside a green, I also put mine down next to theirs, because I was still learning and didn't want to be fired for getting one of the basics wrong.

I became increasingly familiar with how to read a yardage book properly, as well as what players required from a caddie and how to keep your job. Keeping a job was top priority.

Most of caddying was just common sense and simple arithmetic, but what I was most impressed with was the thought that I was the greatest conman in the world. It had been barely a month earlier that I had been caddying for amateur ball beaters who often topped it 50 yards. Now I was getting paid to watch the best golfers in the world from the best seat in the house. And I had a caddie badge to get into every tournament on the PGA Tour. I was in heaven.

Three weeks after my debut with Green, we hooked up again, this time in Memphis for the St. Jude Classic at Colonial Country Club in Tennessee, the course where 10 years earlier Al Geiberger had become the first player to break 60 on tour. It would be another 14 years before anyone else matched the feat—Chip Beck, no less, in Las Vegas.

Green started well and went into overdrive with a sizzling Saturday 65 that left us only one stroke behind leaders Curtis Strange and Andy Dillard, which meant we played with the co-leaders in the final threesome on Sunday. I remember thinking, "How cool is this?"

Green, alas, never got going in the final round and faded with a 74 to tie for 15th.

But I got to observe up close the way champions go about their business, watching Strange, wearing baggy blue pants and a white shirt on a sweltering summer afternoon, nervelessly ram in a six-footer at the last to beat four others by a shot.

Speaking of Strange, he had a reputation of being extremely tight with his money. (See The Gambler chapter.)

Green earned just over $10,000 for his tie for 15th in Memphis, so I pocketed another $500 on top of my $500 weekly wage.

He did not play great for the rest of the 1987 season, though he fired up in the final event for his best finish of the year, a tie for sixth at the Centel Classic.

OPEN ROUND CANCELED

The following year did not start particularly well either, but I loved my new life, especially getting into the majors, and was particularly excited by my first trip to the British Open, or Open Championship as it is known in its homeland.

It was played at Royal Lytham and St. Annes, and I thoroughly enjoyed working on a links course that was very different from the so-called target golf that was the staple of the PGA Tour.

I also stayed in a house walking distance to the course, another rarity in the States.

Saturday dawned to rain of biblical proportions. It lashed down, quintessential Open weather, but I was ready with my Gore-Tex rain jacket with the course crest that I had bought in the pro shop.

Hubert, who started the day 10 strokes behind halfway-leader Nick Price, birdied five of the first seven holes to zoom up the leaderboard.

My legs and feet were wet, hands cold, the clubs were cold and wet. It was miserable weather, but to be five-under after seven holes, I was in all my glory sloshing around. I didn't care how much it rained if we kept making birdies.

Unfortunately, the rain was so heavy that the greens began to flood, so much so that play was stopped, and ultimately the round was canceled.

Saturday's scores were annulled, and we would start the round from scratch the following day, it was announced. It was the first time the Open had taken such a drastic measure, and it meant Hubert's five birdies were all thrown out the window.

I was in the locker room when the cancellation was announced and Pete Coleman, Bernhard Langer's caddie, said, "Cayce, what are your thoughts about that?"

I told him I was "slightly disappointed" and he said that was an understatement.

Hubert took the news philosophically.

He said he had been in the game a long time and had been on both the short end and the long end of the stick many times and that you had to take the good with the bad, or in this case the bad with the good. That was just the rub of the green.

The *New York Times* reported the cancelation thus:

"There were 35 players on the course, strung out from the first through the 16th holes, when play was halted," wrote Gordon White.

"One was Hubert Green, who opened with five straight 3's and birdied five of the first seven holes. Since all today's scores were erased, Green and everyone else must start the third round again.

"The 41-year-old Alabama golfer, who won the 1977 United States Open, had just hit to the eighth green when the committee suspended play. Later in the locker room, Green shrugged and said, 'What can you do? I'm used to it.'"

Farther down, the article continued: "Today's rare suspension came on a day with little wind but very heavy rains that started around midnight. Unlike most other links courses used for the British Open, Royal Lytham St. Annes sits low and flat about half a mile from the coast.

"The greens, many of which are nestled below the fairways, do not drain well. Also, the water table here is quite high and the soil is not very sandy. It was impossible, despite some work with squeegees, to keep the greens at No. 9, No. 10, No. 11, and No. 12 from accumulating water faster than it could be pushed off."

Unfortunately, Hubert could not replicate his form the next day, and eventually finished equal 52nd in what proved to be his final Open appearance.

He had no top 10 finishes in all of 1988, but 1989 was much better, and he almost won again in Memphis, the same tournament where he had been in contention two years earlier, though it was held in 1989 for the first time at the new TPC at Southwind.

Hubert was 10 under par through 16 holes of the final round. At the time it was the best performance I had ever witnessed, though he bogeyed the last two holes and shot 63 to finish second, three shots behind winner John Mahaffey.

JACK AND ARNIE

Two 1989 majors also stick in my memory, not because of what Hubert did, but rather for who we played with.

At the U.S. Open at Oak Hill, we were paired with Jack Nicklaus on the weekend, and what I remember best is a particularly poor shot that Jack hit, and Hubert's reaction to it. Faced with a delicate chip, Nicklaus chili-dipped it with all the dexterity of a 36-handicapper, barely moving the ball a few inches.

"He was never a good chipper," Hubert muttered quietly to me, which I thought was a particularly harsh thing to say about my boyhood hero. I knew the Golden Bear's chipping wasn't as great as that of Hubert, who ranks with José María Olazábal as having the best short game of the 100 or so players I have worked for, but you don't win 18 majors by chipping poorly.

So how did Jack respond to that poor shot? By chipping in his next effort for par. That certainly shut Hubert up. Karma, I thought.

Two months later, at the PGA Championship at Kemper Lakes, I recall the frenzied reaction of fans around the course on the first day when Arnold Palmer's name went up on the leaderboard.

A month before turning 60, Palmer shot an opening 68, and many of the other players in the field, who had grown up worshiping the King, were just as excited as the spectators.

Arnie inevitably faded back into the pack over the ensuing three rounds, but I was almost giddy with delight to find that he would play the final round with Hubert and Jodie Mudd.

As the threesome walked up the final fairway to rapturous applause, Hubert made a wonderful gesture. He quietly suggested to Mudd that they both hang back well behind Palmer so that he could stride up the fairway alone and savor the reception.

PAST HIS PRIME

Hubert unfortunately never came close to winning again after 1989, as age and modern technology inevitably caught up with him. The introduction of metal drivers and woods did him no favors. His ability was built on finesse, not strength, but golf was increasingly becoming a power game. Not that Hubert didn't try to adapt. He belatedly moved to a TaylorMade metal driver but with his unorthodox swing he still couldn't find enough additional length to compete and the game just passed him by.

Ron Streck, by the way, at the 1981 Houston Open was the first player to win a PGA Tour event with a metal driver. Over the next 15 years the entire tour switched from persimmon wood to metal.

The younger guys hit it farther, hit it closer, and putted better than Hubert. Though he still had a silky chipping touch, he was inferior in every other category.

Here's an example of his sublime short game. He was once in a chip-off with Seve Ballesteros, Craig Stadler, and Sandy Lyle at an exhibition Shootout the tour used to hold on Tuesdays of tournament week.

Seve, as expected, almost chipped it in, and gave Hubert a triumphant look that dared him to match it. Hubert promptly chipped his shot in, one of the few times Seve's short game was bested.

Even though Green's appearances on leaderboards became rarer and rarer over our time together, I gained invaluable experience. He helped mentor me and taught me to be a better caddie with good advice, but he was very tough and on occasions mean. I took his advice and was grateful for it but it doesn't mean I ever totally trusted him.

THE DOBERMAN

Even though he did some nice things at times, nobody really liked the guy, and he was called "the Doberman" because a Doberman will turn on his master. You always had to be on your toes with Hubert and could never think you were an ally.

But I admired how Hubert was a fierce competitor with a lot of heart. He was as tough as nails, but not tougher than me, I remember thinking. I tolerated him because he was a big-name

The life of a caddie. Here I am with Steve Jones, lining up a putt at the 2005 Players Championship. (AP Images/Phil Coale)

Here I am (fifth from the left) in the caddyshack at the 1988 Masters.

My old boss Hubert Green watches the ball fly in the early '90s. (Getty Images/Gary Newkirk /Allsport)

With Bob Hope...

...and Andy Williams.

Caddying for Fuzzy Zoeller in 1997. (Getty Images/Stan Badz/PGA TOUR Archive)

Fuzzy and Tiger sitting together, waiting to hit on the second hole during the second round of the 1998 Masters, one year after Fuzzy's infamous remarks. (Getty Images/Timothy A. CLARY/AFP)

Fuzzy, Vijay, and me on the
11th Hole at Augusta National.

Fishing with Fuzzy.

The Van with the Bob and
Tom Show décor.

Viridian Oregon Pinot Noir van.

Having a good
time with Fred
Couples.

With Big Jack.

And with Arnie.

Me and Fred playing in Michigan.

In Abu Dhabi with Ernie Els.

Talking through a shot with Vijay on the second hole during Round 1
of the 79th Masters in 2015. (Getty Images/Timothy A. Clary/AFP)

Enjoying a break in the action with Fred. (Getty Images/ Chris Trotman)

Working with Ernie Els in the first round of the 2016 Masters. (Getty Images/Harry How)

2016 U.S. Open with Ricci Roberts, Ernie Els, and me.

Me, the yardage book, and Fred. (Getty Images/Chris Trotman)

Hanging with Vijay during the first round of the 2015 PGA Championship. (Getty Images/Jamie Squire)

player. And besides, I couldn't afford to be choosy at that fledgling stage of my career.

Along with the aforementioned two major titles he won, Green came close at the Masters too, finishing one stroke behind winner Gary Player in 1978.

His 19 tour wins included three in a row in 1976.

He also tied for third at the 1977 British Open, albeit 11 strokes behind Tom Watson, who beat Jack Nicklaus by a shot in that memorable Duel in the Sun at Turnberry.

A cigar smoker, he died of throat cancer in 2018 at the age of 71.

By the time Hubert and I parted ways in the early 1990s, I had done my apprenticeship and was increasingly confident in my ability to be a good jockey. I just needed a better horse.

I let him know I was moving on to greener pastures, not that I phrased it like that. I just did not want to be around him anymore. He was toxic and I'd learned as much as I was going to from him.

My next job was with Mike Standly, whose lone tour victory was at New Orleans in 1993. I bounced around for a while after that working short-term for a few other players and then received a chance to work for Curt Byrum at the 1995 Players Championship.

I had long wanted a chance to do so, because Byrum was so hard on his caddies, and I thought it would be a great challenge. I'd seen him abuse his caddie and was ready to stand up to him and take no shit. I was up for the challenge and when it presented itself, I pounced.

FORTUITOUS ENCOUNTER

And it was during that Players Championship that a fortuitous meeting with another player's wife led to my landing a dream bag.

The wife's name was Diane Zoeller, wife of Frank Urban, better known as Fuzzy.

I ran into Diane on the 12th hole on the morning of the first round.

She asked me why I was on the course, and I told her I liked to do some early reconnaissance when my man had a late tee time, check out the pin positions, how the course was playing, etc.

She mentioned that Fuzzy was in a furious mood because his caddie, Mike Mazzeo, had been a no-show that morning. Being a no-show, especially at a tournament as big as the Players, is a great way to join the unemployment ranks. Diane later told Fuzzy about our conversation and from what I heard later she suggested that he needed a caddie like me.

To which Fuzzy replied something along the lines of, "No, I don't need someone like Cayce. I need Cayce."

The following week in New Orleans there was a message from Fuzzy's right-hand man Hank Frieda on my hotel phone when I returned from the course.

"Call as soon as possible," he said. "Urgent, but not an emergency."

I promptly dialed Frieda's number, and he said Fuzzy wanted me to work the Masters the following week, and so just like that I started what turned out to be the longest professional relationship of my career.

Breaks like this are not guaranteed, of course, and I was in the right place at the right time. But as Gary Player is so fond of saying, the harder you work, the luckier you get.

From New Orleans, fellow caddie Dave Renwick and I drove all day Saturday to get to Augusta. Renwick was the reigning Masters caddie champion, so to speak, after working for José María Olazábal when the Spaniard won the Green Jacket the previous year, though they had split up by time the 1995 Masters rolled around.

Fuzzy wanted me at Augusta National at 7:00 AM on that Monday, and I arrived with plenty of time to spare, but could not get past the security guard at the course entrance. Because the name of Fuzzy's caddie had not been updated on the list, the club employees had to determine who was and was not allowed to enter the grounds.

Mazzeo was still listed.

I was worried I was going to get fired before I had even started, because Fuzzy was big on punctuality.

I can often talk my way past course security, but not at the Masters. My bullshit wouldn't fly.

Fortunately, the security guard called down to the clubhouse, and Fuzzy was tracked down in the Champions Locker Room, reserved for the select breed of players who have won a Green Jacket. Fuzzy was already there enjoying a hearty breakfast.

He straightened out the matter and I was good to enter the hallowed grounds, and so began what for the most part was a beautiful relationship with Fuzzy that stretched on and off for 14 years. (See Fuzzy chapter.)

11

Rangefinders

*How I cornered the PGA Tour market
with a new device*

Rangefinders are so ubiquitous in golf these days that it's sometimes hard to believe that they were unheard of only three decades ago. Even casual golfers know that a rangefinder, which resembles a small set of binoculars, uses a laser beam to measure the distance to an object, which in golf is usually the flag, though it is used for many other purposes too, such as the distance to carry a hazard, etc.

You simply point the rangefinder at your given target, and it will almost instantly provide a yardage.

The commercial technology had been around well before the 1990s, dating back to the 1960s, when it was introduced for military use.

Modern rangefinders are used for many activities that require precise measurements, including golf and hunting, among other things, but the technology is tweaked for the specifics of these activities. Golf rangefinders, for example, are programmed to lock onto the flag, rather than a tree directly behind the flag.

I first heard of the technology by pure chance, during a practice round with Fuzzy Zoeller at the 1995 U.S. Open at Shinnecock Hills on the eastern end of New York's Long Island.

Fuzzy had hit a drive into the rough at a par-five. I knew he couldn't get home with his second shot—it was a three-wood and change—so I was a little lazy and did not bother calculating the yardage to the hole.

When he asked me, "What's the number?"

I told him, "It's a three-wood, everything you've got."

Which did not satisfy him.

He said, this time more sternly, "I want a goddamn number."

Serendipitously, a couple of spectators were within earshot behind the nearby gallery rope.

One guy said he had a technology I could use: "You push this one button, and it gives the yardage all the way to the flag."

Somewhat skeptical, I replied: "Get the hell out of here," or words to that effect, but I took his contact information anyway and he said he looked forward to hearing from me.

I barely gave the matter another thought until the end of the season, six months later. It was December, my girlfriend had dumped me, so I had the blues, and time on my hands. I recalled that rangefinder conservation and decided to call the guy and remind him of our Shinnecock conversation. I told him I was interested in his product, and he explained the company he worked for that manufactured the device.

It was an Austrian firm called Swarovski, headquartered in the town of Absam near Innsbruck. It was founded in 1895 and is still family owned.

I told the guy of my vision, which was to sell the rangefinder to PGA Tour players who I hoped would be willing to pay a premium price for a product that would offer greater precision than a traditional yardage book.

He contacted Swarovski and explained who I was, and they were interested enough to invite me to their headquarters.

HANDSHAKE AGREEMENT

A few days later I was on my way to Austria. I took along a portfolio of pictures of some of the more famous players I had caddied for—Fuzzy, Arnold Palmer, Payne Stewart, Hubert Green, etc.

I met with five members of the Swarovski family, who told me about their new golf-specific product and how they wanted to test the waters.

I told them I thought PGA Tour players would be the perfect market. They had plenty of money, and rangefinders would help them prepare for tournaments. At the time of writing, the technology was still not allowed during competitive rounds on the PGA Tour or at three of the four majors, the PGA Championship being the lone exception.

As I phrased it to Swarovski, they had a Rolls-Royce product, and I knew Rolls-Royce customers. On nothing more than a handshake, the company gave me a worldwide exclusive for golf for 12 months, agreeing to sell me up to 350 rangefinders for $1,000 a pop. It was up to me to set my own price for the customer.

The way I saw it, the company had nothing to lose. I had a direct pipeline to the world's top players. They hoped I would successfully do their brand building for a year and then they could take it from there.

I flew home the next day and bought 10 rangefinders to take to my first tournament of 1996, in Tucson. I loaded them in my van and spoke with my uncle Charlie, an accountant, who asked me how many I thought I could sell.

I told him my goal was five. It turned out that I underclubbed considerably. I had no idea how much to charge, but Charlie suggested $3,300, a cheeky $2,300 markup.

I headed off to Tucson thinking that if I sold all 10, I'd be a rich man.

FIRST CUSTOMER

My first customer was Sandy Lyle, the two-time major champion from Scotland.

It was on the practice range in Tucson that I pitched my product to Sandy, and anyone else within earshot. There was a hut at the far end of the range, and I demonstrated to Sandy how to use the device. It showed 230 yards to the target.

I suggested he take two steps back, and it showed 232 yards. I did not tell him to move one step backward, because the product only displayed even numbers back then.

He told me that a three-iron was his 232-yard club, so he picked up that club and whacked a ball right into the hut.

He asked me for a price, I told him $3,300, and he said, "Sold."

I had made my first sale.

Bob Tway, another major champion, was my second customer. He was so intrigued by the technology that he used it while riding as a passenger in his courtesy car, to measure the distance to the preceding vehicle.

Tway finished runner-up to Phil Mickelson that week.

A few weeks later, Arnold Palmer bought a rangefinder and that created a lot of buzz on the range, because Arnie was known as being very frugal. The King rarely bought anything.

Word spread like wildfire that I had gotten Arnie to the tune of $3,300.

It wasn't just golfers buying the device. I was on the range at the Pebble Beach National Pro-Am when I encountered Charles Schwab.

If the name doesn't ring a bell, Schwab was the founder and president of the Charles Schwab discount brokerage company, which at last check had annual revenues of about $20 billion.

Guys like Schwab make wealthy professional golfers look like paupers by comparison, and it was hardly surprising that Schwab swaggered up, huffing and puffing and looking pretty happy with himself.

"Hey, Fuzzy," he said, "I'm looking for your caddie?"

"Well, Chuck," Fuzzy replied with a hint of sarcasm, "they normally are standing right next to the bag."

So Schwab turned to me and without any of the usual social niceties got right to the point.

"I want to get one of those rangefinders," he said.

"Yes, sir," I replied, and whipped one out of my pocket for a demonstration.

I gave him one and told him the price was $3,300, thinking to myself that such a trifling amount was peanuts for a man of his wealth.

Then I buttered him up with a comment designed to puff up his already healthy ego.

"I think I know who you are. Aren't you that big name Charles Schwab who I see doing those TV commercials?" I said.

He puffed up his chest and said he wanted to purchase a rangefinder right then and there and would pay me the following day.

Though worth billions, the guy did not carry a checkbook.

"Your credit is good until tomorrow," I said, to which Fuzzy chimed in and told Schwab that I wasn't joking.

Sure enough, Schwab returned the next day with a fancy check signed by Helen Schwab.

I looked at it to make sure it was made out for the right amount and signed properly and couldn't help winding him up and having a little fun.

"I see it's signed by Helen Schwab," I said. "I won't tell anyone who's the real boss in your family."

IRWIN AND WATSON

Business was booming by time the tour hit its annual March Florida swing.

Swarovski kept shipping me more rangefinders whenever I ran out, which was pretty much every week. Not that I let it be known I could get my hands on an almost unlimited quantity.

I created the impression they were in short supply, to force an urgency to buy and I did not give discounts. Many sales were a piece of cake, but some challenged my salesmanship skills.

Three-time U.S. Open champion Hale Irwin said he was in the market for three rangefinders, and initially offered $2,700 apiece, which he reluctantly raised to $2,800 and then $2,900, his final offer, he said.

I told him I'd sell him three for $10,000. When he pointed out that 3 x 3,300 equaled 9,900, I told him I was charging him an extra $100 for costing me precious time. In the end he bought only one.

Another demanding customer was Tom Watson, the eight-time major champion. During a practice round with Fuzzy at Bay Hill, I did my best to pique Watson's interest. That part was a piece of cake. He was clearly intrigued, and I made sure to speak a little louder than normal when I gave Fuzzy a yardage.

Finally, on the 13th hole, Watson asked if he could look at the rangefinder. "Of course you can, Tom," I replied.

I handed it to him on the next tee, the par-three 14th.

He pointed it at the flag, and it showed 214 yards. His caddie Bruce Edwards told him it was 200 to the front of the green.

"So, Cayce," he said, "do you mean to tell me that if I take 14 steps from the front of the green I'm going to be at the flag?"

"In theory, Tom," I replied, "but I'm just not sure how good your steps are."

Old Tom was amiable enough but did not see much humor in the remark. Fuzzy, on the other hand, found it amusing.

Fuzzy and Tom were rivals. They didn't particularly like each other, because Fuzzy beat Tom in a playoff at the 1979 Masters, and Tom always called him Frank, which rankled Fuzzy.

Watson peppered me with questions about the rangefinder, and I told him about the lifetime warranty, the company's prestigious history, and the quality of the glass they used for the optics. And I told him the price.

I thought I was on the verge of making the sale when he pricked my balloon and had the temerity to ask me to leave a brochure in his locker.

I lied and told him I would, but I didn't. I never had any intention of doing so. I had already told and shown him everything he needed to know.

Two weeks later at the Players Championship, Watson was on the putting green with none other than the great Byron Nelson. Fuzzy and I were nearby.

Watson called me over. "Hello, Mr. Nelson, how are you?" I said with deference to Byron.

"Fine, thank you," he replied in his folksy Texas twang.

Courtesies concluded, Watson proceeded to admonish me like a supercilious schoolteacher.

"You did not leave that brochure in my locker like you said you were going to," he said.

I replied that I had shown him the product and had described it in great detail.

Laying it on thickly, I said, "I didn't think a man of your integrity and intelligence needed a brochure to own this kind of quality after you'd demonstrated it to yourself. A brochure wasn't going to change your mind and I didn't want to insult myself or you."

So now I'd made him feel bad.

He hesitated and I knew I was either going to lose him or close him right there, so I said, "Tom, I have one left in my van,

I'll leave it in your locker, please leave a check in Fuzzy's locker for $3,300, and I've got to go."

He said, "Okay." I shook his hand, wished him a great tournament, told Mr. Nelson it was good to see him, and scarpered back to Fuzzy before Watson could change his mind.

"What the hell did he want?" Fuzzy said. And when I told him to expect a check for $3,300 in his locker, Fuzzy said, "Attaboy."

I can't thank Fuzzy enough for his assistance in that whole venture. He must have sold 100 for me on his own, and he never asked for a cent in commission.

"LAST ONE"

There was another amusing rangefinder story from that week at the Players Championship.

I was on the range with Fuzzy, while four other players to whom I'd sold a device were chatting nearby—Tway, Justin Leonard, Joey Sindelar, and Mike Hulbert.

They called me over, and for the umpteenth time during our time together, Fuzzy said, "Go see what the fuck they want."

I sauntered over all cocky, higher than a Georgia pine, thinking I was smarter than Bill Gates because business was so good.

They had a question for me.

"We all really want to know one thing," one of them said, I can't remember who.

"Which one of us really bought the last rangefinder, because you told all of us that it was the last one?"

Thinking as quickly on my feet as I could under the circumstances, I replied that they had "all bought the last one I had on me that day."

I quickly added that I had to get back to work and hustled back to Fuzzy as the four wise men cracked up laughing, delighted at having called out my bullshit.

By the time I got to the Masters two weeks later, everyone associated with the tour knew about the rangefinders and my sales started extending beyond the playing ranks.

Karsten Solheim and Ely Callaway, respective founders of the Ping and Callaway equipment companies, each bought one, as did noted course architect Robert Trent Jones.

Solheim purchased his while we stood under the famous old oak tree in front of the Augusta National clubhouse.

"This is an amazing piece of technology," said Solheim, a great innovator who knew a game-changing new product when he saw one.

THE SHARK

And the biggest name in golf at the time, Greg Norman, put in an order for three, with a request that they be left in his locker the following week at Hilton Head.

This, remember, was in 1996. Know what else happened at the 1996 Masters?

Norman, after several agonizingly close calls at Augusta National, led by six strokes going into the final round. At long last, he had one proverbial sleeve in the Green Jacket.

So I got to Hilton Head Island in South Carolina the following week and wondered what I was going to say when I saw Greg after he'd just blown the biggest 54-hole lead in majors history. I'm sure I wasn't the only one trying to think of an appropriate remark.

I was walking around Hilton Head when I spied a big yacht named *Aussie Rules* docked in the harbor. It was the Shark's 228-foot, custom-built boat, and he was right there on the top deck gazing my way.

Yelling down at me like I was a peasant, he said, "Hey, Cayce, where are my rangefinders?"

"Where's my check?" I barked back.

So he asked me aboard, wrote me a check for $9,900 and I promptly delivered three of the devices to his locker at the course. It was like stealing.

BUSHNELL

Lest you think my deal with Swarovski was too good to be true, it's worth reiterating that it was only for 12 months. The company has not lasted more than a century by making dumb deals.

I would also note that Swarovski was not the only company to launch a golf rangefinder at that time.

Bushnell also introduced a product, and another caddie, Steve Hulka, tried to sell them to tour players, without much success.

Hulka priced his Bushnells at only $350, a pittance compared to my $3,300, but that company had not yet perfected an electronic component called a diode that was an essential part of a rangefinder. Consequently, Bushnell rangefinders sometimes gave inaccurate readings.

In fairness, once Bushnell mastered the diode component, they had a quality product that gave yardages in one-yard increments, as opposed to Swarovski's two yards.

But I was out of the business by then.

I mischievously carried a Bushnell with me throughout 1996 and offered prospective buyers a chance to try both brands, so that they could see the difference with their own eyes.

"Good luck with the yardage if you buy a Bushnell," I would say cheekily.

John Daly and Davis Love bought two each, Jesper Parnevik lost one and had to buy another one, and I heard of a couple getting stolen, which was fine by me, because it led to more sales.

About six months later, Daly complained that the rangefinders only measured in even numbers.

I thought, "How stupid is this country bumpkin if it took him six months to figure that out?"

GOLDEN BEAR

A couple of guys tried to go over my head to get a better price, including none other than Jack Nicklaus. This was during a golden age for golf-course architecture, and Jack being Jack, he figured he could get a rangefinder directly from the company.

Fortunately, Swarovski stood by me and told Nicklaus the device was only available through their representative, yours truly.

So Nicklaus bought one from me. Even Fuzzy was impressed: "How did you do that?" he said.

And it was just as well Swarovski had my back, because I certainly did not want players or any other buyers for that matter knowing how much I paid for the rangefinders and how much I marked them up.

Before the year was out, I had sold my entire quota of 350 rangefinders, and my $2,300 profit per item meant I reaped a total profit of more than $800,000 in the 12 months I had the sales rights.

I had $500,000 in cash at one time in my van that I drove on tour. And yes, I was afraid of being robbed, most likely by another caddie, because they all knew by then that I had made a small fortune with my venture. So I took several precautions. I had an alarm in the van, and a motion sensor that set off a beeper if a door moved.

I also only stayed in motels where I could park right outside my door. And I was packing heat, in the form of a Colt .45 pistol.

SECRET

And then, to make sure all the other caddies knew of the security steps I had taken and so they didn't get any bright ideas, I showed them to Big Artie, and emphasized that they were secret.

"Big Artie" was the nickname of a caddie named Arthur Granfield. If you ever wanted everyone on tour to know something, all you had to do was tell your "secret" to Big Artie. He couldn't help himself and didn't fail me on this occasion. The other caddies were forewarned not to try anything funny.

My year selling rangefinders flew by. I certainly made hay while the sun shined and got out of the business at the end of 1996 when my right to sell them exclusively expired.

I knew the product was good but must admit I did not fully realize the technology would revolutionize the game as much as it did.

And I didn't sell them to donkeys. I sold them to legends of the game.

And at a price they could afford, though I am glad they did not know at the time how much more affordable they could have been.

12

Business

*Booze, hand sanitizer,
and a Nicklaus fiver*

Following a busy and highly profitable **1996** selling range-finders (See Rangefinders chapter), I dabbled in a few other things before getting into the alcohol business by pure chance, starting in 2010.

I knew a woman in North Carolina, Bess Lee, an alcohol distributor I had met at a Total Wine store. She took me to a tasting one night, where I imbibed in a sip of chocolate wine. I almost spat it out, it was so shockingly bad.

I just about fainted when she said she was selling 100,000 cases of the product annually.

I had a sudden idea. If you could sell such a large volume of this awful drink, which was made in the Netherlands, surely there was room in the market for a better-quality chocolate wine.

I vowed to make the best chocolate wine in the United States and between caddie duties went to work.

I previously had an involvement with the Viridian Winery in Oregon (See On the Road Again chapter), but that had been pretty straightforward compared to having to produce a drink myself.

That vineyard association came about when Fuzzy played with the winery owner, Jamie Olsen, in a pro-am in Oregon, shortly after turning 50 at the end of 2001.

Olsen told Fuzzy he needed someone to help sell his wine, and Fuzzy informed him that I was the man.

The 700-acre vineyard produced a nice drop of pinot noir, and Olsen gave me a 10 percent stake in the business on the proviso I could flog his wine. I knew a buyer I had met, again through Fuzzy. I had kept the guy's number just in case, and it came in handy. He facilitated a deal with Costco.

So many of my business deals have been a result of people I have met in golf, usually in pro-ams. I like to say that I have never met a stranger, and neither has Fuzzy.

I called a buddy and told him I had just offloaded 10,000 or 20,000 cases of wine to Costco—I can't remember the exact number—even though I did not know anything about the business.

He said that I did not need to know anything about the business, as long as I knew how to sell.

"You could sell an anchor to a drowning man," he said.

It was a conversation that I recalled years later when the chocolate wine idea bubbled up, and it imbued me with enough confidence to plow ahead.

But now that I wanted to produce an alcoholic drink, as well as sell it, I had a lot to learn.

A neighbor of mine in San Clemente, California, owned a flavor company, so I hired him to produce the first product.

He experimented with a bunch of chocolate concoctions, and I weighed in with my thoughts on what cream to use. I modestly describe myself as a cream sommelier. I knew our market would primarily be female and I figured women generally preferred a product that was a little sweet but did not sit on the palate for too long and did not have an aftertaste, did not cloy.

When I finally tasted a chocolate that was right on the money, I thought I'd hit the jackpot. We finally settled on three flavors—chocolate, mint chocolate, and cherry.

I decided to call it CV Chocolate, the All-American Cream. But that was just the start. My next step was to find a facility to make the drink.

We settled on a co-packing facility in the inappropriately named Temperance, Michigan. The operators there knew how to make cream, bottle and box the booze, and ship it out.

When I finally had my finished product, I got my English caddie friends Ken Comboy and Billy Foster to try it. They are both inveterate beer drinkers, and bluntly said that I didn't have a chance of success, but that didn't worry me, because I knew 90 percent of my customers would likely be women.

But I still didn't have a distributor.

Worse still, people told me that no distributors would take on my brand because I was a nobody and would have trouble even getting my foot in the door to talk.

That's when having so many acquaintances on the PGA Tour came in handy for the umpteenth time. Tour player Howard Twitty knew a distributor in New Jersey and was kind enough to make a phone call for me.

The guy was a golf fan. I later found out he did not have any interest in my product, but wanted to meet me only because he learned that I was working for Fred Couples, and figured I could be his path to meeting Fred.

Golf was the door-opener that allowed me to get my foot in.

From then on, I hit up distributors without appointments, just showed up at their doors. Some thought I was a little crazy and didn't let me in, but others were into golf and happy to talk to a tour caddie.

My alcohol business was truly up and running.

ICED COFFEE CRAZE

After learning the intricacies of the business with CV Chocolate, I had another brain wave, and not for the first time it came while driving my old van around the country.

I noticed billboards for iced coffee popping up on seemingly every freeway exit. Almost overnight, McDonald's, Burger King, Starbucks, Chick-fil-A, you name it, they all started advertising iced coffee.

If there was such a craze for this drink, I thought, perhaps there was a market for alcoholic iced coffee too.

I started investigating further and found a flavor company in North Carolina that had been in business almost a century. Their iced coffee was delicious.

I introduced it to Ernie Els, who had a sip and was hooked. He said, "This is out of this world; I want my name on it." He told his business partners of his desire, and that's how Els Iced Coffee started.

Ernie and I arranged a meeting with Total Wine at their headquarters. The largest chain wine store in the country had already been selling my previous products. I had asked if I could produce a private label so we could increase their profits, and they said yes, they would like a label that was sold only at Total Wine.

There were about 12 of us at the meeting and the guy running it said, "As soon as you give me the labels we can look at them and get started."

I had already made up five labels and had them in my pocket, so I nonchalantly pulled them out and put them on the table.

When we got to the car after the meeting, Ernie wanted to know how in the world had I known they were going to ask about labels?

I told him I didn't know but I wanted to be ready just in case. Total Wine called me the following day, while I was at a printer's office. The graphic arts designers made the adjustments that Total Wine wanted, the label was created, and the Els Iced Coffee was up and running.

I started doing in-store tastings, and distinctly remember my first one. I was at the back of the store, next to the bathroom, which I thought was rude and insulting, but I got down to work in the knowledge that only by demonstrating that I could sell the product would I get to do future tastings prominently located at the front rather than hidden away at the back.

I credit the success of Els Iced Coffee and, more recently, the Total Wine private label IC Iced as largely due to my willingness to travel the country doing in-store tastings and getting to know store managers and their employees.

I thank Lloyd Wrisley, a Total Wine regional manager, for his advice. He told me that offering the personal touch of visiting stores and shaking hands with managers and employees would yield huge dividends, because they would help sell my product even when I was not there.

He taught me how to be a brand builder. Wrisley died in 2023, but his business legacy lives on.

If I was working at a tour event with a Total Wine location, I'd pop in for a visit while I was in town.

I had a one-liner that I used on every manager: "We pour, you score." And I liked to tell them that Cayce Kerr was "coast to coast, like butter on toast."

SELLING 936 BOTTLES IN ONE DAY

I've now visited almost every Total Wine location in the country and have set in-store sales records at more than 200 of them.

But nothing beats the day I had at the Westbury location on New York's Long Island on December 22, 2018.

I had an in-store tasting that day which led to the sale of 936 bottles of Els Iced Coffee, bringing in revenues of $11,222. That's in one day, and it led the store in sales of any single product. I have the invoice to prove it. Gift cards came in second, followed by Johnnie Walker Blue scotch (62 bottles), Tito's Handmade Vodka (144 bottles), Johnnie Walker Black (125 bottles), and Grey Goose vodka (172 bottles).

Normally, if you sell one case in a day you're considered to be doing well, two cases and you're a monster. Last year they sold 650 cases (7,800 bottles) of my IC Iced private label at that same location.

The manager said, "Cayce, you built that brand in our store in one day."

After the success of CV Chocolate and Els Iced Coffee, I decided the next logical step would be to procure a co-packing facility where I could produce the various IC Iced drinks from start to finish, rather than having to outsource production.

The business jargon is being vertically integrated, which simply means that a company brings in-house previously outsourced parts of its business operation.

So I went to work scouting for an ideal location and settled on a building in Baltimore, just off the Interstate 95 freeway.

By then I had brought on a partner, Steven Jackson, and I gave him 50 percent of the company we formed, C&L Imports, which we named for the first letters of our compliance officer's children, Cara and Lincoln.

The story of how Jackson and I met is rather amusing.

He worked for a distributor and approached me while I was doing a tasting, with his stuffy personality, wearing a suit and tie, and wanted to know all about the product. After I told him who I was and what I did, he went home to his wife that night and, according to what she later told me, said that he had met a guy that day who was "full of more shit and lies than anyone he ever met his entire life."

But then he went online to do some basic research about me and next thing he called out, "Honey, come here, this guy's telling the truth."

He came back and said he wanted to go into business. Several people warned me it would be a bad idea. It seemed nobody liked him.

But I saw what he could bring to the table, so I trained him for about a year and gave him half the company. He could do all the things I didn't want to do and, more importantly, all the things I couldn't do. He turned out to be an extremely valuable business partner.

Once we had settled on a 10,000-square-foot Baltimore building that we leased in 2020, we set about installing about $70,000 worth of electricity, bought and installed the necessary equipment, including a forklift and gigantic generators, and then we were ready for business.

We now produce five different IC Iced private label drinks for Total Wine. We do the blending and bottling, and ship all the booze out of one facility, so we manage all of the quality control.

At first, we had no employees.

I lived on-site in my office for about two years before finally getting my own apartment.

We were working from sunrise to sundown, so there was no reason for me to fritter away money on renting an apartment I would rarely use.

We were working our asses off. I'd assemble boxes at night while watching TV, so I didn't need to hire any labor. My son and daughter and three nephews came in to work in the summer, but apart from that, Steven and I ran the whole operation alone. These days we hire a handful of temporary workers.

We love our location because of its proximity to Total Wine's main distribution center in New Jersey, only a couple hours up the freeway.

And the company's corporate headquarters is in Maryland, very handy for meetings.

We also like promoting our product as local at Total Wine's two Maryland stores.

HAND SANITIZER

It was while looking for a co-packing facility that the COVID-19 pandemic swept the world in early 2020.

You no doubt will recall that during the early days, when so much of what caused the infection was not yet fully understood, hand sanitizer was flying off the shelves, so much so that it was almost impossible to find. And if you could find it, you almost had to take out a second mortgage to afford a small bottle.

I spied another business opportunity. What if I got into the business?

Jackson did not want anything to do with it, but I put $50,000 up and convinced him that we go ahead and order what we needed to get started. We procured the alcohol, plastic containers and created a label. I found a co-packing facility in Chicago to produce the product but still did not have a buyer. That's when I got a lucky break.

A business friend of mine was on a family Zoom call during which he found out a family member was looking to obtain a bulk quantity of hand sanitizer.

He told me about the conversation, and I followed the bread-crumbs and found a buyer that had been paid for a shipment that it could not fulfill after losing the previous supplier.

The buyer was in the lurch and urgently needed a new supply.

This company took all the product we had, which had a pleasant fragrance. It was a match made in heaven. We were in and out of the business in three months and turned a gross profit of $850,000.

We used that money to lease the Baltimore plant.

NICKLAUS FIVER

In earlier times while I was working for Fuzzy Zoeller at the 2005 U.S. Senior Open in Ohio, I learned that the Bank of Scotland had issued a commemorative five-pound note to honor the final appearance by Jack Nicklaus at the British Open.

The tasteful bill featured one image of Nicklaus clutching the Old Claret Jug after his 1978 win at St. Andrews, as well as another of him making a swing on the same Sunday.

The business part of my brain immediately started ticking over.

I was watching Golf Channel in a bar with a caddie friend, Brian Staveley, and within minutes I was thinking it might be a good idea to buy as many of the notes as I could get my hands on, use them as part of a tasteful souvenir and flog at a high profit margin.

I decided then and there to go to Scotland and a couple of nights later I was on a plane across the pond, much to the amusement of Staveley, who said that he had never met anyone who came up with an idea over a drink and followed it through without blinking.

"I didn't actually think you would really go," he told me later. "I thought it was just the beer talking."

My policy of always traveling with a passport came in handy on that occasion for that quick trip to Scotland. After landing, I picked up a rental car and made a beeline to a nearby bank, but they would only give me five of the notes.

I later found out about two million had been printed, so it's not as though they were rare.

The next bank also parted with only five of the notes, and I had to acknowledge that my plan wasn't working, so I had to reassess the situation. When in doubt, remember that money always talks.

I asked to see the manager of the next bank I visited. I told him of the meager offerings of the previous banks and that I did not want to be running around all day.

I told him I wanted 400 of the notes. I also slipped him $1,000 cash in an envelope. We call such a surreptitious move "the Vegas handshake." He was a little shocked, but one thing about bribery, it's a global business that knows no borders.

Could he help me?

You bet he could. I walked out with 400 crisp fivers, as the British would say, each with Nicklaus staring back at me, and from there I headed to St. Andrews.

I wanted to buy a Nicklaus print that I thought could comprise part of the souvenir I envisaged. I found one in the clubhouse shop and took it to the counter.

The employee asked if I'd like the print wrapped, and I asked him how many were left.

He said they had received 500 but had sold a few, so I told him I'd take the rest. He raised a bushy eyebrow, clearly surprised if not astonished at my request.

I left with 474 prints, which I shipped back to the States, while I stuffed the Nicklaus fivers into my golf bag.

Upon returning stateside, I took the prints to an English picture framer in Florida and told him I wanted them framed with a Nicklaus fiver inside.

He offered me a good deal, went to work, and when he was done, I had a unique souvenir that I proceeded to flog primarily to players, many of whom hung them in their dens or man caves.

Fred Funk bought 10 and had them signed by Tiger.

I had bought the Nicklaus prints for the equivalent of $350 each and sold them for an average of $1,800.

I ended up offloading them all.

Even accounting for my expenses—the trip to Scotland, the framing costs, etc.—I made a more than tidy profit. You can do the math.

More important than the money was the priceless expression of gratitude I received from the Golden Bear himself.

I personally presented a print to him on national TV at the Father/Son Challenge in Florida in 2005. I had no advance warning that the broadcaster had gotten word of what I was planning to do, so I just ran with it, grateful for the free nationwide publicity.

Jack's wife, Barbara, located me on the range the next day and said Jack had been so happy to receive the souvenir and that they had reminisced long into the night over that famous 1978 Open victory.

She asked me if there was anything Jack could do, and I promptly handed over a thick wad of the fivers I still had. She returned them the following day, all 100 or so signed by Jack.

I then had more souvenirs framed with the Nicklaus signature, which added an extra touch.

One of them sold for $50,000 at a charity pro-am.

I later received a letter of gratitude from Jack, and to my surprise also got a Christmas card from him for the next five years. My mother was impressed.

"I see Jack Nicklaus is sending you Christmas cards now," she said.

PART FOUR

LIFE ON TOUR

13

On the Road Again

How I sharked Seve and delivered Fred
on time to a presidential date

I **rarely fly when traveling in the United States,** preferring the freedom of the road in my trusty old 2003 Chevrolet van no less. It had more than 724,000 miles under its belt at the time of writing, and has seated some two dozen major champions, including Fuzzy Zoeller, Darren Clarke, and Fred Couples.

And my previous van, which I owned for nearly a dozen years starting in 1992, also transported some famous cargo, none more so than the late, great Seve Ballesteros, whose story I will detail later in this chapter.

I purchased my old van from a guy I met in a pro-am at the now defunct Buick Open held at Warwick Hills in Michigan. He owned a local dealership and charged me only $500 over what he paid for it. Even better, he put me up for free at his home adjacent to the 18th fairway for the next few years.

I eventually retired that first van to a vineyard in Oregon, after 350,000 miles or so. I had a small stake in the vineyard, whose owner I met through Fuzzy. (See Business chapter.)

I donated the van because I figured the vineyard could put it to use one way or another, maybe to ferry the workers out to pick the grapes and whatnot.

SHAGGIN' WAGON

Some people call my current 2003 model the Shaggin' Wagon or the Passion Pit (more on that later). I just call it my second home.

It's where I often sleep, eat, and sometimes, er, well you get the picture. These days I use it as my office too.

While it's still common for many who work the tour to drive between tournaments on the eastern seaboard where distances are manageable and relatively comfortable, I prefer to drive coast to coast.

I should thank Hubert Green for showing me the advantages of a van. He was my first regular player back in 1987 (See Tour Beckons chapter) and made me an offer I could not refuse.

I could drive his van from tournament to tournament. All I had to do was drop him at the airport, get his clothes dry cleaned, and transport his luggage and clubs. That way he could travel lightly by air with only carry-on luggage.

It seemed like a pretty good deal to me, and so by the time Hubert and I split I was so used to getting between tour stops without the hassles of dealing with airports, flights, and rental cars that I had already bought my own van.

I have always felt so comfortable on the road and would be hard-pressed to name an Interstate freeway I haven't been on. I know just about every exit on Interstate 10, the freeway that traverses all the way across the southern part of the country from Los Angeles in the west to Jacksonville in the east.

Los Angeles to Miami, Seattle to Boston, San Francisco to New York, no problem. I'm coast to coast like butter on toast.

It's when I do my best thinking and ponder business ideas, many of which have first come to me on the open road.

That's why I rarely even play the radio. And forget about Bluetooth. This van dates from George W. Bush's first term as president.

As one caddie quipped, "Cayce's van—engine: worn out; tires: worn out; radio: brand new."

Soon after starting on tour, I managed to pick up a few handy bucks by transporting players' clubs, earning $50 per set.

Many players fly by private jet these days, but back then, when they mostly went commercial, misplaced clubs were an occupational hazard.

I also transported the radios that PGA Tour officials used for on-course communication. I charged $100 a week, cash on delivery, and looked forward to that crisp new bill every week.

Another reason I liked carrying the radios was because they were easy passengers. They did not talk back to me, did not tell me how to drive, or make me pull over because they were hungry or needed a bathroom break.

And I also developed friendships with many tour officials, such as Slugger White, guys who work insanely long hours, have an encyclopedic knowledge of the rules, and are always on hand to help any player with a ruling. Rules officials are at the course from before sunrise to after sunset, and they were invariably exhausted on Sunday afternoons when I would go to their trailer to collect the radios.

They had beer on ice and certainly deserved a drink or two to celebrate the end of a work week that could stretch to 100 hours, no exaggeration.

I couldn't help but recognize how underappreciated they were. Players had a running joke that on-course officials had an unwritten contest to find the biggest tree with the most amount of shade and breeze to park under. But you could hardly blame them when they had to sit in their golf carts all day, sometimes in stifling heat, timing players, and waiting to be called upon for an occasional ruling.

NETWORKING

I would also transport human cargo in the van, mainly in the form of other caddies. I wouldn't charge them per se, but my unwritten rule was that a first-time rider had to buy the first tank of gas. After that we would split the cost of subsequent refills if any were needed.

When the distance between tour stops was relatively close, and required less than a tank, I didn't even have to open my wallet the entire trip. Cheap is good, but free is even better.

The van has helped me make friends with numerous caddies, which has served as a way of introduction to their respective players. Like any business, caddying is as much about networking and who you know as what you know.

I did not see race or nationality when it came to my passengers—international caddies, American caddies, the brothers, they all rode with me. When you get the reputation of being a good guy, other caddies seek you out. The more people you know the better.

It helps you keep an ear to the ground, to know who's getting hired or fired, who's looking for a job and which players are looking for a caddie. You're always in the loop.

My passenger on one trip was fellow-caddie Steve Duplantis, a great guy who I've also written about elsewhere. (See Caddies Behaving Poorly chapter.)

I entrusted him at the wheel while I took a nap in the back, only to wake up and find the van stationary in the emergency lane. The idiot had run out of gas.

While I was threatening him with grievous bodily harm, he jumped out and, as luck would have it, we were close to an exit and a gas station. He jogged off into the distance and returned a little while later with a can of fuel, the crisis averted.

BENJAMIN FRANKLIN

As you might notice is a common theme throughout the book, a lot of my caddie friends were British. That's largely because when they first started coming over to the PGA Tour in droves they had few connections. I befriended many of them with offers to ride in my van and they invariably responded with gratitude.

Some of the American caddies were not too thrilled at the British influx, perceiving it as a job threat, and I suppose there was some truth to that, but I never looked at it that way.

Englishman Billy Foster was among the foreign caddies I quickly bonded with, and that's how five-time major champion Seve ended up in the van during the famous March Florida swing in the early 1990s.

Foster had already lined up a lift with me for the short trip of two hours or so up the Florida Turnpike from the Honda Classic in Fort Lauderdale to the Arnold Palmer Invitational in Orlando.

Seve was in the States with his wife, Carmen, and their two very young boys, Javier and Miguel, and they were all planning to fly, so Billy suggested to the Spaniard that the family ride in the van instead. Seve was sold on the convenience of being able to load all his luggage into the van and getting dropped off at his Orlando hotel.

It was a great experience for me, being a relatively new caddie at the time. I recall Seve's boys watching the passing scenery as their father sang them a lullaby in Spanish. As fierce a competitor as he was, I'd never seen that soft side of him before.

I had hung Seve's clothes in a closet in the back of the van, and when we pulled up to the hotel the bellhop hustled out and the two of us put all of Seve's and his family's luggage and clubs on a cart.

Seve didn't have to do anything except stand there and watch.

I hadn't discussed a fee with Seve, and did not plan to ask him for payment, but when he reached into his wallet my eyes lit up.

He had a large stack of bills and as he reached for one, up popped a $100 bill, otherwise known as a Benjamin Franklin, so named because it sports the face of the former president. Quick as a flash I grabbed it and thanked him profusely.

I thought I'd hit the jackpot, especially for such a short ride that had probably cost no more than $20 in gas. As successful as Seve was, I thought $100 would be no problem for him.

But according to Billy, his boss never planned to pay me that much.

Seve did not exactly have a reputation for splashing the cash with abandon, shall we say, and Billy said he almost had a heart attack when I grabbed the $100 note, but was too embarrassed to ask for it back.

There was no doubt, Billy said, that Seve had been searching for a $20. Instead, Cayce sharked him for five times that amount.

Billy and I got a kick out of reminiscing over that story for a long time.

Seve died of a brain tumor in 2011, while Foster was still going strong at the time of writing and rode Matthew Fitzpatrick to victory at the 2022 U.S. Open.

MAGNOLIA LANE

Not long after parting with Seve, Foster picked up another prized European bag in the form of Darren Clarke.

At the 2004 Masters I offered to collect Billy and Darren at the Augusta airport and take them directly to the course, where Darren could collect his courtesy vehicle for the week.

It was certainly worth the effort because having Darren on board meant I was granted permission to drive what was then a brand-new van down Magnolia Lane, the famous 330-yard stretch of pavement that transports one figuratively and almost literally to another world.

Washington Road is perhaps the most unappealing road in Augusta—mile after mile lined with garish neon signs and just about every restaurant chain in the country, along with assorted tattoo parlors, dollar stores, pawn shops, payday lenders, etc.

Having said that, I love TBonz Steakhouse, where you can find me nearly every night of Masters week, schmoozing with fellow caddies and seemingly everyone who's anyone in the golf world.

As noisy and busy as Washington Road is, once the security guard opens the gates to Magnolia Lane, a sense of peace and tranquility envelops the senses as the bustle recedes almost instantly to the background, little more than white noise.

The caddie parking lot is situated on the opposite side of Washington Road, but the presence of a Masters competitor in the van was all the security guard needed to grant us admission at the main entrance.

And so down Magnolia Lane we trundled, and as we approached the circle in front of the clubhouse, I spotted my boss, Fuzzy Zoeller, on the adjacent practice range.

I beeped my horn to get Fuzzy's attention and cheekily yelled, "If you get lucky, I'll give you a ride in this one day, Fuzzy."

Darren just cracked up.

There was virtually nowhere the van couldn't go.

In the words of caddie Ken Comboy, "Only Cayce Kerr can get where smoke can't."

No wonder the van was famous on tour. Not only did I use it to transport caddies, clubs, and tour radios, but it eventually became a traveling billboard.

BOB & TOM

I had my first van painted in the livery of the above-mentioned vineyard, while I later enjoyed a two-year deal with a syndicated sports radio program from Indianapolis called *The Bob & Tom Show*.

Fuzzy knew these guys, told me their show was lucrative, and introduced me when the opportunity arose.

I pitched them on the idea of having my van advertise the program, and sure enough they liked it. We lined up a detailer in Indianapolis to paint the van with the *Bob & Tom Show* logo etc., along with the words "Honk If You Listen to Bob & Tom."

The guys gave me some swag so that if someone approached me during my travels and commented on the van, I gave them a key chain or T-shirt or some other small memento.

Bob & Tom paid me $50,000 a year for two years. When they signed for a second year I was over the moon, because I thought I was one and done.

It sounds like easy money, but you've got to get the deal done in the first place. That's the hard part people forget.

NAKED AND UNAFRAID

The van has also been the venue for some fun and games over the years.

Once, while staying at a doctor friend's house in Des Moines, Iowa (see Vijay chapter), he not only was a gracious host, but was good enough to introduce me to an attractive female friend. Not that he was trying to set us up, but we hit it off immediately.

Her car and my van were both parked in the driveway, one thing led to another and we started making out in her car, before switching vehicles and spending the night horizontal jogging in my roomier van.

When she awoke naked the next morning, she asked me where her clothes were.

I said, "Sweetheart, when you climbed into my van last night, you didn't have any clothes on."

I told her that we had removed every stitch of her clothing while we were in her car and I had then talked her into moving over to my van naked.

The doctor was not amused at the happenings in his driveway, especially since the woman in question had a boyfriend, who, to my good fortune, was absent that night.

I told the good doctor that it was not my fault the woman had been so willing to play around with me (pun intended). It was too good an opportunity to turn down.

DELIVERANCE COUNTRY

But I've saved my best van story for last, and it revolves around none other than Fred Couples.

I was working for Fred at a Champions Tour event in Savannah, Georgia, in 2013.

He missed a couple of short putts down the stretch and only finished two shots out of a playoff, so his chili was running hot, so to speak.

But he did not have much time to stew on what might have been, because he had a date the following morning to play with former President George H.W. Bush in a charity pro-am in Houston.

Fred's agent, Lynn Roach, was on hand to transport Fred to the local airport for a flight by private jet to Houston. But the weather in Savannah was so bad the flight was canceled, and there was no way of knowing when the airport would reopen, so now Fred was really in a pickle.

How in the world was he going to get to Houston for an 8:30 AM tee time with the president?

That's when I stepped in with a suggestion.

I said, "Look, why don't you get in the van? I'll drive you to Atlanta airport. It's only about three hours and you can get the first flight out in the morning, be in Houston at 7:30 and the tournament will pick you up and get you to the course in time to meet the president and make your tee time."

"That's a fucking great idea," said Roach.

Fred was not quite so enthusiastic at first, but he agreed nonetheless, climbed in, and I started hightailing it to Atlanta.

He soon warmed up and realized it was the best option available.

Before long, two women in a car pulled up next to us and started screaming at Fred in the passenger seat.

He immediately thought it was a couple of fans. "What the fuck do they want?" he said.

Turns out they were good Samaritans trying to let us know we had a flat tire. They did not recognize Fred as far as I know.

Anyway, the tire lasted just long enough for us to limp to the nearest exit and park in a gas station, officially in the middle of nowhere.

And I had to break the news to Fred that I did not carry a spare tire, because it weighed down gas mileage. I was so nervous my hands started to sweat.

It did not help when Fred said: "Great. Now what the fuck are we going to do?"

He calls his agent, Roach, who reminded Fred he had a AAA membership card in his wallet. Fred did not drive, but was a AAA member, nonetheless.

So Fred fished out the card, I called AAA, and a guy arrived in a tow truck an hour or so later.

He hitched the van onto the back of the truck, and Fred and I climbed into the truck, Fred wedged into the middle seat. My goodness, a photo of that would have been priceless. I can guarantee you that Fred had never been in a tow truck before and has not been in one since.

Anyway, luckily there was a 24-hour tire center not too far away, so the driver took us there and we bought a new tire. It was dark by then.

Let's just say the scene was a long way removed from the cloistered gated community setting that a player of Fred's stature had become used to over the years. He really had a chance to see how the other half lived.

And he couldn't wait to get back to his half.

There were Black guys, White guys, rednecks, Mexicans, just about every culture you could name, and Fred had this "Get me out of here" look on his face. He did not even know 24-hour tire places existed in the United States.

The AAA guy took the van off the tow truck, jacked it up, put a new tire on, and we were on our way again, a most relieved Cayce Kerr at the wheel.

Better late than never, we got to Atlanta. I dropped Fred at his hotel and then received a phone call from his agent, who wanted me to call again in the morning to confirm I had gotten Fred onto his flight.

After a few hours of sleep, I picked up Fred, dropped him at the airport at about 5:30 AM, and then called Roach to let him know Fred was on his way to the gate.

He said, "Cayce, you're unbelievable," and I thanked him for the compliment and asked, by the way, what had Fred said about the eventful journey the previous night?

According to Roach, Fred said, "This Cayce takes me to places I had no idea existed in this country."

More importantly, Fred made his tee time with the president.

14

Celebrity Encounters

*Visiting Kevin Costner's home
and other celebrity tales*

Meeting celebrities is one of the perks of being a tour caddie, and I can't speak well enough of most of them, but there are exceptions to every generality.

Celebrities are used to being in the public eye, of course, so most handle the attention on their golf game with poise and class, humbling as it can be to hit a poor shot in a public setting, though I encountered one egregious example at the other end of the behavior spectrum, which I detail later this chapter.

One thing so many golf-playing celebrities have in common is an absolute love of the game that sometimes borders on an obsession. I think there are several reasons for this. Firstly, many celebrities are by nature type-A personalities who would not be where they are without being driven perfectionists.

Secondly, they usually have enough money to afford top instructors, as well as membership to the best clubs around, and who wouldn't enjoy playing an immaculately manicured layout with perfect greens?

Thirdly, they often have schedules that allow for plenty of downtime, and golf is a game that requires a significant time commitment.

Because so many celebrities love golf, I've had the opportunity to meet dozens of them in pro-ams over the years, from superstars of yesteryear such as Andy Williams, Bob Hope, and Ginger Rogers, to those more of the modern era like Geoge Lopez.

OSCAR-LEVEL KINDNESS

But nobody, and I repeat nobody, has ever impressed me as much as Kevin Costner, and when you finish reading this you'll certainly appreciate why.

I was working for Fuzzy Zoeller at the 2005 Outback Steakhouse Pro-Am Champions Tour event at TPC Tampa Bay, at which we played with Costner. The event was hit by such torrential rain that the tournament was rained out after only 36 holes.

I was living in Southern California at the time, San Clemente to be exact. Though I usually drove between tournaments, on this occasion I had flown to Florida, and was booked to return home on Monday morning.

By Saturday afternoon it was obvious that no play would be possible on Sunday.

The thought of spending an extra day in town unnecessarily did not thrill me, and nor did the thought of paying for an expensive change of ticket, but not for the first time, Fuzzy went to bat for me. He asked Costner, who also lived in Southern California, whether he would mind giving me a ride home on his private jet.

Costner agreed.

I have been fortunate enough to fly privately often with players, but this was the biggest private jet I'd ever seen at the time. It had about 20 seats, and only three passengers—Costner, his caddie/friend, and me, along with two pilots and one flight attendant.

I was in seventh heaven until a few minutes into the flight, when we struck severe turbulence and I started to feel queasy, so I eased myself down onto the floor and lay in the aisle. It's not as though I had to worry about getting in the way of other passengers.

I was in bad shape, so I closed my eyes, and moments later the flight attendant, or so I thought, put her hand on my head and a wet towel on my forehead to cool me off.

I said, "Thank you, dear," and a deep voice replied, "I'm not your dear."

It was Costner who had placed the towel over my head.

I thought, "How cool is this guy? He's pretty down to earth for a global movie star."

Once we emerged from the turbulence, I started to feel better, and eventually got back into my seat, only for Costner to joke, "If I knew you got sick on planes I wouldn't have given you a ride."

To which I cheekily replied, "That's why I didn't tell you."

We still had several hours ahead of us, so the two of us enjoyed a long conversation while Costner's friend slept soundly. Costner was very inquisitive about the nature of professional golf and caddying, and I was happy to educate him as well as I knew how.

When we landed at Santa Monica Airport and jumped into Costner's car, his friend took the wheel and said he would drop Costner off at his home first, before transporting me to Los Angeles International Airport (LAX), where I had left my car.

We made our way from the Los Angeles plain up some winding roads, where we finally pulled up at his La Canada house, which was discreetly tucked into the foothills near the end of a quiet cul-de-sac that saw little traffic.

I told Costner I was feeling okay when he enquired about my condition, and he promptly asked me whether I would like to come inside for a while. It was an invitation I was not going to decline. Caddies are used to doing what they're told.

It was a beautiful double-level property. It wasn't gigantic but it was gorgeous, and had a pool, all in all very tasteful. He took me inside and started showing me around. In the kitchen was a large black-and-white photograph of a herd of elephants, maybe more than 100 of them.

There were also some pictures of his kids, but none of himself. He went up in my estimation even further, because some of these celebrities take themselves so seriously. Then he asked me into his bedroom, which I found a bit strange at first, but he just wanted to show me a gigantic picture that took up the whole wall behind his bed.

The picture captured a lion jumping over a member of a camera crew during a shoot, and he told me the story of when it was taken and how dangerous a stunt it had been.

Just then he received a phone call, so his friend took me downstairs to the home theater, where Costner had the two trophies for the Academy Awards he won for the 1990 film *Dances with Wolves*, which he'd produced, directed, and starred in.

The movie captured seven Oscars all up, with Costner receiving two of them for Best Picture and Best Director. I had always wanted to hold an Oscar, so I grabbed both of them and clutched them briefly. If only I had a photo of that, but this was the pre-smartphone era and I did not have a camera on me.

Costner soon reappeared, asked me again how I was feeling, and when I said I was well enough to head home, promptly opened his freezer and gave me a huge piece of foil filled with juicy salmon, which he had caught on a recent fishing trip to Alaska.

I eventually departed after about an hour at his house, and his friend dropped me at my car at LAX, from where I made the one-hour drive home.

My then-wife could hardly believe it when I told her that the salmon was courtesy of a certain Mr. Costner.

Unfortunately, my son, Matthew, and daughter, Caroline, who were born in 1999 and 2001, respectively, were too young at the time to appreciate the story, but they sure do now.

My mother was already a big Costner fan and was delighted to learn of how down-to-earth he was off-screen. Sometimes a star's public image is not merely an illusion.

RHINESTONE COWBOY

Around the same era, Fuzzy was joined in the Tucson Open pro-am by a legendary trio of singers, Glen Campbell, Alice Cooper, and Michael Bolton.

There was plenty of time to shoot the breeze between shots, and I recall Campbell talking about how he had once received a royalty check for $7.5 million for his 1975 smash hit "Rhinestone Cowboy."

I can't vouch for the accuracy of that figure, and it sounds a bit high to be honest, but I thought that if one big hit could bring in that kind of wealth, I should try writing one myself.

"All I need is to be a one-hit wonder and I won't have to carry this bag anymore and you can kiss my ass," I joked to Fuzzy. But I had no musical training, so it did not take long for me to acknowledge that writing a tune, let alone a hit song, was beyond me, and admit defeat to Fuzzy. My caddie career continued.

Also around this time, I accompanied Fuzzy to Utah for a Robert Redford pro-am charity event.

After the golf we had the pleasure of visiting Redford's Horse Whisper Ranch near Sundance, and Fuzzy mentioned that I was a keen horse rider, so one of the employees saddled up a mare and out I went for several exhilarating hours just the equine and me in the beautiful Wasatch Range.

I returned just as the sun was setting over Mount Timpanogos and had the pleasure of meeting the great actor before we departed.

Redford sold the ranch for $6.5 million in 2022.

KENNY ROGERS AND FRIENDS

Earlier in my caddie career I had an opportunity to work at a gala charity outing at the Georgia home of country singer Kenny Rogers.

Rogers lived at the time on his 400-acre estate, Beaver Dam Farms, just outside Athens, and the magnificent property included an 18-hole golf course.

Kenny did not have to venture far when he felt like playing. The first and 10th tees were located directly outside of his master bedroom, one on each side. He also had tennis and basketball courts and a helipad, all of which were put to good use in the charity event.

This was no small charity event with B-list celebrities.

Rogers invited four golfers—including my then-boss Hubert Green—four tennis players, four basketball players, and four singers.

Two of the tennis players were John McEnroe and Vitas Gerulaitis, while the singers included Kris Kristofferson, Smokey Robinson, and Dionne Warwick.

I was asked to do the yardage book for the course, a first for me at the time, and after spending a day compiling it I was ready to meet the rich and famous and see how the other half lived. I quickly realized that they lived high on the hog.

Hubert's partner was Kristofferson and shortly after flying in on a chopper, the man whose hits include "Me and Bobby McGee" made his way to the range wearing corduroy pants that lacked a cord to keep them up properly.

I introduced myself as Cayce, and Kristofferson, who died in 2024, said that he had a daughter by the same name, though spelled differently.

"I'm a friend of Kenny's and he asked me to come, but I have no idea how to play golf, so any assistance you can provide so that I don't embarrass myself would be greatly appreciated," he said.

Not that I instantly turned him into a good player, but he was grateful for a few basic tips, and we enjoyed our day on the course.

At one stage during the day, we had a little break, and our little group was killing time when Jerry Pate asked his partner Smokey Robinson if he'd mind singing for us.

"No problem," Smokey said, and promptly belted out a few a capella bars of his megahit, "I Heard It through the Grapevine."

Excuse the cliché, but I had to pinch myself to see if I really was in the close company of such music royalty.

BO KNOWS

Years later, while I was working for Fred Couples, he played with Bo Jackson in a pro-am on the Champions Tour in Alabama.

Jackson, the only person selected to play in both the NFL Pro Bowl and the Major League Baseball All-Star Game, was great company, and he regaled us with a story of how he had felt dissed as a young man by the legendary New York Yankees owner George Steinbrenner. Jackson had been in high school when he was drafted by the Yankees in 1982, but he turned down a lucrative signing bonus offer from Steinbrenner to wear the famous pinstripe uniform.

Instead, Jackson attended Auburn University before eventually turning professional four years later and joining the Kansas City Royals.

Jackson told us he was upset when he heard that a jilted Steinbrenner had speculated that he was going to use his big contract to buy everyone in his family a Cadillac.

Bo thought it was unnecessarily stereotypical.

He was determined to show Steinbrenner just what he had missed out on, and sure enough did so in a big way during a visit to Yankee Stadium in 1990, where he hit three homers in one game. Jackson said that he made sure to tip his bat at the owner's box because he wanted Steinbrenner to know that those home runs were just for him.

That same week Fred played with Jackson in Birmingham, we also enjoyed the company of another keen golfer, Condoleezza Rice, the national security advisor and, later, secretary of state for President George W. Bush between 2001 and 2009.

She was an absolute sweetheart, if I may say so, and I was hardly surprised when one of her security detail walking with us said what a delight she was to work for.

MOONSCAPE

Early in my career, while working for Green, we played with astronaut Alan Shepard at the Bob Hope Classic pro-am at Indian Wells in the Californian desert. The course was surrounded by stark desert mountains that provided a sensational backdrop.

We were playing the back nine, the 14th or 15th hole as I recall, right up against the Santa Rosa Mountains, and Shepard couldn't help but notice a similarity to somewhere he had visited.

Noticing that Hubert and I were looking up at the mountains, Shepard said, "That's what the moon looks like."

It was hard to argue, given that neither Hubert nor I had been to the moon.

Shepard, in 1971, became the fifth man to step foot on the moon. A keen golfer, he made four swings on the lunar surface, though he only made decent contact with his final effort.

MOON RIVER

Speaking of the moon, even earlier in my career, in 1988, I had the pleasure of meeting famous crooner Andy Williams, whose many hits included the famous "Moon River." Williams was also a huge golf fan who hosted the San Diego PGA Tour stop at Torrey Pines from 1968 until 1988.

I had been a tour caddie for less than a year and was on my first West Coast swing when Williams played with my then-boss Green at the Bob Hope Classic, which in those days was a pro-am for the first 72 holes, before the pros played a fifth round alone.

Many celebrities seek a swing tip or two whenever appearing in a pro-am. Not that I am a swing expert, but I at least know enough to help out now and then and was happy to give Williams a little advice. I can't remember exactly how much he tipped me, but I do recall it was generous.

Hubert had planned to skip the following week's Andy Williams San Diego Open, so I was looking for a bag. Not being bashful, I asked Williams if I could caddie for him in the pro-am.

"That would be great, Cayce," he said. I eventually ended up lining up a bag in San Diego with George Burns, but he was not in the pro-am, so I got to caddie for Williams for a day.

He gave me a bunch of swag, including a sweater and a hat with his name on it, and he invited me to dinner. He couldn't have been any nicer. Though it was only a one-day gig, it got the attention of the other caddies.

I was always aggressive in chasing work. As they say in the United Kingdom, you've got to get stuck in there.

Those celebrities had plenty of cash, so I made sure they shared some of it with me. They always paid a little bit more than anyone else, especially if you were a tour caddie and did a good job, because they thought they were getting a bit of extra expertise.

Back to the Bob Hope Classic for a minute, that was also where I encountered another celebrity who was playing with my boss Green in the pro-am.

I did not recognize the man when he approached me on the first tee, shook my hand, and surreptitiously handed me a folded $100 bill during a handshake.

He said he did not want to embarrass himself and wondered whether I would mind giving him a bit of help with yardages, etc.

"Yes sir, no problem," I said as I opened the palm of my hand and saw my favorite American, Benjamin Franklin.

I found out from someone that the generous amateur was Donald O'Connor, the singer and dancer who won a Golden Globe for his dance routine in the 1952 film *Singin' in the Rain*.

O'Connor, it turned out, was a decent player, and after a few holes Hubert started wondering why I was giving this amateur so much help, instead of focusing on my primary responsibility.

Hubert knew something was up.

"Why are you being so nice to this guy?" he said.

"When we were on the first tee, he slipped me $100 and asked me to help him out," I replied, figuring I might as well be truthful.

So Hubert did his best to embarrass me with a little humor by yelling to O'Connor with a query as to whether he was going to pay me another $100 for the back nine.

Professionals want you to give them your undivided attention, but it's pretty common to help amateurs where you can. It doesn't cost you anything and it helps keep the pace of play moving.

It was also at the Bob Hope Classic pro-am a few years later that NASCAR driving legend Jeff Gordon played with Fuzzy.

Gordon was pleasant enough, but the only thing he spoke about all day was how much he wanted to win races. He repeated the thought over and over. That was the extent of the conversation. He said nothing about his life.

It was such single-mindedness that helped Gordon win 93 races and four NASCAR championships.

He mentioned to me that if I ever wanted to attend a NASCAR race he would make sure I was taken care of. I had never been to a race, so the following year when I was in Atlanta, I took him up on the offer and with fellow caddie J.P. Fitzgerald enjoyed a day at the storied Talladega track in Alabama.

The noise was on a vastly different scale compared to the hushed tones at golf tournaments, but I immensely enjoyed the contrasting experience.

CHARGERS

The Pebble Beach National Pro-Am was another good place to meet celebrities. I once was introduced to Dean Spanos, owner of the San Diego Chargers in the NFL.

Spanos won the amateur section of the tournament and gave me a $1,000 tip.

Though I grew up a Dallas Cowboys fan, I switched my allegiance that day, and have been a Chargers fan ever since. I sometimes joke that I wouldn't have switched for $100, but $1,000 was another story.

As another mega-wealthy businessman Kerry Packer once said, "There is a little bit of the whore in all of us."

I lived in Southern California for a while, so it was good to support my home team, even though the franchise has since moved to Los Angeles.

BUNKER TROUBLE

Not all celebrities I met behaved well.

I knew of George Lopez from TV's *George Lopez* show, among other programs, but had never met him before the day I am about to describe, when he lost his temper while playing in a pro-am and proceeded to do something that could have had dire consequences during a Champions Tour stop in which I was caddying for Fuzzy at TPC Tampa Bay.

Not that Lopez is Robert De Niro or Leonardo DiCaprio, but he was famous enough that many people knew who he was. Lopez was not exactly a single handicapper, and like a lot of mediocre amateurs, bunker play was not exactly his forte.

So we got to the par-three 17th and his tee shot found a bunker, left of the green, from where he hit too far behind the ball with his first attempt to extricate himself from the sand, and left his ball in the trap.

That was when the trouble started.

A lady in the peanut gallery started laughing, which, to be fair to Lopez, was not something anyone would like. I have an old saying that whenever people are laughing at someone it's always funny—unless they are laughing at you.

Anyway, it all could have passed without any further issues except that Lopez also left his second sand hack in the bunker.

By now the woman in the bleachers previously laughing alone had been joined by a handful of others who found the celebrity's predicament hilarious.

Lopez was certainly not amused though, and he simply snapped, turned around, took his stance facing the grandstand, and took dead aim at the lady.

Surely, he's only bluffing, I remember thinking. I thought wrong.

Lopez took an almighty swing, made clean contact (at last) and his ball came off the clubface like a rocket and whistled at a rate of knots past the stunned woman's face, missing her by inches.

I swear I am not exaggerating when I state it could have killed her. It could have been a disaster in so many ways, and there were so many witnesses that Lopez could not have denied it.

We had all seen the spectators laugh at him.

Fuzzy and I had never seen anything like that before in our entire careers, nothing even remotely close. Fuzzy always has something to say but on this occasion he was speechless. Everyone in our group was in shock. You could have heard a pin drop.

An obviously ashamed Lopez did not say anything to us, and we did not say anything to him. He just held his head low, and we finished out the hole and went to the 18th tee.

As far as I know, Lopez faced no repercussions from the PGA Tour, but he lost my respect that day, and I am sure I can say the same for everyone else who saw it.

Golf is a game that can drive you half-crazy with frustration, but you have to hold it together when you are in the public sphere, no matter what the circumstances.

The game is a test of character, and Lopez failed the test.

15

Crime and Punishment

*Carrying $1 million cash for a Japanese
high roller, and a Mexican heist*

The name **Ken Mizuno might not mean** much if anything
to you, but three decades or so ago he was one of the biggest high rollers in both his native Japan and the western United
States. When I first met Mizuno, I thought he was just a superrich golf fan and businessman who enjoyed sharing his wealth.
It wasn't until much later that I discovered it was a little more
complicated than that.

I met Mizuno in 1989 while working for Hubert Green.

Mizuno had been interested in adding a professional golfer
to his payroll for some course-design work, and from what I
heard targeted Fuzzy Zoeller, due to Fuzzy's charismatic nature
and gregarious personality.

But he instead ended up with Green, who upon their introduction in Las Vegas initially was cool to Mizuno's approaches,
though he quickly warmed up when he realized how financially
lucrative the relationship would be. Mizuno at the time owned the
Ibaraki Country Club in Japan and was in the process of buying

several expensive properties, including Indian Wells Country Club in the Palm Springs area of California.

On the first night they met, Mizuno gave Green an envelope that had thousands of dollars in it, and Hubert couldn't shut up about it.

Their relationship kept growing and I was soon a beneficiary of Mizuno's largess too.

One day I was caddying for Mizuno and Green at the old Tropicana course in Las Vegas, land that is now occupied by the MGM Grand, and while forecaddying on a par-three was struck by Mizuno's errant tee shot.

I was standing under a tree with my arm on a branch, and the ball hit me in the chest and knocked me down.

I wasn't badly injured, and any thoughts about the large bruise that was likely to develop dissipated when Mizuno handed me an envelope as a way of apology.

It contained $10,000 in cash. I kid you not.

When a sugar daddy starts handing out money like that, he quickly becomes your new best friend.

I'd only been caddying on tour for a couple of years, and $10,000 was a very big deal for me. Not about to look a gift horse in the mouth, I said, "Thank you very much, Mr. Mizuno." He even sent a doctor and a nurse to my hotel room that night to check that I was okay.

Mizuno was very ostentatious with his wealth. He had money coming out of his ears, owned a DC-9 jet, drove a Rolls-Royce, and handed out cash like candy on Halloween night. He did not do things by half measures.

One time he sent Green on a mission to buy 1,500 palm trees he wanted planted on his Indian Wells golf course. He did not care how much they cost. Remember that Green was a two-time major champion, yet here he was schlepping around Palm

Springs for his benefactor, like a common day laborer. That's how generous Mizuno was.

He even put me up once at one of his Hawaiian properties when I was there to caddie at the Sony Open. There's hardly a better place on tour to get a free room than Honolulu, where hotel prices in what passes for winter are exorbitant.

On another occasion I ran into Mizuno at the 1991 Bob Hope Classic, where Mizuno was playing in the pro-am at the Indian Wells course he had just purchased. Mizuno was on the range looking for a couple of tips, so I gave him a few pointers for maybe five minutes at most, nothing any other caddie wouldn't do, and watched him hit a few balls.

He said, "Thank you, Cayce-san."

He had his interpreter ask me where I was headed next, and I said Phoenix, at which point Mizuno reached into his pocket and peeled off $1,500 to help me pay for the drive. That was enough gas money to get much farther than Phoenix.

I told Fuzzy and Hubert the story and they joked, "Why didn't you tell him you were going to Miami?" I guess I wasn't thinking fast enough.

MYSTERIOUS BRIEFCASE

I also once stayed in a penthouse suite at the then-new Mirage in Las Vegas, courtesy of Mizuno. For a caddie more used to sharing rooms with another caddie at budget motels, it was a lovely treat.

And it was at the Mirage where my best Mizuno story unfolded.

Mizuno's friend, a guy named Frank Tatura, asked me to carry a briefcase from the Mirage to Caesars Palace next door. I wanted to make sure I wasn't carrying hard drugs, so when I expressed my concerns, Tatura quietly told me the briefcase contained $1 million in cash.

"I'll meet you over at Caesars Palace, by the cage," he whispered, referring to the area of a casino where cashiers exchange money for chips, etc. "That's all you need to know."

So a few minutes later I took the briefcase from the penthouse suite down the elevator, went outside, and walked to Caesars Palace, where I met Tatura, handed him the briefcase, and returned to the Mirage.

Part of me wondered whether instead of making my rendezvous I couldn't have jumped into a cab and hightailed it to the airport with the money, never to be seen again.

I'm not joking.

But as tempting as that was, I figured someone would track me down sooner or later. And who knows whether Mizuno had me under surveillance?

So why was I asked to carry $1 million from one hotel to another?

To this day I do not know, and I never asked for details, other than to be assured the briefcase did not contain drugs. To be honest, I never really wanted to find out.

Mizuno had been very generous over the short period of time I'd known him, so when he asked me for a quick favor, I had no hesitation agreeing.

Who knows if Tatura wasn't also carrying a similar sum?

It was definitely a covert operation, and not the sort of assignment many caddies get.

Of course I couldn't help telling my caddie buddies about it, and their reaction was invariably identical.

"When can I meet this guy?"

TOO GOOD TO BE TRUE

By now you're probably wondering whether Mizuno's generosity was too good to be true, the answer to which is an unequivocal yes.

Below is part of a wire story by United Press International in October 1993.

"Ken International Co, formerly owned by Japanese golf tycoon Ken Mizuno, agreed Tuesday to forfeit about $65 million in U.S. assets as part of a plea bargain on criminal charges.

"The firm pleaded guilty to laundering millions through expensive pieces of U.S. real estate that were fraudulently obtained by over-selling memberships at a golf course in Japan.

"Ken International also agreed in its plea in U.S. District Court to forfeit $260 million of assets, although the government can currently account for just $65 million of them.

"Federal prosecutors said Mizuno, now on trial in Tokyo on separate fraud and tax-evasion charges, used Ken International to transfer about $265 million in 'fraudulently obtained proceeds' from Japan to the United States between 1989 and 1991."

The story went on to report that Mizuno used $52 million of those funds to buy Indian Wells Country Club. At the time it was the second-biggest forfeiture case unrelated to drugs in U.S. government history.

No wonder Mizuno thought nothing of handing out a few thousand dollars to a caddie occasionally.

Mizuno was eventually sentenced to 11 years in prison in Japan.

Green, however, was never charged with a crime, despite his three-year business relationship with Mizuno until the latter was indicted in the U.S. in 1992. From what I heard, Hubert was interviewed at length by the FBI, but he had been smart and honest enough to report all his income from Mizuno.

So was I surprised to find out Mizuno was a crook? Not exactly. But he was a generous crook.

"NOBODY MOVE"

Speaking of crime, my first visit to Mexico City was certainly memorable, but not in a good way.

When the Champions Tour announced it was going south of the border for a tournament in 2003, it did not take long for word to get around for those who weren't already aware that it wasn't the safest city in the world.

I did not even search for my own accommodation, staying instead with Fuzzy at the official tournament hotel. He let me sleep on the floor in his room, which was fine by me. I was no stranger to that.

As was the custom at every tour stop, one of the first orders of business for players was to find a good nearby restaurant.

An up-market steakhouse within walking distance of the hotel seemed to fit the bill.

The PGA Tour security detail warned players not to walk alone to the restaurant, and not to wear expensive watches or flashy jewelry that might attract the eye of criminals.

On the evening after the first round, Fuzzy and I sauntered down to this highly recommended Rincón Argentino Steakhouse with Fuzzy's two pilots. He had his own jet at that time. The four of us were offered a big table next to the front entrance. It was an unusual layout, with only one table in that part of the restaurant. It was the place to sit if you wanted to be seen, with the bonus of being near the kitchen, all the better to get your steak served hot off the grill.

As it turned out, it also made the occupants of that table sitting ducks.

The remainder of the restaurant was off to the right, down a few steps, far enough removed that you couldn't hear or see what was happening upstairs near the entrance.

Fuzzy did not want any attention, so we asked to be seated near the back, and were quietly just about finishing our meals when another player, Rodger Davis, came up to us looking as white as a ghost, which is saying something if you've ever seen the deeply tanned Aussie.

Davis said he'd just had a gun pointed right at his head, actually touching it at one stage, and he asked Fuzzy, "Can I please ride out of here with you on your plane?"

Fuzzy acquiesced immediately and when we heard the details of the robbery that had just unfolded, Fuzzy in his own inimitable way said, "Well I'll be damned."

We sat gobsmacked as Davis, who was almost a major champion by the way, finishing one shot behind Nick Faldo at the 1987 British Open at Muirfield, told us the full story.

Rodger told us that two guys had entered with guns, shouted, *"Manos en el aire, nadie se mueva"*—hands in the air, nobody move—and then pulled the weapons back and cocked them.

Wallets and watches were flying off the table then. These guys weren't playing around. They took their haul and scarpered, the ordeal over in seconds.

The criminals fled with six expensive watches, one from every player at the table, and thankfully nobody was physically hurt.

After hearing the full story, Fuzzy commented that he was sure glad that we had not been seated up front, not only for the obvious reason that at least we weren't the victims, but also because he suspected I would not have been as cooperative as the robbed players.

"If we'd been there, Cayce, I know you. You'd have whacked the mother and then they probably would have shot me," he said.

I replied that I certainly wouldn't have taken their shit. What exactly I would have done I'm not sure. It would have been an instinctive reaction. And I added that he could thank me for requesting a table at the back of the restaurant.

A couple of days after the incident, Davis offered some more detail of the robbery to the Australian Associated Press.

He said that when the men initially demanded everyone's watches, he had told them to get lost, only to realize the seriousness of the situation when one of the bandits pointed a

9mm pistol at the head of fellow player Butch Sheehan. The other players at the table were Jim Thorpe, Bob Gilder, Bobby Walzel, and Walter Hall.

"A second later the other guy clipped me over the head with the butt of the gun," Davis said. "Then he cocked the gun and clicked it back and forward. I unclipped my Rolex and flung it in the air, ducked, and put my hands over my head."

Mexican authorities immediately upped security for the players and provided a police escort to the course for the rest of the week. Nevertheless, pretty much every player and caddie spent the remaining days counting down the time until we could get the hell out of town.

INSIDE JOB

Mexican authorities later determined that the heist had been an inside job.

Other players had sat at the same table on previous nights, and staff had learned that the visitors were rich pro golfers in town for a tournament.

The *Los Angeles Times* reported that two of the restaurant's security guards were arrested for the crime, along with three waiters.

As we jetted out of town a couple of nights later at the end of the tournament, accompanied by a still shaken but by now slightly less stirred Davis, Fuzzy told us to look down at the massive city below.

"This will be the last time we'll ever see this place," he said.

The story, for Davis at least, had as good an ending as could be hoped for under the circumstances. Two weeks later, the Aussie recorded his first and only victory on the Champions Tour.

16

The Gambler

"If you're gonna play the game, boy,
you gotta learn to play it right"

It's hardly a secret that many professional golfers love a bet, most famously Phil Mickelson, who lost almost $100 million over three decades, fellow sports gambler Billy Walters claimed in his 2023 memoir *Gambler: Secrets from a Life at Risk*.

In earlier times, Raymond Floyd loved to bet on golf, and back in the 1960s he arranged for a big money match in El Paso, Texas, against a young local boy named Lee Trevino.

Floyd had no idea what Trevino looked like, because Lee was not yet on tour.

So when Floyd pulled up to the clubhouse in his car, a hardworking young man quickly scurried over and politely welcomed Floyd to the club.

"I'm looking for Lee Trevino," Floyd said.

Turned out that the young man Floyd was speaking to was none other than the Merry Mex himself, who hoisted his opponents' clubs over his shoulder and took them inside. What's more, Trevino well and truly whipped Floyd in their match and took the money, the first of many money games the pair played over the years.

Trevino told me this story.

OUTHUSTLING A HUSTLER

There are a couple of other gambling anecdotes involving an inveterate gambler of a later era that I can certainly vouch for, because I was the one accepting the bets.

I'm talking about Garrett Willis, a flash-in-the-pan player who bobbed up to win the 2001 Tucson Open. He had only four other top-10 finishes his entire, otherwise lackluster career. I caddied a couple of tournaments for Willis back in 2001. He was a player with whom you did not make a long-term commitment. If you hit it off with him the first week, great; if not, you just moved on.

My first time with Willis was at the Los Angeles Open at Riviera, and he quickly discovered how much he wanted to gamble.

We had a few side bets during a practice round, whether he would par or birdie a hole, that sort of thing, and by time we got to the 18th tee I had him stuffed pretty good, up around $750, not bad for a day's work.

As we were walking down the 18th fairway, I challenged him to a double or nothing bet on how many stairs there were on the climb from the 18th green up to the clubhouse.

The stairs are clearly visible from the fairway, and he quickly started counting. I said, "Whoa, whoa, whoa, you don't get more time than me to count them."

He agreed that we would both have 10 seconds. This guy thought he was a total hustler, but what he did not know was that I already knew the answer.

I had read about those stairs in the *Los Angeles Times* that very morning, in an article that stated that there were 53 of them. I figured, correctly, that Willis would not have seen the story.

So when our 10 seconds were up and Willis guessed 56 steps, I went with 55. I knew that would win me the bet without raising his suspicions. Alarm bells might have gone off in his head had my guess been exactly correct.

We duly counted the stairs on our way up to the clubhouse, and I must admit I was slightly relieved that the number was indeed 53. After all, I had not actually counted them beforehand. Rather, I had given the author of the article credit for getting his facts right, which fortunately he had.

It was so satisfying to outhustle a guy who thought he was such a good hustler, and he never knew that the fix had been in from the time I had baited that hook back in the fairway and suggested the bet.

There's nothing better than making a bet when you already know the answer.

RINSE AND REPEAT

We missed the cut that week, but against my better judgment I picked up his bag a few months later at the Buick Classic at Westchester Country Club in the leafy suburbs north of New York City.

He again missed the cut by a country mile.

After several bets during the second round, I again was up by $750 as we got to the final hole, an easy par-five that even my grandmother could par.

His performance had been pathetic. He couldn't hit the broad side of a barn, so I made a double-or-nothing bet that he would make bogey or worse. Much to my delight, and a bit of surprise, he completely butchered it and I doubled my money. He proceeded to write me a check for $3,000 in the scorer's tent—$1,500 for my salary and $1,500 to cover his gambling losses.

We had played that day with Paraguayan Carlos Franco, whose caddie was Bradley Whittle, one of my best friends. Whittle said that Franco had been surprised if not downright shocked that Willis and I had bet during the round.

Was that against PGA Tour regulations? Hell yeah, but back then there was not as much scrutiny paid by the tour to strictly enforcing those rules. It was a different era.

Whittle said that Franco had asked him in broken English: "Caddie and player gambling?"

Whittle: "Yeah."

Franco: "Caddie betting against player?"

Whittle "Yeah."

Franco evidently could not believe it, but Willis just loved the action.

I used some of that bonus Westchester money to take Whittle—that's Whittle the caddie, not to be confused with Willis the player—to dinner that night at the Rye Bar and Grill, a rather expensive local restaurant.

Whittle and I joked for years after that about how I had taken Willis down on the West Coast and then again on the East Coast.

If he wanted to donate, the Cayce Kerr Foundation was happy to accept his money.

FRUGAL KING

As happy as I was to take Willis to the cleaners, few bits of hustling have given me more pleasure than the time I got a famous and famously tight superstar to open his wallet.

It was all for a good cause. I was chosen as fundraiser one year for the annual caddie tournament, and my good friend Eric Schwarz, affectionately known as Big E, oversaw the event itself,

Our record purse up until then had been $12,000, which I set out to beat, so I hit up a bunch of players. Fuzzy Zoeller kicked it off with $1,000, and I ended up getting six others to also contribute $1,000, and 24 others to give $500.

With others giving smaller amounts, we collected $40,000.

Many tournament directors contributed too. I told each one that a donation would encourage caddies to urge their players to enter their event the following year. I lied to them all, because it's not as though a caddie has any influence on his player's schedule.

The superstar who gave us $1,000 was none other than Arnold Palmer, and I took considerable pride in getting the King to part with a four-figure sum, because he had a reputation of being one of the cheapest guys around. He certainly was not overly generous to his caddies.

So here's how we hit him up. During the PGA Tour's Disney World Classic in Florida in October, Schwarz and I drove up to nearby Bay Hill, where Arnold lived and had an office in the clubhouse. We planned to go inside looking for Arnie, but upon arrival saw him hitting balls on the range, so we sauntered on over.

"Arnold, how are you?" I said.

"Fine, Cayce," he replied, and I introduced Big E, explaining that he was the chairman of our caddie tournament for which we were raising funds.

"Fuzzy kicked it off with $1,000, and we're here to see how much we can put you down for," I said, deliberately framing the question in that manner.

Arnold did not reply immediately, and Big E and I stayed silent awaiting a response.

Finally, after a few seconds, Arnie said, "How much did you say Fuzzy kicked in?"

I repeated the figure and Arnold without any great joy in his voice said, "Put me down for the same amount."

We thanked him, picked up a personal check from his secretary the following day, and were so proud to extract such an amount from Palmer that we pinned the check up in the caddie trailer for the rest of the week.

One even more frugal player proved a tougher nut to crack.

Curtis Strange had a reputation of being even tighter than Arnie. I once saw him having breakfast in a Waffle House, the inexpensive chain restaurant that the caddies call Awful House.

I thought to myself, "This guy is a two-time U.S. Open champion and he's eating at a Waffle House! You've got to be kidding."

A few years later, when I asked Curtis to contribute to the caddie event, he reluctantly removed a thick wedge of $100 bills from his pocket, at least 100 of them by my estimation.

He peeled one off and handed it over.

"Can I have another one?" I asked, figuring I had nothing to lose.

"Don't press your luck," he said sternly, and I knew he wasn't joking.

With $40,000 for our tournament, we found sudden interest from caddies who in previous years had been lukewarm about playing.

We routinely had a bunch of no-shows, or caddies who were late for their tee times, but guess how many entrants did not turn up on time that year?

Exactly none. Money talks.

17

Superstitions

Habits and idiosyncrasies of top players

Just as with life in general, some golfers are highly superstitious and some not at all. Among the players I worked for, Payne Stewart and Charl Schwartzel belonged in the latter camp. Ernie Els, on the other hand, had a most interesting superstition. For reasons that I'm unclear about, he insisted on replacing his ball whenever he made a birdie. He believed that a ball had only one birdie in it. Ernie is no dummy, so he must know deep down that a ball is an inanimate object, but you don't argue with your boss. You just accommodate his wishes.

So whenever Ernie birdied a hole, I would immediately hand him a new ball when he walked off the green and made his way to the bag.

If he made nine birdies in a round, I had better make sure I had nine balls. So when I worked for Ernie, I would not give any balls to kids in the gallery because I could not afford to take any chances.

Sometimes I would give one to the standard-bearer or the scorer, but I knew in those cases that I could ask for it to be returned in an emergency. I could just promise to get the volunteer a souvenir ball once the round was done and dusted.

So why did Ernie have such a superstition? He never told me, and if he did not want to tell me, I was not going to ask.

Which leads me to the question of how many balls I usually started a round with? When I first began caddying, I would always have a dozen in the bag, but as I got older I often went down to nine, or even less. It would depend on the player. You always want to keep the bag as light as possible, without leaving out anything that might be needed.

With someone like Fred Funk, for example, you did not even need nine balls, because he played the whole round with one ball. And because he was such a relentlessly straight hitter, he rarely lost a ball in a hazard.

But every player is different. Some change their ball every three holes or so—Jack Nicklaus springs to mind—some every six holes, and some rarely at all.

ONE BALL REMAINING

I've come close to running out of balls, but not as close as Steve Williams, who did not have a single one left in the second round at the 2000 U.S. Open at Pebble Beach.

Tiger Woods had to complete five holes of his second round on Saturday morning, and his caddie Williams did not check how many were in the bag before they resumed.

There had been six balls in there when they left the course on Friday night, but it turned out that Tiger had removed three of them to practice putt in his room and had forgotten to put them back.

Williams had neglected to check the number of balls before the resumption, which meant Tiger had only three balls remaining, and he gave one to a boy after scuffing it on the 14th hole.

Therefore, when Tiger hooked his drive onto the shore-line rocks of the mighty Pacific Ocean at the par-five 18th, he unleashed a profanity-laden tirade that no doubt would have been even worse had he known he was down to his last ball.

Williams had his heart in his mouth, and, as he said in an interview with the U.S. Golf Association, it was the most nervous he had ever been on the golf course. He knew he would be at risk of being fired if Tiger lost another ball and tried to talk him into foregoing the driver and hitting an iron off the tee instead, words that fell on deaf ears.

Fortunately for Williams, Tiger's drive found the fairway and he negotiated the hole without any further trouble, thus allowing the caddie to avoid a nasty recrimination.

Williams did not tell Woods the story until after the tournament, and Tiger told him that he knew something was up at the time and, yes, he would have sent the caddie packing had that last ball been swallowed up by the ocean.

If he had lost that last ball, Woods would have had two options, both of which would have incurred a two-shot penalty. He could have scrounged a ball from another player, but this would have violated the one-ball rule that requires players to use the same type of ball the entire round. Woods was the only player in the field that week using the then-new Nike Tour Accuracy ball.

Alternatively, he could have waited for one of his entourage to retrieve another of his balls from his locker, or wherever he kept them.

Either way, the two-shot penalty would not have mattered too much in the bigger picture given that Tiger won by a record 15 shots. It would have been a helluva story, however.

But the episode demonstrates that even a caddie as professional as Williams is only human.

Nobody can be good at everything, all the time, especially when your job is so demanding. Working for Tiger, knowing that every second of your day at the course is being scrutinized by television cameras, professional photographers, and thousands of spectators, is big-time pressure.

OTHER MAJOR CHAMPIONS

Fred Couples also had a superstition of sorts, in that while I worked for him on the Champions Tour, he used a shiny black driver with no scratches and was determined that it remained that way. He said that I would be fired should I get so much as one scratch on it, so you can imagine how careful I was with that baby.

Even worse, he added that I would be fired even if *he* was responsible for a scratch. In those circumstances, it would be my fault for not having gotten the club out of his hands quickly enough.

He wanted the head cover placed back on the driver immediately after a shot, and I was happy to oblige. I stood closer to him than usual on his tee shots to make sure I could grab the driver without delay. Fred was very attached to that club. It looked so beautiful to him, and he wanted it to remain perfect. I'm happy to report it remained scratch-free during my two-year tenure.

Another major champion, former PGA Championship winner John Mahaffey, would not allow his caddie or anyone else to touch his grips, ever, under no circumstances. You could only touch the shaft.

He did not want to risk anything that might change the way the grips felt.

Mahaffey also never took off his glove during a round, which is unusual, because most players remove the glove to putt, but a small percentage do not.

Vijay Singh always played a ball with the same number, 19, the date of his son Qass' birthday. The balls were stamped by Titleist specifically for Vijay, and it was a great way to ensure he would never get his ball mixed up with another player's, because most balls are numbered between one and four.

Vijay was not particularly superstitious for the most part, but I do recall one oppressive day at the John Deere Classic in the Quad Cities when I threw away his towel at the end of the front nine, which he played in six under par. He had been hanging the towel around his neck and it was soaked with sweat and other moisture and was downright disgusting.

As we walked off the 10th tee, he wanted to wipe his face, so I fetched a fresh towel out of the bag, only to be asked where the old towel was.

He said, "I don't want this towel. That other towel's six under par." He made me scurry back and retrieve it from the trash can where I had discarded it.

He promptly birdied the next hole and then parred the 11th, at which point he figured the towel's magic had worn off and that he was finally ready for a new one.

"Throw that towel away now," he said.

I couldn't get rid of it fast enough.

IDIOSYNCRASIES

Many players had what might be termed idiosyncrasies or unusual habits, rather than superstitions.

Former U.S. Open champion Steve Jones, for example, did not want to be handed his putter until he was one yard from the green: Not two yards, not 10 yards. Not until he was about to take that first step on the green would you hand over his putter. The only other player I worked for with the same approach was Andy Bean. Jones and Bean preferred not to switch their brains into putting mode until they arrived at the green.

A lot of players want the putter as soon as their approach shot finds the putting surface, no matter how far away, but not Jones and Bean.

David Frost also had a policy that he wanted a 10-minute and a five-minute warning before his tee time, no exceptions.

If he was still on the range at the 10-minute warning, he would immediately hustle over to the putting green.

And he used the five-minute warning to allow himself ample time to get from the putting green to the first tee. He was such a great putter that he did not feel the need to spend much time working on his stroke before teeing off.

Frost was not the most popular player on tour. There was not a lot of love for him, and he is not someone who will ever be missed. He wasn't one of Els' favorites. Let's just say they did not exchange Christmas cards.

But as a golfer, Frost gets huge respect. He won 10 times on the regular tour and when I worked for him on the Champions Tour, he still had heaps of game. I had the pleasure of being on the bag at the Minnesota TPC for his first win on the 50-and-over circuit in 2010. He shot 61 in the final round, starting birdie, par, birdie, birdie, eagle, and won by seven strokes.

He lost a three-way playoff that same year at the Senior PGA Championship at Colorado Golf Club. Fred Couples was also in the playoff, which was won by Tom Lehman.

To illustrate how obsessive golfers can be about their profession, Frost sometimes texted me in the middle of the night with a message about something in his swing that he wanted to work on the next day. I had to make sure to remind him. Those texts showed that instead of sleeping peacefully, he was thinking about his swing.

I used to text back a patented answer, "Will do," or something like that, so that he would know I had received the message and would not resend it.

People might think Frost must have been crazy being so obsessed with his swing that he would go to those lengths in the middle of the night, but in fairness to him, pretty much all players are crazy one way or another.

EVEN NUMBERS

And last but certainly not least, Fuzzy Zoeller used only even-numbered irons—2, 4, 6, 8—during his warm-up.

He did not hit a 3-, 5-, 7-, or 9-iron until it was necessary during a round.

The backstory to this was that when Fuzzy was a boy his father bought a full set of clubs and gave Fuzzy all the odd-numbered irons and his brother the even numbers.

Contrary to what many believe, Fuzzy hailed from a very modest background. He married into money, to which I say, good for him. As the old saying goes, it's just as easy to fall in love with a rich woman as a poor woman.

After hitting odd-numbered irons all through his upbringing, Fuzzy had had enough, hence he switched to hitting even numbers.

It's probably not necessary to hit every iron in the bag before a round anyway, so even-numbered irons allowed him to work his way through the bag in a timely fashion.

18

Odds and Ends

*From the best haircut of my life
to a not-so-golden bear*

NICK FALDO

My late British journalist friend Billy Blighton made a career out of covering basically one player on the PGA Tour. I'm talking about Nick Faldo, the winner of six major titles and for many years the best British player by the length of the Ascot straight.

Blighton moved to the United States in the early 1990s and attended nearly every American tournament Faldo played for nearly a decade, until the writer's premature death at the age of 54 in 2001.

He freelanced for half a dozen British newspapers, and interviewed Faldo without fail after every round, whether the player shot 66 or 76. The pair became quite close, so much so that Faldo started to confide in Bill in 1995 that he was having an extramarital affair with a young college golfer. Blighton could have had a big scoop that the British tabloids would have paid handsomely for, but Bill instead told Faldo he did not want to hear about it, leaving it for a competitor to ultimately land the story.

One day at the Players Championship, I was caddying in the same group as Faldo, who hit a beautiful tee shot that set up a tap-in birdie at the par-three 13th. After the round, while the players were signing their cards, I quietly mentioned to Bill that Faldo had hit a lovely five-iron fade for that birdie and suggested it would be a good way to start the conversation.

Moments later, Faldo came over to talk to Bill, whose first words were, "That was a terrific fade with your five-iron at the 13th, Nick. Tell us about it."

Faldo was mightily impressed that Bill knew not only the club, but the ball flight. When players think a reporter has walked the course with them and paid such close attention to detail, they usually afford the writer more respect.

Little did Faldo know that Blighton had never left the media center all afternoon, but Bill said that Faldo could not shut up about the shot as soon as it was brought up.

JOHN DALY

Drives of 300 yards are commonplace these days—the average on the PGA Tour in 2023 was 299.9 yards—but three decades ago they were pretty much unheard of, except in specific conditions.

Unheard of that is until a 25-year-old guy named John Daly appeared seemingly out of nowhere to win the 1991 PGA Championship at Crooked Stick in Indiana.

The story has often been told of how he was the ninth alternate for that championship and drove through the night to get to the course once he heard he was in the field following a spate of withdrawals.

Taking a gigantic backswing that brought the club almost to vertical, he generated enormous power with his aggressive "grip it and rip it" philosophy, and his victory was greeted raucously by golf fans who bonded instantly with a new blue-collar hero who smoked on the course—a rarity these days—and chugged beer off it as though worried that they weren't making any more.

Daly wasn't an instant success story to me, though. He had already played a bunch of practice rounds with my man at the time, Hubert Green, and a future boss in Fuzzy Zoeller.

I remember his then-wife, Bettye Fulford, walking in the middle of the fairway with John, attached to him like superglue, and telling us her age. She was 13 years Daly's senior, and we immediately gave her the nickname "Fast Bettye."

When you were on the outside looking in, it was easy to see this woman was taking full advantage of John. She had hooked this young guy who she probably thought was going to be a superstar. The tumultuous on-again/off-again relationship produced a baby girl, before the couple finally called it quits for good in 1995.

Daly bought two rangefinders from me when I was selling the then-new hot golf item in 1996. (See Rangefinders chapter.) He lost them and then wanted me to give him a free one, but I declined.

It wasn't my fault he couldn't keep track of them.

MARGARITAVILLE

Fellow caddie Ken Comboy and I were entering the upmarket Aunt Chilada's Cafe on Hilton Head Island in South Carolina once and by coincidence arrived almost simultaneously as Ben Crenshaw.

I held the front door open for Ben and we exchanged pleasantries.

I told him I was well and added, "Our timing couldn't be any better. We're just in time for you to treat us to dinner."

I was joking, but Ben said, "Well, I'm by myself, so I'd be happy to buy you guys dinner." We got a table, enjoyed a pre-dinner margarita, and talked about nothing but the Ryder Cup.

Ben loved discussing the Ryder Cup and Comboy did too, as you'd expect from an Englishman.

Eventually, our sizzling hot meals were placed in front of us and Ben eagerly cut into his first enchilada, stuck his fork into it and was just about to take a delectable first mouthful when a boorish fan stuck a pen in Ben's face and asked for an autograph.

Gentle Ben did not say a word, but I could tell he was steaming. He put down his fork, signed the autograph without saying a word, and the solipsistic fan wandered off after offering a perfunctory thank you.

Comboy thought it was pure class by Ben to accommodate the request with such poise and as much graciousness as one could reasonably expect under the circumstances.

EQUIPMENT

I've worked for some players who never (or rarely) changed their equipment and some who switched all the time.

Fuzzy, for example, used the same driver for seven years. He had been searching for a long time for something he really liked, and must have tried about 100 drivers, but nothing felt perfect.

Then, one day, he picked up a new club and it was almost love at first sight. He hit one ball, and his eyes lit up. He asked for another ball, and the second practice shot confirmed what the first one had told him. He had found his new Betsy.

Tour players have an amazing touch and feel that separates them from your average golfer. They need something with exactly the correct weight, length, shaft, loft, and lie, and they can feel a minute change in specifications.

That's why the tour companies' trailers are so busy early in tournament week.

Some players stick with the clubs they like, but others are seduced by the telephone numbers that manufacturers throw at them to switch.

That does not make them bad people. It just makes them whores. They all think the same thing, that if the price is right, they will learn to hit it, but it's not always that simple. There are so many examples of players losing their game after switching equipment that you would think it would have served as a reality check by now.

There is no better recent example than that of the then-world No. 1 Justin Rose, who in 2019 signed a lucrative contract with Japanese clubmaker Honma to use 10 of its clubs. Rose was the first tour player contracted to Honma, and though he won in San Diego in his second start with the new clubs, his game soon went south, and barely a year later he played the Bay Hill Invitational without a single Honma club in his bag.

He had slipped to 14th in the world by May of 2020 when he and Honma announced their divorce, and Rose returned to his old lover, TaylorMade, whose clubs he had previously played for 20 years.

ENTOURAGES

When I first came out on tour in the late 1980s, entourages were non-existent. The only people accompanying a player most weeks were his caddie and occasionally his instructor and/or agent for a day or two. But as players began making more and more money, their entourages expanded almost as quickly as their net worth.

Most modern players have so many people on their payroll it's hard to keep track. The list is seemingly endless: agent, full-swing instructor, short-game instructor, putting coach, fitness trainer, psychologist, masseuse, chef, club-fitter, and so on and so on. Hey, let's just include a flower girl and invite everyone to the party.

Every pig has his snout in the trough, to coin an old phrase. Some of these people I see as valuable, others not so much.

The agent is obviously there to make money, for which he takes a healthy cut, usually about 20 percent or so for any contract negotiated.

An instructor can bring value by helping a player play better, which, it never should be forgotten, is what it really is about.

And sore backs are a perennial issue for many players, so there is value to having a massage therapist who knows your body.

Trainers, however, I'm not so sure about. Having one on the payroll is not necessarily a bad idea, intrinsically, but I noticed over time that these guys often started to get a bit full of themselves and thought they deserved major credit for the success of their players.

I wish they would just do their job and be happy to have a job that pays very well and stop thinking that they are the ones actually hitting the shots.

GREEN-READERS

Learning to read greens is a highly valuable skill. Some caddies excel at it, while others never master it.

Thankfully, green-reading books were banned by the PGA Tour in 2022. They had been introduced in 2008 and offered far more detail than the traditional yardage book, which simply showed general information of how a green sloped. Green-reading books were far more detailed, providing an exact percentage of slope in different sections of greens.

They turned putting from part science and part art into an almost exact science, and many players were dismayed that the art of reading a putt had become to an extent a redundant skill.

So how were green-readers so accurate?

Golf Digest described them perfectly.

"The process begins by placing an optical scanning laser directly on or close to the green. Some scanners cost about $120,000 and are used to take impressions of oil rigs, industrial spaces, and even car-accident scenes.

"The unit shoots a laser beam at a mirror that is spinning rapidly within the housing of the device. Millions of beams, reflected by the mirror, are projected onto the landscape of the green, scanning as the device rotates to encompass the entire surface.

"As each beam is redirected at the green, it is measured precisely. Very precisely. Minute differences in height are measured and fed into storage. Typically, three million to four million bits of data are collected, all in the 10 minutes it takes to scan a green."

They cost more than $100,000, so the technology is obviously not cheap.

My observation was that the devices helped players make more putts. Player still had to put a good stroke on the ball obviously, but the devices gave them more confidence because they did not have to second-guess themselves.

When you see a player leave a medium-length putt short, it is usually because he is not confident in his read. Interestingly, green-reading books were never allowed at the Masters.

VOLUNTEERS

Volunteers are the lifeblood of the PGA Tour and all other tours for that matter.

Without them, there would be no tour. Even the most cashed-up tour event would be hard-pressed to operate if it had to pay everyone needed to make a tournament function. Volunteers have also been very generous to me over the years, often offering me complimentary accommodation for the week.

But there is one volunteer who I recall most fondly of all, a woman I met at the Players Championship. She was a hairdresser and kindly offered to come to my ocean-front hotel room one day to give me a trim.

When she arrived, I cheekily told her that one of my fantasies was to get a cut by a naked hairdresser on the balcony while I gazed out to sea.

She happily obliged, and I can honestly say it was the most memorable haircut I ever received.

AMERICA'S GUEST

Volunteers are not the only locals who have generously put me up during tournament week.

In Hartford, for example, a married couple who used to follow Fuzzy every week at the PGA Tour stop there invited me to stay in their townhouse.

The guy was a character. He owned two funeral homes and one night when I was tired of telling golf stories, I passed the baton to him to regale our audience. He told a couple of stories that were so outrageous that I vowed never to give him a chance to make me listen to them again, stuff about bodies, embalmings, and whatnot.

On the other side of the country, I met an amateur at Pebble Beach who became a good friend and invited me to stay at his house within walking distance of the range. Now that's some prime real estate, and there is hardly a better place to stay for free than the Monterey Peninsula, where accommodation usually costs a small fortune.

Farther down the California coast, I often stayed with a doctor friend in Bel Air for the Riviera tournament that I still like to call the L.A. Open.

In Tucson I stayed on a 3,000-acre ranch for 25 years. Some of these relationships went on for decades.

I'd get my guests tickets for the tournament and they enjoyed hearing fresh stories over dinner every night of what really happened at the course that day that they would never find out through the media coverage.

Another advantage of staying privately was avoiding those sometimes-awkward encounters in hotel lobbies or elevators with strangers who figured out you were a looper and asked you to confirm as much, before peppering you with questions.

As much as I like to say I've never met a stranger, there are occasions after a bad day when I just wanted to be left alone and retreat to my room.

The question among caddies when you arrived at every tournament was, "Where are you staying this week?" It was always nice and posh to say, "I'm staying privately," even more so because caddies invariably shared a room.

In the early days I couldn't afford to stay alone, and that was an old habit that died hard even after I started accumulating some wealth. I have always been a minimalist.

I was fortunate enough to stay privately at other tour stops in Washington, Houston, and San Antonio, among other places.

In Washington, I stayed with a friend I'd made during my time caddying at Congressional. This guy was a fanatical golfer and his house was big enough that I was able to invite a few of my caddie friends to stay as well. We all gave him enough free balls—slightly used, as most pros change balls every few holes— that he had enough to last the entire year.

In Louisville, Fuzzy had a friend named Steve Wilson, who owned a farm, and one year when the PGA Championship was there, he put up several of us. We all brought him back memorabilia from our players, often balls, but sometimes even clubs. The guy loved the caddies.

In Houston I'd stay with an aunt, while in San Antonio I enjoyed the company of my dear mother, or sometimes my uncle Charlie.

FAVORITE COURSES

Pebble Beach is my favorite course. The design of every hole is brilliant, and the views of the Pacific are just a bonus.

It's about the only course where caddies want to stay out there longer. I've talked to a lot of my peers and we all agree it's a place where you never count down the holes, unlike a lot of other venues where you can't wait to get done.

My second favorite is the new course at Sunningdale outside London. I played there once with 1996 U.S. Open champion Steve Jones while we were in the area for another tournament. The new course is hardly new, designed more than a century ago by Harry Colt, who used the terrain to fashion a beautiful masterpiece that stands the test of time. British links courses are more famous, but Sunningdale is proof that it has some inland gems too.

I also love two other courses with greens just as fast if not faster than those at Augusta National. One is Royal Melbourne, where I caddied for Vijay Singh in two tournaments in 2013. The other is the Taiheiyo Club Gotemba course in Japan. Talk about a hidden gem. The greens when I worked there were like greased lightning, and the location, at the base of snow-capped Mount Fuji, the tallest peak in Japan, was about as close to golfing nirvana as I've experienced. A quick glance at the photo on the club's internet home page is all you need to know I am not exaggerating about the view.

ELS CENTER OF EXCELLENCE

After Ernie Els and his wife Liezl's son Ben was diagnosed with autism, they devoted their time and resources to developing the Els Center of Excellence, which opened in 2015 in south Florida.

A friend of mine from Maryland called me a few years ago and said that he could not get his son into the school, which caters to autistic children. All it took was one phone call from me to Liezl and it was a done deal. My friend's son was admitted to the school.

My friend moved his family to Florida to accept the offer and he called me in tears later to say he was eternally grateful to the Els' for their help.

It shows what a quality couple Ernie and Liezl are.

INSTRUCTION TIPS

Everyone seems to go to YouTube for instruction tips these days but I can think of no better simple advice than that offered by Steve Elkington. He said that there are three fundamentals of the game that require no athletic ability—stance, grip, and posture.

I got that verbatim from Elkington and it was probably the smartest thing I ever heard him say.

Once you get those fundamentals down and get yourself in an athletic position, you can start playing the game and become a solid player. I've given lessons focusing on those fundamentals and have had people say they learned more in an hour than in several lessons with their local pro. That's how I know they are effective and important.

GOODNIGHT JIM

Jim Goodnight, the co-founder of the SAS Institute software company, perennially tops the list of the richest person in North Carolina, with an estimated net worth approaching $10 billion.

Goodnight is also a keen golfer and owns the Prestonwood course in Cary, where the Senior Tour's SAS Championship is held.

I worked for Fuzzy Zoeller when he played with Goodnight in the tournament pro-am.

As Fuzzy and I were making idle chit-chat walking down a fairway, I jokingly asked Fuzzy whether he thought Mrs. Goodnight would say, "Goodnight, Jim" to her husband before turning out the light at bedtime.

The mischievous Fuzzy promptly threw me under the bus.

"Hey, Jim," Fuzzy yelled out, "Cayce wants to know whether your wife says, 'Goodnight, Jim' before you turn out the light at night."

Goodnight fortunately had a good chuckle.

NOT-SO-GOLDEN BEAR

It's common to see wildlife during professional tournaments, usually squirrels, turtles, birds, deer, the occasional snake perhaps.

But sometimes an animal sighting creates quite a stir.

Such was the case at the 2008 U.S. Senior Open at the Broadmoor in Colorado Springs, where there was a bear sighting, and I'm not talking about the Golden Bear.

I was in the caddyshack when my friend Tommy Lamb entered excitedly after his morning round. I thought he might be wanting to talk about his round with Jay Haas, but that was not foremost on his mind. Lamb instead told us that a black bear had wandered onto the course and, no doubt sniffing the smell of frankfurters that had wafted across the premises, had raided a hot dog stand in search of an easy meal.

It just goes to show you the popularity of hot dog stands. The bear evidently disappeared after realizing it could not access the dogs.

"I've seen a lot of things on a golf course, but never a bear," Lamb said.

PART FIVE

THE CADDIES

19

So You Want to Be a Caddie

Advice on becoming a looper

Being a PGA Tour caddie is hard work, and while the rewards for those with good players make it financially lucrative these days, that does not mean that it's easy money. It's certainly not a nine-to-five job. The hours are long, job security non-existent, and you work seven days a week, sometimes for long stretches at a time.

A typical week unfolds thus: Sunday night is for traveling between tournaments, sometimes stretching into Monday, depending on the distances involved, while Monday is also a day to walk the course. Tuesday is practice day, Wednesday pro-am day (or a long, boring day on the range if your player is not in the pro-am), and the starting gun finally goes off on Thursday.

If your player makes the cut and is playing the following week, there is no time for a breather. As soon as you get done on Sunday, hopefully with a little money in your pocket from a good finish, you immediately hit the road. It does not happen so much these days, but back when I first started it was common for a player to compete four weeks straight, so if he made the cut every week you went almost an entire month without a day off.

And I used to try to pick up another bag when my regular boss skipped a tournament, so working 28 days straight was par for the course.

And you can forget about public holidays. You're invariably away for Memorial Day, July 4, Labor Day, and often Thanksgiving.

I recall being in Japan for eight consecutive Thanksgivings. I almost forgot what it was all about because I was always out of the country.

Christmas is about the only time of year you are guaranteed to be at home, because there are no tournaments that week.

It was fairly easy to get a job when I first started caddying, because there was not a lot of quality competition for good bags, to be brutally honest.

You probably know the old saying that a caddie needs to do three things—show up, keep up, and shut up, but you'd be amazed at how many caddies could not manage even those basics, especially the showing up on time bit.

As I've detailed elsewhere (see Caddies Behaving Poorly chapter), the quality of the loopers 35 years ago wasn't always top notch. The average caddie was broke, uneducated, would frequently turn up late and hungover, and often did not show great attention to detail.

Engineering graduates generally did not make their way to the PGA Tour caddie ranks back then. There simply was not enough money for the average rank-and-file caddie to earn a decent living. And caddies were not always professional and savvy enough to say the right thing at the right time, or perhaps more pertinently not to say the wrong thing at the wrong time.

I remember reading a 2007 *Golf Digest* interview with David Graham about his bad experience with his caddie at the 1979 PGA Championship.

Graham detailed the story of how he had a two-shot lead playing the 72nd hole at Oakland Hills in Michigan, but after hitting his drive wide right had too many spectators in the way to figure out his yardage to the hole. So Graham said he asked his caddie Willie Peterson for a number. Now Peterson was no novice, having worked for Jack Nicklaus many times at the Masters, but his answer was not exactly what the player expected.

"Willie's answer was shocking: 'You haven't asked me one question all the way around. I don't know. Figure it out for yourself,'" Graham recalled in the interview.

A flabbergasted Graham made an educated guess, but clearly got his number wrong and hit a six-iron over the green. He made a double-bogey to fall into a playoff with Ben Crenshaw.

Now here's the kicker.

On the way to the scorer's tent, Willie said, "Don't worry, boss, we'll get 'em in the playoff."

To which an understandably livid Graham replied, "Don't even speak to me. The farther you stay away from me the happier I'll be. Just carry the clubs."

The story had a happy ending for Graham when he won the playoff for the first of two major victories, but just imagine how much bad blood there would have been if the playoff result had been reversed.

Willie might have been miffed that Graham had been doing his own yardages and not relying more on his looper, but his response was still stunning and unprofessional, something that I cannot believe would happen in a major championship today under any circumstances, no matter how extenuating.

STARTING OUT

So if you still want to be a tour caddie, first you must learn the trade by working at either a private club or an upscale resort.

Sadly, fewer clubs in the U.S. have caddie programs than when I was starting out, but it wouldn't hurt to do a bit of research to find out if there are any in your local area that use caddies and, if so, try to start there.

If you present yourself as respectable, chances are you will get your foot in the door.

If there is nothing available locally, and you are prepared to move, resorts such as Bandon Dunes in Oregon and Pinehurst in North Carolina need a lot of caddies.

Pinehurst uses lots and lots of caddies for their 10 courses, and if you're keen and behave professionally, it probably won't matter if you've never caddied before, so long as you show a willingness to learn.

The base rate for a round is not great, but with tips it can add up to a half decent living for a young person without a family or huge overheads.

Work as often as you can and gain as much experience as quickly as possible.

Learn how to read a yardage book, learn etiquette, interpersonal skills, green reading, everything that is relevant for a job that is part art and part science. You need hard skills and soft skills.

There is a big difference in the quality of golf between a 22-handicapper and a professional, but the basics are the same, no matter how good or bad the player is.

TOUR CADDIE

If you subsequently want to become a tour caddie, I'm afraid to inform you that it is more challenging to break into the business than it used to be. Apart from the red-hot competition to get a bag, due to the quality of those already employed being so professional, there are fewer opportunities to pick up a job in the players' parking lot at tournaments.

As detailed later in this chapter, that used to be the prime spot to find employment, but modern technology has largely put paid to that.

LOMBARDI TIME

But if you do somehow graduate to the pro ranks, remember the mantra that you are only ever one shot away from being fired on any given day. The day you forget that is the day you'll be in trouble.

Never rest on your laurels. I had a basic rule that I got to the course an hour before I'd been told to be there. They call that Lombardi time, after the legendary Green Bay Packers NFL head coach. The quickest way to be fired by a pro is to be late, and players often show up early because they get tired of sitting in their room if they have a late tee time.

I got my job with Fuzzy Zoeller because of his previous caddie's tardiness. (See Tour Beckons chapter.)

Another important thing to remember is to always count the clubs on the first tee to ensure there are no more than 14 in the bag. Don't worry about counting them before you get to the tee, because it's possible a club could be slipped into the bag at the last moment.

I once allowed Fuzzy Zoeller to tee off with 15 clubs, a costly mistake that I have detailed elsewhere in the book. (See Masters chapter.)

WRONG BALL MISTAKE

And identify what ball your playing partners are using, because it is not rare for pros to hit the wrong ball. I'm thankful it happened to my man only once, but once was enough.

The occasion was a long-ago Players Championship at Sawgrass when I was working for Hubert Green, who was playing the same type of ball as Dave Rummells.

At the par-five second, both players hit drives down the middle of the fairway and their balls came to rest about 10 yards apart. They subsequently played their second shots and Hubert found the green. Once we got to the putting surface, Hubert threw his ball to me to clean. I tossed it back and he looked at it and said, "This isn't my ball."

Pretty much every player marks his ball uniquely with a Sharpie for the very reason to minimize the chances of hitting the wrong ball, and Hubert noticed the mark was not his.

Both he and Rummells received two-stroke penalties and we all had to trudge back to the spot on the fairway where the error had occurred, and we resumed playing the hole from as close as possible to where our tee shots had ended.

While the player is not totally blameless in such situations, it is primarily the caddie's fault. There were four idiots in our group—two players and two caddies—and I was one of them.

CHECKLIST

Another caddie basic is a checklist of things you need in the bag or your pockets.

The basics include yardage book, pin sheet, balls, gloves, ball marker, tees, towels, rain gear, sweater, umbrella, Sharpie, and pencil. The quantities of balls, etc. depends on the player and conditions.

The caddie is in charge of the entire bag and must let the player know everything that is and is not in the bag.

And it is important to house every item in the correct bag pocket, and to know what is where. For example, you don't want to have to unzip every pocket in a panic looking for a new glove when your boss asks for one.

I also have a personal rule that I put a player's personal non-golf items in the same pocket in the bag—usually a wallet, phone, credential, and often a watch.

As soon as the player hands them to me before a round, I tuck them away and zip up the pocket. I don't unzip it for the rest of the round. That way, I cannot be accused of any shenanigans.

Every player has unique requirements about what he wants in his bag. Most pros require you to carry two or three gloves, but Fuzzy loved having a couple of dozen. He used a new one every day.

He was very finicky because he said the stitching could be different on every glove.

Sometimes he would try on two or three just to get the right one. My friends certainly liked that, because I always had plenty of gloves to give them.

Fuzzy also wanted a tube of Krazy Glue in his bag, because his thumb often split, while Ernie Els wanted a couple of Nutri-Grain bars. He was very specific about this. A different type of bar was not acceptable.

The yardage book is perhaps the single most important item and I never went anywhere without it during a tournament. Many caddies kept it in the bag, but I preferred to always have it on me because I figured I would be less likely to lose it.

I had a lot of valuable information in my yardage book—notes detailing the clubs my man had hit the previous day or days, sometimes even the previous years, what the wind had been doing, and assorted other tidbits.

"LISTEN, YOU IDIOT"

Another important requirement, the pin sheet, is supplied on the first tee, and I always picked up two, just in case, along with a handful of tees. You never knew when a pin sheet would get wet or blow away or whatever, so it was handy to have a backup.

These days you can get the pin positions online the night before, so you can plan your strategy well in advance, but we still get good old paper pin sheets on the first tee as well.

At the 1988 U.S. Open at Brookline in Massachusetts, I was working for Green, while Scottish caddie Dave Renwick was with José María Olazábal, at the time a rising Spanish star. While walking down the first hole on the first day, Renwick suddenly started panicking. He had forgotten to get a pin sheet.

He said, "Cayce, on the European Tour they hand us one on the tee box. I failed to get one."

I replied, "Listen, you idiot, you're not on the European Tour now."

I gave him my extra pin sheet and said a good caddie always carried two. It saved him from getting what would have been untold grief and perhaps even termination from Olazábal.

Little things like that last a lifetime when you help a brother in arms out. Renwick and I were great friends from that day onward, until his death of cancer at the age of 62 in 2016. (See Caddies Behaving Poorly chapter.)

Knowing the hole locations is all well and good, but nothing beats actually walking the course before a round to see how it is playing and specifically how the greens are rolling.

It's not always feasible to do this if you have an early tee time obviously, but there is no excuse otherwise.

By watching the early starters, you can often see things such as specific areas of greens that repel approach shots, because of a swale or a false front, to use a couple of examples.

And importantly, you can see how specific putts are breaking.

I've lost count of the many times I have heard the TV announcer in the tower at the 17th hole say something along the lines of, "I've been sitting up here all afternoon and every player with this putt has allowed too much break," or vice-versa.

Or that everyone has left a specific putt short, or vice-versa.

And if you get to know TV commentators or even marshals, little bits of information they impart can help.

For example, former tour player Bob Murphy used to call the 10th hole at the Masters. He had been there for years and perhaps knew the green better than anyone. Talking to him, he might say something along the lines of, "Cayce, I've seen that putt a hundred times. Everyone thinks it breaks right but it breaks a little left, toward Rae's Creek."

Tiny things like that, you don't know if they are going to be useful, but they just might be.

All these nuggets of data can go into the memory bank to be brought up as needed. Only 10 percent or less of what you notice will likely be of any use, but you never know what 10 percent that will be.

It's a bit like the old advertising expenditure adage that, "We know half of it will be wasted; we just don't know which half."

OCTOPUS

Another caddie tip is to make your bag as light as possible without cutting corners, so I would usually ditch the umbrella and rain gear if working a desert tournament in Palm Springs, Las Vegas, or Dubai and the forecast ruled out wet weather.

But if I removed the umbrella, I had to remember where you left it, in case it needed to go back into the bag the following day.

I also considered extra towels to be necessities, especially in the heat or rain.

The toughest time to caddie is in rain and wind. You literally do not have enough hands to hold everything you need. Sometimes you need to be an octopus.

PERFECT LIE

You also need occasionally to use a bit of ingenuity and, dare I say it, a touch of deception to land a bag at times.

I'll give you an example. I was at the 1993 British Open at Royal St. George's, but found myself without a job when my man Russ Cochran withdrew after injuring his wrist at the previous week's Scottish Open.

I love caddying on links courses because of the unique challenges involved, so I was keen to pick up a job for the week and at least make my trip financially worthwhile.

I had already rented a car and gave some other caddies a lift for the long drive down to the south of England.

Royal St. George's is the only course in southern England on the current Open rota. The others are all in northern England (Royal Birkdale, Royal Lytham & St. Annes, and Royal Liverpool), Scotland (St. Andrews, Royal Troon, Muirfield, and Carnoustie), and Northern Ireland (Royal Portrush). Turnberry, which Donald Trump bought in 2014 and renamed Trump Turnberry, last held the Open in 2009, when 59-year-old Tom Watson lost a playoff to Stewart Cink. Royal Dornoch in the north of Scotland would no doubt be on the Open rota if it was not so far off the beaten track.

But back to my story. I arrived at St. George's bright and early on Monday morning seeking a bag, and bumped into my old friend Dave Musgrove, the outstanding English caddie who worked for Sandy Lyle among others.

Muzzy, as he was affectionately known, whispered in my ear that Tom Purtzer had not yet hired a caddie, so I set my sights on getting his bag.

Purtzer was a five-time PGA Tour winner with a beautiful swing, so I knew the competition for the job would be fierce.

Caddies looking for work back in the 1990s would traditionally wait in the players' car park, where word would invariably get around as to which players were still looking for a bagman. And when these players pulled up, they would invariably be swarmed as soon as they exited their vehicle by caddies offering their services.

But I had a crafty trick up my sleeve. The car park was packed with about 30 rats looking for a job, because every European caddie wanted to work the Open.

Guys kept asking, "Cayce, who you got?" and I replied Purtzer.

"We were wondering who was caddying for Purtzer," a couple of guys said.

"Well, now you know," I replied.

It was a long day watching like a hawk to see who was in every car that arrived, because I needed to be the first to Purtzer's car, or my scheme would be busted.

He finally pulled in at about 3:00 PM, having just stepped off a plane from a trans-Atlantic flight, and I made my way to him briskly before anyone else could do so.

I bid him hello and explained that I was looking for a bag because my scheduled man Cochran had pulled out.

"Tom, I know you are obviously under no obligation to hire me, but hear me out," I said. "I've got to be honest. See all the caddies over there? I told them I am caddying for you this week. If you engage my services, I will pick up your bag and we can peacefully make our way to the clubhouse. If I walk away, half of them will attack you looking for a job and the other half will attack me for lying."

After what seemed like an interminable second or two while he thought it over, Purtzer said, "Okay, let's do it. Pick up the bag."

My devious tactic had paid off. I was employed for the week.

Coincidentally, we played the first two rounds with Greg Norman, who at the end of the week clinched his second Claret Jug. I could tell Norman had his A game, not that that was anything unusual at that stage of his career.

Purtzer finished equal 69th, but at least he made the cut and made my trip worthwhile.

Caddies no longer loiter in car parks, at least not on the PGA Tour—notice I have picked up a lot of British lingo from having so many friends from across the pond during my years on tour—but instead try to text or call players in advance, or sometimes make an approach through a player's agent.

But back in the day you had to really hustle to get a job. We didn't have cell phones and internet and communication with managers, all the different methods that caddies who already know their way around the tour find work now.

Jobs are rarely facilitated in the car park these days. The vagabond existence has largely gone.

STEVE WILLIAMS

One aspect of caddying that can only really be learned from experience is when to speak up and when to stay quiet.

I'll use Steve Williams as an example. Williams had a great career with the likes of Greg Norman and Raymond Floyd and, most famously, Tiger Woods, who he worked for from 1999 to 2011.

Williams has often said that he was never afraid to give his opinion, and that certainly worked for him. He had a strong presence and a powerful inflection in his voice. And when you had the caliber of players that he had, it gave him the freedom to speak up. And he never feared losing his job, because there would always be another great bag waiting for him.

He worked for players who valued his opinion, which is why what you say and when you say it is dependent on the relationship you have with the player and the confidence he has in you.

If you have a player who's a bit fragile, it's a different kettle of fish. You must pick your spots and know how to pick them.

The hardest part of the job is caddying for someone who's struggling. That's when you've got to be a motivator and tell your player to dig deep when he starts feeling sorry for himself.

"Listen, get a grip on yourself, you've got your name on your bag. Pull yourself out of this and let's go," you might say, or words to that effect.

Always try to frame advice positively. If there is a creek running down the left side of a hole, you could either say, "Don't hit it left" or "Keep it right." Which is better? The latter, of course.

I found that my confidence to speak my mind increased if the player had confidence in me.

Vijay Singh once said on the Golf Channel that I was the best caddie he ever had. It was at the Frys.com Open in California in 2013 (see Couples chapter), the first time I caddied for him, and he finished second. I asked him why he had complimented me so effusively. He was curious as to why I had not been more flattered.

"I can only go downhill from here," I jokingly replied.

Fred Couples was another player who instilled in me the confidence to speak up, even at the risk of being wrong. Fred paid me a compliment one night when the guy we were staying with during the Senior Players Championship at Westchester Country Club asked me what the turning point of the round had been.

Fred said it was at the par-five ninth hole. He had driven into a bunker, before hitting his lay-up fat. He was steaming after two bad shots in a row, and when I gave him the yardage to the hole for the third shot, he quickly grabbed a seven-iron.

I had only a couple of seconds to decide whether to say anything. I wanted him to hit a six-iron, because if he came up short there was a real danger his ball would roll back down the slope in front of the green and he would end up 40 yards from the hole and would have a very difficult time getting up-and-down.

I decided to weigh in gently by showing him a diagram of where I feared his ball would end up if he hit a seven-iron.

"I guess you want me to hit a six-iron," he said.

"I just know where I don't want this ball to end up," I replied.

He heeded my advice, switched to a six-iron, hit his shot to 20 feet and two-putted for par. It doesn't sound like a particularly dramatic moment, but Fred told our host it was the turning point of his day. He subsequently won the tournament in a playoff.

The point is that, as Ben Hogan once observed, a caddie will nearly always have a chance to weigh in and impact his boss' day. You rarely know in advance when this will be, but you've got to be ready.

It could happen on the first hole, the 13th hole, or the last hole.

So whether to speak up is really only something that can be learned on the job. There are no instruction manuals.

CHAMPION CADDIE MOVE

A good caddie also does what he can to look after his boss off the course, or in the following case get him onto the course in the first place.

My old Irish friend J.P. Fitzgerald was disappointed in 2019 when his player, Victor Perez, did not get into the field for the Dunhill Links Championship, a lucrative European Tour event held on three courses in Scotland, including St. Andrews.

J.P. did, however, from his days caddying for Els, know the tournament owner and director, South African businessman Johann Rupert. So J.P. went in to bat for his man, contacted Rupert, told him that Perez was an up-and-comer, and requested that Rupert consider giving the French player a sponsor's exemption.

The lobbying effort was successful, because Rupert granted the request and Perez more than justified the decision by doing nothing less than winning the tournament.

If that's not the greatest caddie move ever, I'd like to know what is. J.P. went above and beyond the call of duty by leaps and bounds by using the relationship he had developed with Rupert to ask for a favor.

He was rewarded for his efforts with a nice payday of roughly $80,000 for the standard 10 percent cut of the winner's prize money, and it is hard to imagine it being more richly deserved.

STAYING IN THE GAME

The money on the PGA and LIV Tours is great these days, but many caddies in the old days wanted to quit because they were poor and had trouble staving off poverty.

I know it still can be difficult to turn a profit on the other tours, both domestically and around the world, so mental fortitude and a determination to keep going through tough times can be paramount.

I recall my old friend Eric Schwarz, better known as "Big E," wanting to give up because he was battling financially. He drank too much for his own good, but that did not prevent him from being an outstanding caddie. When he confided in me once I tried to give him a motivational speech of sorts.

"Big E, you are one of the best," I said. "You can never leave."

A year later he won the 1995 U.S. Open with Corey Pavin at Shinnecock Hills, and he has been one of my best friends ever since.

He thanked me profusely for giving him the confidence to stick it out until better days arrived. Big E thankfully cut down on the booze on his doctor's orders and his health was all the better for it.

Big E also had a hard to believe but true experience a few years ago when he was staying with a friend for a Champions Tour event in Hickory, North Carolina.

One morning Big E wandered downstairs into the kitchen to find his host sprawled out on the floor, as dead as a dodo.

Big E literally fainted with shock and broke a leg in the process.

When he regained consciousness, he dragged himself to the phone and dialed 911.

The paramedics arrived promptly, confirmed that the host was dead—he apparently had a massive heart attack—and transported Big E to the hospital.

As if the ordeal was not bad enough, Big E was briefly a suspect in his friend's death, until the cops determined that the deceased had died of natural causes.

WILLIAMS THE G.O.A.T.?

Being a caddie, you've got to stay on top of your game 24/7, and one thing about Steve Williams, he was on his game every day of his life. But as assured as he was of his own abilities, he never sought to share the limelight with Tiger. It was not his fault he became the most famous caddie in the world. That came with the territory.

As the old saying goes, there are three things that don't last: "Dogs who chase cars, pros who putt for pars, and caddies who think they're stars."

Was Williams the best caddie in the world? That's an impossible thing to quantify. It's safe to say he was certainly great for Tiger.

Do you know how to be a great caddie? Work for a great player, and Steve always had great players.

There are caddies I consider to be outstanding, but have never gotten their due, because they have always worked for donkeys.

That's just the nature of the profession.

It's a bit like horse racing in that you could say that the best way to become a great jockey is to ride a great horse.

There is probably no such thing as the "best" caddie. So much depends on the chemistry. Some caddies are probably best suited to working for introverts, others for extroverts.

Two other caddies that served as great role models for aspiring caddies were Jim "Bones" Mackay and Joe LaCava.

Bones made a meteoric rise from an assistant pro at Columbus Green Island Country Club in Georgia to working for Phil Mickelson for an astonishing 25 years—more or less the entirety of Lefty's career as the second-best player of his generation.

Bones learned the caddie trade by working for three major champions, Scott Simpson, Larry Mize, and Curtis Strange, before Mickelson hired him in 1992.

Jim was making peanuts at his club job, around $12,000 from what I've heard. Speaking of peanuts, that's less than former president Jimmy Carter made farming them.

Like most of us back then, Mackay had not grown up dreaming of being a tour caddie, but rather had fallen into the job.

What was so impressive about Bones was not that he got hired by Mickelson, but that he kept the bag for an eternity, until he was ready to move on. I think he managed that not only by being very good at his job, to state the obvious, but also by doing it very quietly, if that's the right word.

Was I jealous of Bones? Yes.

Here he was, not long out on tour, working for one of the world's best players and winning tournaments prolifically, while I was grinding my ass off but not having half his success.

LaCava lasted almost as long with Couples as Bones did with Mickelson.

As with Bones, LaCava had almost instant success, winning three times with Ken Green before being picked up by Couples in 1990. Two years later they won the Masters together and remained an item until Couples was old enough to play the Champions Tour.

Bones and LaCava became really good friends, and while LaCava was something of a mentor early on, I think they both learned a lot from each other. They lasted so long because they knew what great gigs they had and they weren't going to mess up, so they kept their noses clean and very much to themselves.

Tellingly, both men parted on their own terms. LaCava left Couples for Dustin Johnson in 2011, before taking the most coveted bag of all with Tiger Woods a few months later. While Bones quit for a TV job with NBC in 2017, before later returning to caddying to work for Justin Thomas.

RICCI ROBERTS

I am loath to name all the outstanding caddies for whom I have the utmost respect, out of fear of missing someone, but would be remiss if I did not also mention Ricci Roberts, who caddied for fellow South African Ernie Els for two decades, including a couple of separations and reconciliations.

Ernie was incorrigible, perhaps the hardest player to work for on tour. It was a miracle Ricci lasted so long and was on the bag for all four of Ernie's major championships.

Every player-caddie relationship has a different dynamic, but Ernie and Ricci had a special sauce that worked for them.

It doesn't mean Ricci was the best caddie on tour, but he was the best for Ernie, and in the end that is all that mattered.

20

Caddies Dumping Players

*The time I switched players
in the middle of a U.S. Open*

Players fire caddies way more often than vice-versa, but sometimes the boot is on the other foot.

I've lost count of the number of times I've been fired, and vice-versa. If you haven't been sacked at least a few times, it probably means you haven't been on tour for long. There are a few exceptions, but it's unusual for a caddie to survive more than a few years on a bag, especially when the player is out of form, which is virtually every player sooner or later.

The player can't yell at his agent because he brings in money. He can't yell at his wife, because she'll take half of that money in a divorce. He can't yell at the crowd or volunteers, or he'll get fined or suspended.

The caddie is about the only person in his entourage he can yell at, so guess who so often takes the brunt of a player's sour mood? Is that unfair? Some would say so, but it comes with the territory.

A player usually spends more time with his caddie than his significant other, so it's hardly a wonder that things often go south.

Even if player and caddie have compatibility, the relationship inevitably comes under immense stress sooner or later and when a player screws up, it's inevitable that nerves will fray, and we must eat that shit sandwich.

Our days are usually numbered.

And whenever a caddie gets fired, the player invariably reels out the old line when breaking the news that it's only business, nothing personal. It's a bit like the golf equivalent of the old romantic breakup line that "it's not you, it's me."

But the boot is sometimes on the other foot. Caddies fire players either because they've had enough of their abuse or have received a better offer, or both.

I vividly remember one occasion when I did the ditching, in the middle of a major championship no less—the 1996 U.S. Open at Oakland Hills in Michigan.

I was working for a guy named Anthony Rodriguez, a fringe player who played in 37 PGA Tour events. I got the job because neither of my employers at the time, Fuzzy Zoeller and Don Pooley, were in the field.

I worked 46 tournaments in 1996, caddying for both Fuzzy and Pooley. Their schedules clashed only a handful of times, which worked out well for me. As far as I know, no caddie has ever worked so many events in a year.

Rodriguez asked Fuzzy if he could use me for the Open and Fuzzy gave the request his blessing. I jumped at the chance. Rodriguez was an up-and-comer, was playing well, and I didn't have a job.

I wanted to caddie in as many tournaments as I could back then, to make as much money as I could. A week off could wait until the end of the season.

I was delighted when Rodriguez started with a 71, but he shot 77 in the second round to make the cut with nothing to spare. He was gagging at the end.

David Berganio, meanwhile, made a good start and was only three strokes behind halfway-leader Payne Stewart.

Berganio had a friend from Los Angeles on his bag, but decided on Friday night that he needed a full-time professional looper for the weekend. The friend had been too excitable for Berganio's liking and was making him nervous.

When I spoke with Berganio he vividly recalled the subject.

"It was my first year on tour and I was using an old friend, David, from high school," Berganio said. "We grew up together playing a par-62 executive course.

"Unfortunately, he was too emotional on the course. On Friday I hit a ball into the water, took a drop, and then hit my next one onto the green, but it spun back and it stopped in the fringe.

"I had a 40- or 50-footer, and as the ball makes a beeline to the hole, [caddie] David jumps up screaming with excitement instead of removing the flag from the hole. I had to yell at him to pull the flag in time before the ball rolled in. It was embarrassing.

"So he comes over to the back of the green and I'm like, 'What's wrong with you?' He'd reacted as though I'd just won all four majors. I hurt his feelings so badly he was like a little wet puppy dog who I'd just beaten down.

"It got me thinking that this ain't the guy I need if I'm going to have my best chance this week. I wasn't doing it to be an asshole but it was my business and I needed a change. It was hard to break the news to David. I said, 'I'm going to pay you whatever percentage [of prize money] you would have made but I have to do what's best for me.' He was hurt for sure, but I told him he wasn't really being fired because he was welcome back for the next tournament.

"Changing caddies mid-tournament cost me twice because I paid David and Cayce their wage plus the usual percentage of prize money, but it was worth it.

"Cayce did a really good job, just as I expected. He remained calm and gave me no pause to think I had made a rash decision changing horses in midstream."

I had been surprised when Berganio approached me that Friday afternoon and asked whether I could work for him the following day.

Rodriguez and Berganio had tee times that were far enough apart for me to caddie for both in the third round. It is customary at pro tournaments for weekend tee times to be made in reverse order of positions at the time. So those who make the cut on the number with nothing to spare tee off first, and so on, until the leaders head out in the final pairing or threesome.

Berganio was equal 10th and so had a late tee time, while Rodriguez had played poorly on Friday and was one of the first out on Saturday morning.

I was up early, caddied for Rodriguez, who had another bad day, shooting 76. I then went to the caddyshack, got a quick bite to eat, changed my clothes, and returned to the course to do it all over again, this time for Berganio.

One advantage of going 36 in a day is that you know how the course is playing and among other things can hopefully put into the memory bank a few instances of putts that are deceptive, for example.

I won't say nobody has ever caddied for two players in the same round, but the other caddies could not remember it ever happening.

U.S. Golf Association official Jeff Hall was in the scoring area when I entered after my second round of the day. He asked me hadn't I already gone 18 holes for someone else that morning?

I wasn't 100 percent sure you were allowed to work for two players in the same round, so I told him that there was another caddie who looked just like me, and that he must be thinking of the other guy.

Hall and I chuckled about this when we spoke on the phone in 2024. He clearly remembered the story I've just recited, and also confirmed that it is indeed legal to work for more than one player on the same day.

Berganio carded 72 and on Saturday night he and I were talking about having a good final round and hopefully getting in position to have a chance to win.

We were all jacked up because we were only five strokes behind 54-hole-leader Tom Lehman. Sure, our odds weren't great, but that is close enough to the lead to have a genuine chance if everything goes your way. An outside chance of winning, that was pretty exciting, certainly better than having no chance.

Berganio said, "Look, I've got to have you fresh. I can't let you caddie for Rodriguez in the morning and me in the afternoon." So I canned Rodriguez for Sunday and caddied only for Berganio in the final round.

I had to break the news to Rodriguez that I wasn't going to work for him. He was unhappy, of course, his ego deflated, but I just gave him the facts, no sugarcoating it or dancing around the truth.

I said, "Listen, here's the reality, if you were in the situation Berganio is in, I would do the same thing for you. You're in last place. Nothing against your ability, you could have a great round tomorrow and I hope you do. Your goal was to make the cut and now my goal is to help a guy win the tournament."

I told him that he didn't have to pay me, that Berganio was going to take care of me. It wasn't a subject that was up for negotiation.

It was just business.

As it turned out, Berganio never really challenged for victory, but played well enough to shoot a respectable 72 and finished equal 16th. He collected $33,188, a pretty good check in those days.

More importantly for Berganio, he made a four-footer on the last hole to qualify for the following year's Masters. It was only his second appearance at Augusta and he missed the cut, but at least he got to play there again, and as we packed up to leave Oakland Hills, he thanked me for my effort.

Berganio, born to a single teenage mother, grew up poor in Los Angeles, light years removed from the country club life. He was only 27 at the time of that U.S. Open and while he never became a star on the PGA Tour, he was good enough to play in 158 events and make nearly $2 million in career prize money.

His best result was a runner-up finish at the 2002 Bob Hope Classic, where he lost to Mickelson in a playoff.

LECTOR

While I've canned a player during a tournament, I've never quit mid-round. That is a drastic step that isn't generally advisable if you want suitable employment elsewhere, because you don't want to get that sort of a reputation. But it does happen.

Robert Allenby, a high-strung Australian player who won four times on the PGA Tour, was renowned for wearing his caddies out. He wasn't nicknamed "Lector" for nothing. (Hannibal Lector was a fictional serial killer made famous in the blockbuster 1991 film *Silence of the Lambs*.)

At the 2007 BMW Open at Cog Hill near Chicago, Matthew Tritton—"Bussy" to all his friends—dumped Robert Allenby's bag near the seventh tee, took off his bib, and walked back to the clubhouse, leaving a shocked and embarrassed Allenby wondering what to do.

Tritton is one of the most easygoing blokes you'll ever meet, so if he had had enough, things must have been bad.

Fortunately for Allenby, his fitness trainer Vern McMillan was in the gallery, and the guy got some extra weight training by lugging the heavy bag for the rest of the round.

"It's not the first time and it won't be the last time," Allenby quipped at the time, prophetically as it turned out.

Proverbial lightning struck again eight years later at the Canadian Open at Glen Abbey, when another caddie parted company with Allenby during a round. The fireworks started after the four-time PGA Tour winner hit an approach shot into Twelve Mile Creek and made a triple bogey.

"Robert's a pretty highly strung individual and he hasn't been playing great of late," the caddie, Mick Middlemo, told Australian radio station SEN at the time. "We had a discussion about a club, then of course I copped the wrath of that. Then, unfortunately, the personal insults started. I've been called a bad caddie … but when the personal insults come in and you're being called a fat so-and-so … I got a little bit peeved by it and then the third time he said it I walked up to him and basically said, 'I dare you to say that to me again.' He didn't say it again. There was never going to be any violence … I was just going to put the bag down, get my gear, and leave."

There was also the time at the 2007 Canadian Open when caddie Mike Mollet, nicknamed "Buddha," quit his man Jay Williamson on the 15th hole.

Mollet marched straight back to the clubhouse, stopping only to let a rules official know of the situation. Mollet also revealed that he had thrown into the water all the balls that Williamson had in his bag.

As Michael Collins detailed on ESPN.com, the official asked, "Well, how many does he have left?"

Mollet replied, "Just the one in his hand. I couldn't get that one from him!"

THE POSTMAN DOES NOT RING TWICE

Farther back in time, J.C. Snead's caddie once packed it in during the Texas Open at Oak Hill Country Club in San Antonio.

The caddie's name was Harry Cadell. He was a retired postman who loved golf. I was working for Hubert Green at the time and we were in the same group as Snead for the first two rounds. We had an early tee time on Thursday and after 11 holes of the first round, Snead was already eight over par and Harry had seen enough bad golf.

On the third tee, which was our 12th hole, he walked off so that he could caddie for Lon Hinkle in the afternoon.

The third tee was a very short walk back to the clubhouse. If you were ever going to leave a guy, it was a perfect place to do it. A humiliated J.C. had to call upon the services of a volunteer to carry his bag the remainder of the round.

Hubert didn't like J.C. to begin with, so Hubert thought it was hilarious.

Then, as we were walking off the tee, J.C. said to me, "Cayce, can you believe that motherfucker left me right here on the tee box?"

I just shook my head and didn't respond.

I can talk with the best of them, but sometimes silence really is golden. There was no good response in that situation.

If I had said, "I don't blame him, you're eight over," then I would have looked terrible.

Another reason that caddies sometimes quit their player is because they are not playing often enough.

This was the case with my old friend Joe LaCava, who resigned from Tiger's bag in 2023 simply because Tiger was playing so infrequently. Like most caddies, LaCava just loves being inside the ropes, and even though Tiger was no doubt paying him a handsome retainer to do nothing, it just got old after a while.

Most of us lifelong caddies love what we do. It's in our blood. As much as any of us would love to work for Tiger, when Patrick Cantlay came knocking in 2023, Joe answered the call.

I'm not privy to the financial details, but I'm sure Joe earned more working with Cantlay that year than he would have if he had remained with Tiger.

The chance to caddie for a top player, and the subsequent remuneration that comes with doing so, is usually too good to turn down.

"GOT YOU"

I'll conclude this chapter with my very favorite story.

Russ Steib, an attorney from Ohio, was working for Gary Koch at the Honda Classic in Fort Lauderdale one year. It was a breezy South Florida day, and Koch's driving was almost as out of control as many of the drivers on the nearby Interstate 95 freeway. As the front nine wore on and there was no sign of improvement, Koch's temper started to fray.

Not that that is anything out of the ordinary. Pretty much every pro's got a temper, and some play better in that state. Lanny Wadkins was a great example. He was at his best when he was steaming.

Caddies are used to taking a player's shit, but Koch crossed the line of what is acceptable after another drive sailed way right. He snapped and threw his driver at Steib, hitting the caddie between the legs, squarely in the crown jewels.

Steib's legs buckled as his eyes watered with pain, but he manfully carried on working as he waited for the excruciating feeling to subside.

He was still in some discomfort on the next tee when Koch hit another terrible drive.

He made out to throw the driver at Steib again, but faked him instead, keeping the club in his hand. He had lost his mind.

"Fooled you, didn't I?" Koch barked at Steib, who did not take kindly to the remark.

So when Koch handed the driver to Steib, the caddie calmly placed it across his knee and without saying a word snapped it in half.

He then had perhaps the greatest caddie comeback in the history of the PGA Tour.

"Fooled you, didn't I?" Steib said.

This happened on about the eighth hole, which meant Koch had to play the rest of the round without a driver.

I know this story is 100 percent true because my good friend Tommy Lamb was caddying in the same group for Jay Haas and came straight to the caddyshack to regale those of us there with the incredible story.

Technically this wasn't a story of a caddie firing a player, because Steib did not quit, but his action amounted to the same thing in reality. He was not given his marching orders instantly, but never worked another tournament for Koch, and struggled to get hired by other players after that, once word got around on the grapevine.

And while it was a bad career move by Steib, it made him an absolute hero in the caddie ranks. We've all dreamt of doing something like that at one time or another, but it takes a guy with major cojones to actually do it.

Though he would not have done it if he had not been hit square in the cojones in the first place.

21

Caddie Nicknames

From Last Call Lance to Shitty,
we were a colorful bunch

As I detail in the next chapter, Caddies Behaving Poorly, the money on offer today has made the business of caddying a lot more serious than when I first arrived on the scene in 1987. It is a serious business now with the potential for life-changing paydays, which has largely put paid to late-night drinking and carousing.

You can't stay out with the owls and get up with the roosters without paying a price, and you're more susceptible to being late for a tee time if you're making last call at the bar, not to mention you are probably not feeling great or as sharp as you'd like.

So we don't have as many colorful characters today; caddies are more robotic, as though cloned by artificial intelligence.

For example, a caddie might speak thus. Imagine a robot talking:

"Hi, my name is Michael Smith, I have a yardage book, you have 142 to the front and 160 to the hole. You always hit an eight-iron here but it's downwind and might be a nine today."

I'm not trying to disparage the modern looper.

The guys are very professional, have an image to uphold, mostly do a great job, and I hope they continue to make good money. It's just a different world compared to the old days.

Almost everyone used to have a nickname based on his character or appearance. And when I say "his," I'm not being disrespectful to women, because they were 100 percent men, or at least 99 percent on the PGA Tour.

Nick Faldo's erstwhile Swedish caddie Fanny Sunesson apart, I can't think of another regular female caddie on the PGA Tour, except the occasional wife or girlfriend carrying the bag.

I won't list all the hundreds of nicknames that have come and, in many cases, gone during my time on tour, but will detail some of my favorites.

There were the self-explanatory ones, such as "Thirsty," "Last Call Lance," "Gypsy," "Carl No Truth," "Bald Al," "Reefer Ray," "Weed," "Disco," "Edinburgh Jimmy," "Scottish Dave," "The Russian," "Rick at Night," "Skyscraper," "Akron Trash," and "Shady Grady."

Then there were those whose nicknames were a little more cryptic. Names such as "Shitty," "Britty," "True Temper," "Asbestos," "O-just," and "Oops" spring to mind.

Let me tell you more about a few of these guys.

THIRSTY

Thirsty is a South African named Basil van Rooyen, who after taking out American citizenship, delighted in calling himself an "African American," even though he is White.

He was (and still is) always thirsty, as long as the drink contains booze.

I remember that Thirsty used to call Frank Nobilo "Front Edge Frank" when he worked for the likable Kiwi, who had a reputation of leaving a lot of putts short. Thirsty didn't use the slightly disparaging name to Nobilo's face, of course, but trust me, all the caddies knew who you were talking about when Front Edge Frank was mentioned.

Nobilo is such a nice guy I hope he never knew.

LAST CALL LANCE

Last Call Lance was former tour player Lance Ten Broeck, who after losing his tour card made a very good living as a caddie, most famously with Jesper Parnevik.

If the caddie watering hole of choice at any given tournament was still open, chances are that Lance would still be there at closing time. He died in 2023, aged 67.

At the 2009 Texas Open, Lance pulled off a double that earned the respect of every caddie, by both playing and caddying on the same day. As far as I know, he is unique in having done so.

He still had some playing status as a tour member due to having made 162 cuts in 355 career starts, so he often entered tournaments where he was scheduled to caddie, on the off chance that a spot would become available and none of the higher alternates in the pecking order would be on-site.

Sure enough, on the first day at La Cantera in Texas, Lance caddied for Parnevik in the morning as per usual, and then learned that a player in the afternoon half of the draw had pulled out at the 11th hour.

So Lance figured he might as well give it a shot. Never mind he did not have his golf clubs with him, or that by his own admission he had drunk enough to sink a battleship the previous evening. He quickly bought a pair of pants, borrowed some clubs, and shot 71. The next day he fired a 70, and missed the cut by only two strokes, pretty damn good under the circumstances, playing with unfamiliar clubs. Imagine what he could have done with his own clubs.

I was there that week and can assure you that every caddie and player in the field was talking in awe about Lance.

Some caddies over the years were also handy players, but none were better than Lance. He even beat his own boss that week.

"Guys bring in their instructors, mental coaches, and practice 10 hours a day, and he beats half the field hungover and tired," Parnevik told *Golfweek*.

SHADY GRADY

Shady Grady was a nice guy. Though, as the name implies, he was a little shady.

He often accompanied me in my van between tournaments, and regularly took the wheel in the wee hours of the morning so I could grab 40 winks in the back. The first time he hitched a ride he offered to take over the helm of the ship at about 3:00 AM—and promptly fired up a joint.

When I objected, he said, "Grady's got to have his medicine. Without his medicine, Grady can't get the White Lightning down the road."

I reluctantly let him smoke and he drove as stoned as bejesus and never missed a beat. It's not something I'm proud of, but it's true.

SHITTY

There have been plenty of unflattering caddie nicknames, but the moniker assigned to Mike Boyce just about takes the cake.

He was known far and wide as "Shitty," and you would understand if you had ever met him. Not that he was a bad guy, but let's put it this way, you'd never confuse Shitty for a debonair James Bond. Shitty didn't go a day in his adult life without drinking and smoking as far as I know, and there was hardly a strip club in the United States that he wasn't familiar with.

I once visited a downtown Houston club called Baby Os. I was by myself and figured I was most unlikely to run into anyone I knew. I entered the establishment, and the girls were drop-dead gorgeous.

Then I noticed four of them dancing for this one guy. These girls were all over him, and when I say all over him, I mean *all over him*.

Holy cow, it was Shitty. I called out, "Shitty!"

He was clearly hammered and without missing a beat said, "This is the way I want to die."

He eventually married a stripper, which shocked exactly nobody, and I believe they were still an item on the day he died a few years ago.

Shitty had some good bags over the years, most notably a long partnership with seven-time PGA Tour winner Gil Morgan.

And I remember with a touch of amusement that Shitty somehow stumbled onto Greg Norman's bag for a week as a temporary replacement after Bruce Edwards had quit the Shark's bag following the previous tournament in 1992. As luck would have it, Norman promptly ended a two-year-plus drought by winning the Canadian Open and was inevitably asked whether he would consider giving Shitty the job full-time in view of their success that week.

Without directly answering the question, Norman demurred and implied that he would be moving in another direction, as they say.

It would have been hilarious to think of someone with the Shark's polished image having a caddie named "Shitty." Norman had a reputation to protect, and it was beneath him to have a caddie with that name.

Besides, Norman had so many offers for his services he could afford to be choosy. He came out of the locker room at Glen Abbey with about 25 notes of phone numbers of caddies. Norman threw them all in the trash. It turned out he had already decided to hire Tony Navarro and the pair had a long and fruitful partnership.

Despite making decent money, Shitty was often broke, which to be fair was not exactly rare for a caddie in those days.

At the 1990 PGA Championship at Shoal Creek in Alabama, he asked to borrow $100 and promised to pay me back the following day.

I responded by letting him know that he had to find me, that I would not be spending time looking for him. And, I added, I would charge $25 interest for every day he was late. That was the price of the money.

I did not see him the next day, but 48 hours later he located me, handed over $100, and came up with a bunch of excuses about why he had not been able to find me the previous day. I did not budge, telling him he owed me another $25, which he threw at me in a huff while barking that he would never borrow money from me again. Like I was bothered by that threat.

I calmly told him that he knew the rules of engagement before accepting the loan, and that rather than being upset at me for simply enforcing our verbal contract, he should be upset at himself for not paying it back promptly.

"Friends don't charge friends interest on their money," he pouted.

To which I replied, "I don't charge my friends interest."

I don't mean to imply that I did not like Shitty, but he was an acquaintance rather than a friend.

BRITTY

Rhyming with Shitty was Britty, a caddie named Alan Bond so named because he was British, with a typically dry British sense of humor to boot.

Britty worked for a long time for the Australian player Brad Hughes, and one day Hughes, or "Hugo," as he was known affectionately, went on a birdie tear that prompted the tournament broadcaster to send a camera crew to catch up with the proceedings.

Britty noticed the crew approaching on the 14th hole and had a quiet word in Hugo's ear that he might want to make himself look presentable for TV. He informed Hughes that he had a booger hanging out of one of his nostrils, to which a grateful Hugo offered Britty a huge thank you.

"No problem," Britty replied. "It's been there since the sixth hole."

There is more about Britty in Caddies Behaving Poorly.

REEFER RAY

Reefer Ray not only smoked weed but, from what I was told, had some legal troubles pertaining to selling it and was always trying to stay one step ahead of the law.

I only found out about Ray's fugitive status after he was stopped for speeding while we were driving from California to Florida following the competition of the tour's West Coast swing more than three decades ago.

I drove as far as Houston, by which time exhaustion was starting to take over, so I let Ray take the wheel, giving him firm instructions not to speed. Which he ignored, of course, and an hour or two later I was woken from my slumber by a siren and the unmistakable flashing blue light of law enforcement.

Before the cop walked up to the window, Ray hurriedly told me that his name was in fact Bob Hobday.

I was puzzled but had no time to get the full story out of him before the officer appeared and asked Ray for his license.

The officer took the license bearing the name Bob Hobday back to his car to verify, I assume, and upon returning to the van asked Ray to exit the vehicle. He then requested my license, which read my real name, David Anthony Kerr, not the name Cayce that everyone knows me by. I must have also mentioned Ray's name, because the officer by now was getting most suspicious as to our identities.

"Your friend is calling you 'Cayce' and you're calling him 'Ray' and I'm just trying to get to the bottom of it and find out who you guys are," he said.

I told him I was a professional caddie on the PGA Tour working for a double-major champion named Hubert Green, who owned the van and whose clothes in the back were embossed with his name. We caddies, I added, often had CB-like handles, so it was not uncommon for us to use something other than our real names.

After a cursory glance at Green's clothing, the officer seemed somewhat satisfied with my story, which from my end was 100 percent true. I was Green's caddie and it was his van.

The officer issued Ray a speeding ticket and left us to continue our journey. As soon as we took off again I exploded at Ray. I was upset because I was driving my boss' van and worried I might get fired if we got into trouble with the law, even if it wasn't my fault.

"Would you mind telling me what's going on?" I barked.

It was only then that he told me his whole backstory, that he used to live in Chattanooga and sell weed out of the music store where he worked. He said he was eventually busted, charged, and found guilty, but before being sentenced decided to skip the country for Canada.

A friend with a similar appearance, Bob Hobday, had given Ray his driver's license, but Ray only got as far as Washington State, where he met a local lass and fell in love.

He never made it to Canada, instead marrying the woman and remaining in the U.S. Ray did not even tell the poor lady until their wedding day that his real name was Ray Reavis.

With a warrant out for his arrest, Ray continued to travel with Hobday's license, which he successfully used at that traffic stop in Texas to avoid being taken into custody.

Ray caddied for a long time but most of the guys he worked for couldn't play dead in a western. Therefore, he never had any money and eventually became known as "Reeferless Ray," because he was so broke that he had to bum weed off other caddies.

As far as I know, the law never caught up with Ray, who died in 2013 at the age of 65.

TRUE TEMPER

Then there was an Australian bloke nicknamed "True Temper," because he was always shafting someone. Are you with me? True Temper is the famous maker of golf shafts.

There was also Smiley, real name Tim Thalmueller, who is still on tour. His nickname is a bit of a misnomer, because he is not always smiling, but once a name was assigned it tended to stick. Smiley was shot and critically wounded in a parking lot in Miami at night during the 1990 Doral Open, but fortunately recovered.

One of my favorite nicknames was "O-just," so named because when someone asked who he worked for, the answer from other caddies invariably was "Oh, just about anyone who'll have him."

At the other end of the spectrum, a more well-regarded caddie was called "Sponge." He was an amiable Kiwi by the name of Mike Waite, who worked for fellow New Zealander Michael Campbell when the latter won the 2005 U.S. Open at Pinehurst No. 2, staving off none other than Tiger Woods down the stretch.

But Waite was nicknamed "Sponge" not because he could soak up alcohol—unusual for a caddie he was only a light drinker—but because of the state of his hair when it got wet. It looked like a sponge.

Then there was Jeff Medlin, nicknamed "Squeaky" because of his high-pitched voice. He had an outstanding career, working for Nick Price in his prime. As well as winning three majors with Price, he pinch-hit for John Daly when Long John burst onto the scene winning the 1991 PGA Championship.

But Medin's life was cruelly cut short by leukemia. He died in 1997, aged only 43.

There was also a Native American we called "Chief." Political correctness had not filtered into the caddie ranks back then. Come to think of it, it still hasn't for the most part.

A caddie nicknamed "Gypsy" was a pleasant character, though his was a name that could have been attached to almost any caddie, given our itinerant lifestyle. For some reason, however, it stuck to a guy named Joe Grillo. He ran the caddie trailer and cooked for the troops. He also worked for Curtis Strange and Steve Elkington for a while.

When he wasn't caddying or preparing meals, the best place to look for Gypsy was the nearest horse track. He was always broke, because there was not much money to be made cooking for a bunch of cheap caddies.

One of the best names was "Asbestos," assigned to Steve Duplantis because he seemingly was fireproof, no matter how often he turned up late for his longtime boss Jim Furyk.

I've shared my favorite Duplantis story in Caddies Behaving Poorly.

OOPS

A guy from Oregon who did not last long on tour said he was a point guard in college and a great basketball player. Every second word out of his mouth was "I." Let's just say he loved talking about his favorite subject.

The way he spoke you would have thought he was in line to be the No. 1 NBA draft pick.

He told us his nickname was "Hoop" because of his ability to drive to the hoop and score, but he was such a bad caddie that we nicknamed him "Oops." And made sure he knew about it.

THE STALKER

Say what you want about caddies, most of them had deliciously dry senses of humor.

For example, a caddie nicknamed "the Stalker" was working for a journeyman on the Champions Tour once when his player, after another mediocre round, said that he was just popping into the locker room to change.

The Stalker, frustrated after another day of witnessing bad golf, replied, "Why don't you change into Hale Irwin so that when you come out you can make some money."

Ouch.

I never even found out why this caddie was called "the Stalker"—or his real name for that matter. I called him "the Stalker" to his face once without realizing that nobody referred to him that way—except behind his back.

He was very embarrassed. I think he knew of the unflattering name, but it still wasn't nice to hear it.

"C'mon man," he said, "I thought we were friends."

If the Stalker's put-down of his player was quick-witted, another classic came from Bob Burns, nicknamed "Bullet," who was working for Fulton Allem at the Heritage tournament in South Carolina.

At the short par-three 14th at Harbour Town, Allem's tee shot found a water hazard.

"I'm so angry right now, Bullet, that I could break something," said an exasperated Allem.

To which Bullet replied, "How about par?"

The other two members of the group, Nick Price and Davis Love, could not stifle laughs, and even Allem acknowledged that it was a pretty good line.

Other caddie nicknames I liked over the years included "Bambi," "Broke Brad," and "Steve the Liar."

TELL-A-CADDIE

Some guys did not have particularly interesting nicknames but were nonetheless interesting characters.

Johnny Buchna was simply called "Bucky." He was a guy you needed to know because he knew everything that was going down on tour. If you wanted to make sure you were up to speed, it was worth investing in a drink with Bucky, who was always in the bar. Bucky also features prominently in the Caddies Behaving Poorly chapter.

As the old saying, now outdated, goes, there are three forms of communication—telegraph, telegram, and tell-a-caddie. And there was no better tell-a-caddie than Bucky.

He caddied for Joey Sindelar for nearly two decades, which tells you both that Sindelar was a pleasant boss and that Bucky knew his business. But he never seemed to get much respect. I guess you could call him the Rodney Dangerfield of caddying. If you're too young to get that reference, please look it up.

Friday was a particularly good time to go to the bar, not only to catch up with Bucky but with caddies who were drowning their sorrows after missing a cut. You could almost guarantee that someone would reveal they were ready to quit their man. It was good to hear of jobs that might become available as soon as the next day. There was always someone in the bar who would say something like, "I've had enough of Steve Pate. I'm getting rid of him tomorrow."

Of course, sometimes it was the booze talking, but not always.

STAR CADDIES

Then there were the caddies to the stars, such as Fluff, real name Mike Cowan, so named because of his bushy mustache. He worked for Peter Jacobsen for nearly two decades before receiving an offer no caddie could refuse—to work for Tiger Woods when Tiger turned pro in 1996.

Phil Mickelson's caddie of 25 years, Jim Mackay, got the nickname "Bones" courtesy of Fred Couples more than three decades ago. Mackay was at a restaurant with a group of players, caddies, and wives at a tournament in France when Couples, trying to get the attention of a skinny caddie whose name he did not know, instead called him "Bones," and the name stuck.

And finally, how can I not mention Steve Williams, who does not need any introduction to golf fans after working for Woods from 1999 to 2011.

The New Zealander had great bags almost his entire career, working pre-Tiger for the likes of Norman and Raymond Floyd, and post-Tiger for Adam Scott, for whom he gave a great read for the Aussie's winning putt in a playoff at the 2013 Masters.

Even without Woods, Williams would have had a great career. He wisely did not go out drinking with his peers. A quiet dinner maybe, but that's about all.

Players aren't stupid. They learn which caddies are out until all hours.

Laying low at night was a good career decision if you wanted to work for Woods. The last thing Tiger needed was the internet blowing up with stories and photos of his caddie downing shots at closing time.

That said, every caddie should behave, because we are an extension of our boss in some capacity, and his reputation for integrity will take a hit by association if we step out of line.

But that's in theory. In reality, poor behavior was hardly uncommon back in the day.

It's said quite correctly that nobody comes to a golf tournament to watch a caddie, but Williams really was a superstar, better known than half the players on tour. Which is why we sometimes called him the "Fifth Beatle," though not to his face, I must confess.

I knew well-established players who were a little jealous of Williams, because he got more airtime than they did, but when you were standing next to Tiger, you were going to get airtime. It came with the territory.

And other caddies were extremely jealous, with good reason. He had the job the rest of us coveted, and for good measure did not care whether he made friends with us. Steve walked around looking very powerful and cocky and did not make small talk with anyone. He kept to himself, so the mystique made people dislike him.

Williams really led by example and worked for great players. It was a win/win all the way around. Tiger was so good in his prime, he could have won with a volunteer, but Williams never got lazy and always made sure he was on top of his game. Though he did not go out of his way to befriend his peers, you've got to remember that it's lonely at the top, and I had a lot of time for Steve after he once did me a big favor.

An old caddie nicknamed "Irish," who lived in New Zealand, was quite an accomplished craftsman, and he used to make beautiful bowls from wood that he sourced locally. He sold them for several hundred dollars, and I thought they were beautiful and decided to buy one, so I gave Steve the money, and after his next trip home to New Zealand he returned to the U.S. with my bowl, which still sits in my Masters cabinet.

The quality of the bowl is striking, but that's not the point of the story.

The point is that Steve cared enough about a colleague to help. There was no obligation to do so, but he did it willingly anyway.

I'll end this chapter by mentioning arguably the most appropriately named caddie of all time. His name was Tom Watson, not to be confused with the great player of the 1970s and '80s, who won five British Opens, two Masters, and a U.S. Open. Watson the caddie was an Aussie who worked for women's world No. 1 So-Yeon Ryu among others.

His nickname was "Eight Majors."

Caddies Behaving Poorly

Tales from the good (and sometimes bad)
old days on tour

Caddies on the PGA Tour these days are largely a but-toned-up breed, more likely to while away the evening sip-ping sparkling water and watching Netflix than closing the nearest watering hole. But for my first decade or so on tour there were some wild times that for better or worse will probably never return.

I think the largely exemplary behavior of modern caddies is due to the magnitude of purses on tour these days. A seven-figure purse was considered a big deal when I started on tour in 1987. Fast forward to 2024, and most purses for regular tournaments were close to $10 million, while the eight designated limited-field events offered $20 million. There was also the little matter of $25 million handed out at the Players Championship.

Take Jack Nicklaus' Memorial tournament for example. The event is held on Memorial Day weekend or thereabouts, on the first course Jack designed, Muirfield Village in Dublin, Ohio, which he named after Muirfield, Scotland, site of his first British Open victory in 1966. The Memorial has been one of the most prestigious and richest events since I arrived on the scene. In 1988, the purse was just over $1 million, which would be worth a little under $3 million in 2024 dollars, according to the U.S. Bureau of Labor Statistics CPI inflation calculator.

Curtis Strange took home $160,000 for winning the 1988 Memorial.

The 2023 winner, Viktor Hovland, collected $3.6 million.

The winning caddie usually gets a 10 percent cut, so Hovland's looper probably received $360,000, compared to $10,000 for Strange's caddie in 1988.

Hubert Green, my first regular boss in 1987, paid me a basic wage of $500 per tournament in addition to a 5 percent cut of prize money for anything other than a win.

Three decades later, I was getting a base wage of $3,000 a tournament.

Even allowing for inflation, that's a big increase, and an example of why caddies these days just aren't going to risk their jobs by turning up for work hungover.

I know many caddies, and players for that matter, who still enjoy letting their hair down on a Sunday night, but that's about it. You simply cannot afford to get a reputation as a drunk these days if you want to remain viable in the profession.

I used to enjoy a drink as much as the next man, as long as the next man isn't Steve Duplantis, to steal a line that British comedian Ricky Gervais used about Mel Gibson when hosting the Golden Globe Awards in 2010.

But more on Duplantis later.

I do not drink much these days. I guess part of that is that I'm no longer a spring chicken, but it's also because most of my hard-drinking caddie friends are dead. There is nothing like watching a bunch of your closest mates succumb to various ailments to prompt some serious reordering of your priorities.

CROSSBAR MOTEL

So many caddies were arrested for drunk and disorderly conduct that we called jail the "Crossbar Motel," though I want to make it clear that I never ended up there—unless it was to bail someone out, which I've done more than once.

When I started on tour, I tried to quietly learn the ropes and find my feet like everyone else in such a situation. It can all be a bit bewildering in those first few weeks and months, and while it's hard to believe now, I didn't know too many people back then because I was so new to the scene. What I did have was my boxing skills, honed from a teenage amateur career in which I won five national Golden Glove titles, and only lost five times in 107 fights.

That ability to deliver a punch, or at least threaten to do so without showing any fear, stood me in good stead one night early in my career in Hartford, Connecticut, where I was sitting quietly by myself at the end of the bar minding my own business as I sipped on a scotch.

There were several other caddies at the bar, some already three sheets to the wind. The guy sitting next to me, who I later found out was named Johnny Buchna, challenged me to an arm wrestle.

He was a scrawny looking thing back then and I had no interest in his challenge. I said, "Listen, pal, mind your own business. You don't want to mess with me."

And then a guy known as "Budweiser Paul"—nicknamed for obvious reasons—jumped into the conversation and said he did not like the way I was talking to his buddy and challenged me to a fight.

He said, "I'll take your ass outside and whip it for $500 right now."

I replied, "You don't have to do that. I'll whip your ass right here for free and if you feel froggy, just leap. I'll give you the first one."

I was thinking to myself, "Who the hell is this guy? Does he know I've been around a few fights?"

He backed off so quickly I like to joke that he won the gold medal in backstroke.

There were about 30 rats (caddies) in the bar while this verbal sparring was going down, so it was a big commotion; a new guy, and bully Budweiser Paul pushing his weight around like he always did. He had a reputation for getting everyone he challenged to back down, and here I was ready to knock him out right there at the bar had he taken a swing at me.

Fortunately for his sake, he did not throw a punch.

I didn't think too much further about the matter until the next day, when several caddies who had been at the bar came up and introduced themselves.

They said they had seen how I had put Budweiser Paul back into his cage and told me not to pay attention to him, as they did not like him either because he was always trying to bully someone.

I said, "I don't mind if he tries to bully someone but I ain't backing down, not for some hillbilly I've never met before."

Plus, I enjoyed knocking people out, because I was good at it. That's human nature, I guess.

I hadn't caddied in many tournaments, and I thought, "This is a rough crowd, right up my alley. I'm going to feel at home out here."

WRECKED AT NIGHT

Word had gotten around quickly, and from that moment the caddies on tour knew who I was. I didn't have any further trouble for the best part of a decade, when out of nowhere a guy named Rick Hippensteele had a go at me at a bar in Atlanta.

There was an old TV programming block called "Nick at Nite" and Hippensteele's nickname had started out as "Rick at Night," which eventually morphed into the even more appropriate "Wrecked at Night." (See Caddie Nicknames chapter.)

He threw a haymaker at me and fortunately I was able to move my head back like Roberto Duran and his fist just barely grazed my chin. Thank God, I slipped the punch, because it was delivered with plenty of force.

I was not amused. I told him, "If you ever do that again, if you ever make that mistake again, I'm going to knock you out." I did not retaliate because he was drunk, behaving poorly, and it wouldn't have been fair. I gave him an honest chance to stay away. He had fair warning, but some people just can't take a hint.

The following week I was at the Colonial tournament in Fort Worth, Texas, sitting with my crusty old Scottish caddie friend Dave Renwick, at the caddies' regular watering hole near the course. We were absolutely slaughtered, when this same caddie came in, sat right next to me, and started giving me an earache.

Rick was upset because I had gone to work for Don Pooley, soon after Rick had been fired. That year, 1996, I worked for both Pooley and Fuzzy Zoeller. Their schedules only conflicted occasionally, so I caddied virtually every week.

Anyway, I had no interest in listening to Rick have a go at me, so I got up and left. You would think that would be the end of the story, but some guys just can't take a hint.

Rick came scurrying after me and while my back was turned tapped me hard on my right shoulder and hissed, "You don't walk away when I'm talking to you, boy."

He jolted me and I turned around and gave him a left hand that was so fast he never saw it coming. The punch left him knocked out and lying on the ground. I kicked him in the ribs for good measure because I'd hit him so hard I had jammed my thumb.

The bar called the paramedics because they wanted to get him out of there. Having someone prostrate on the cement in front of your establishment is never great for business.

He went to hospital by ambulance and was certainly Wrecked at Night that night.

Once Rick came around, he called Pooley from the hospital and told him he had been beaten up by yours truly. Rick was working for Kirk Triplett by that stage, and clearly wasn't going to make his tee time the next day.

The news spread like wildfire and Fuzzy heard about it in no time and wanted me to apologize to Triplett for being responsible for his caddie's absence.

Fuzzy also asked why, if I'd only belted Rick once, did the guy also have two broken ribs? I had to confess that I'd also kicked him in the ribs. Fuzzy said it was the Mexican coming out in me. (My grandparents on my mother's side were Mexican.)

Other players must have found it amusing, judging by the way they teased me the rest of the week. A couple even left notes in Fuzzy's locker joking that Don King wanted to promote my next fight.

The following week I was back on Pooley's bag, and when Don got to see the state of Rick's face, which was pretty bad, he wondered why I had hit him so hard.

I told Don that fighting was not like golf. In golf you can just feather a little seven-iron in if you don't want to hit it hard. When you go to battle with someone in a fight it's all-out war. It's life or death, or at least it seems like it at the time.

At first, we thought Rick was going to lose his eye, it was so bad. Some said it was the worst black eye they'd ever seen. He was in hospital for a couple of nights, and showed up on tour the following week looking like crap. I wouldn't even have come to the golf course looking like that, I would have been so embarrassed. He was a tall guy, over six feet, and he had to swallow his pride and tell people who asked about his injury that it had been inflicted by me.

We never really spoke afterward because we didn't have anything in common. I didn't apologize and he didn't come around and harass me anymore.

He struggled to get a bag and last I heard was working as a club caddie at former PGA Tour commissioner Tim Finchem's course in Jacksonville.

In the words of Fuzzy, I put the myth of whether I could really fight to rest, because everyone was wondering if I had a left hand. They all knew the answer when they saw Rick's black eye.

So you might be wondering: Why did Rick not press charges?

It just wasn't the way caddies rolled back then. We didn't want to bring any extra attention to ourselves by getting the law involved. And besides, he hit me first, so I was acting in self-defense. I can't help it that he was messing with the wrong person.

IF IT'S FREE, TAKE THREE

There have been so many incidents of caddies behaving poorly that trying to decide the best is rather like picking your favorite golf course. I'll tell you one thing. Never offer to pick up the tab for a caddie's booze unless you're prepared to incur a hefty bill.

That's the lesson a casino manager in Reno discovered one year during the tour stop there, a second-tier event that, by extension, also gets a lot of second-tier caddies. The Peppermill Casino kindly offered caddies free accommodation and complimentary booze for the entire week. Talk about a rookie mistake by the hotel management.

It was the late 1990s and I was there working for Jay Williamson.

At the end of the week the casino hosted a caddie party, and the hospitality coordinator duly gave a speech thanking the loopers for providing so many free tickets to the golf tournament.

But he then added a kicker. "I've got to let you guys know, I've been in business for 35 years and I've had every group of people come to our casino: doctors, lawyers, salesmen, rednecks, you name it. But nobody, I repeat, *nobody* has ever come close to drinking as much as you guys."

When you think of all the groups he'd hosted, that was a huge statement. To which the caddies spontaneously gave the guy a standing ovation and ordered more drinks. Caddies were crazy back then. There were so many who just drank and drank until they could no longer stand.

As the old saying goes: "If it's free, take three; if you're near the door, take more."

STRANGERS IN THE NIGHT

Speaking of too much alcohol consumption, there was a bizarre happening during what was back then known as the PGA Tour qualifying school, a tense and grueling six-round tournament after which the top 35 players earned their cards for the following year.

I was there and, fortuitously, so was my close Canadian friend Bradley Whittle. He had previously worked for Wayne Grady during the underrated Australian player's heyday, highlighted by an emphatic and perhaps underappreciated victory at the 1990 PGA Championship at Shoal Creek, Alabama (which, by the way, that week had the toughest rough I have ever seen).

Grady was always a great friend of caddies. One time he invited a dozen of us around for a little party at his Orlando house during the 1995 Walt Disney Classic.

He kindly supplied ample beer for the attending loopers, one of whom couldn't handle it and vomited in a toilet. That wouldn't have been too bad, except that the caddie's aim was about as accurate as a 30-handicapper's drive.

The embarrassed caddie did not own up to it, and when Grady discovered the disgusting state of his toilet, he proceeded to try to identify the culprit. Nobody ever fessed up.

Anyway, a few years later, Grady sold his house and moved back to Australia but purchased a townhouse in Orlando that sat empty most of the year.

Grady, or "Grades," as he is universally known, and Whittle were good friends and Grady, being a generous man, offered Whittle use of the townhouse during qualifying school.

There was one explicit condition, Grady insisted. Nobody else was to stay there. *Nobody.* Do you think Whittle assured Grady he would abide by that rule? Yes, he did. Do you think Whittle kept his word? Of course not.

There were four of us there that week, but Grady had provided Whittle with only one key.

We decided the most convenient way to handle that would be to leave the door unlocked.

So one night we all went out, came home late (and not completely sober), and crashed in our respective bedrooms upstairs.

Most of us left for the course early the next morning, and by coincidence, Whittle was the last to depart. He stumbled out of bed, got dressed and ready, descended the stairs, and was about to close the front door when he heard someone snoring in the nearby living room.

Investigating further, he entered the room, only to see three strange men sleeping on the floor. Whittle had no idea who they were, or how they had gotten there, but they certainly weren't caddies.

Whittle woke them up and asked them to explain. It turned out that the guys said they were staying next door but had come home so discombobulated and hammered in the wee hours that they had stumbled into the wrong townhouse.

I mean, what were the chances of that?

I suspect you are probably thinking this story is too good to be true, that the men were perhaps homeless or whatever, but I swear this is the way Whittle told it and has continued telling it to this day.

Whittle, already thinking of how badly this would look if it ever got back to Grady, told the trio politely but firmly that they had to leave quickly, which, fortunately, they did.

Whittle pleaded with the other caddies to keep quiet about the incident, lest Grady ever find out.

But it's hard to keep a secret for long on the PGA Tour, and Grady learned the truth eventually. Thankfully he did not suffer a cardiac arrest. Such is his forgiving nature that he and Whittle remain friends, and to this day catch up whenever their paths cross.

That bizarre incident with the strangers sleeping on the floor was preceded a couple of nights earlier by a situation in which we lost one of our housemates.

Alan Bond, known to everyone on tour as "Britty," because of his British nationality, was a good friend of both Whittle's and mine. Britty spent a night behind bars that week after being arrested for drunk and disorderly behavior, but we couldn't find out where he was.

We all drank mostly at the same watering hole, but for some reason weren't drinking with Britty that night.

Despite everything I have written that would make you think caddies were out drinking every night, that was not quite true. Sometimes we would take a night off, especially if we had a morning tee time the following day. It's good not to drink in that situation if you want your performance up to par.

I think it was Britty's boss that week, the brilliantly named Duffy Waldorf, who picked up Britty at the slammer. Duffy is a great guy, and he also needed his caddie to report for work again.

Sadly, Britty died of leukemia in 2017.

When you partied with Britty, anything could happen. There was always drama wherever he was drinking and the more you disliked Britty, the more he enjoyed taunting you. He was a true Brit.

Whittle and I had dinner at his house in Dallas shortly before he passed. His wife fixed us a nice meal and, knowing Britty's sense of humor, I asked for his caddie guest pass.

After all, I said, he wouldn't be needing it and there was no point wasting it.

Britty got a kick out of it. At least I think and hope he did.

SCOTTISH DAVE

Speaking of jail, I've bailed quite a few guys out of the slammer, including the aforementioned Renwick at the 1994 Southern Open at Callaway Gardens in Pine Mountain, Georgia, a small town about 70 miles south of Atlanta. In 1994 it had an official population of 1,102, so when I say there were no cars, no people, and only one place to drink, I'm exaggerating only slightly. The main strip through the town, US Highway 27, which even today is a single-lane road, was so devoid of traffic that it was almost impossible to get into trouble.

Or so I thought.

I was sharing a motel room with Renwick and knowing the Scotsman's predilection for a drink or 12, I would not even countenance lending him my van.

Except for this one time. Big mistake.

Renwick wanted to drive to the bar a mile down the road—when you've already schlepped a bag seven or eight miles on a golf course, the thought of walking home with a skinful of booze in one's system isn't exactly appealing—and I thought, what could go wrong out in the boonies?

I was having a quiet night in, so against my better judgment loaned Renwick the van.

I was just dozing off to sleep when I was awoken by someone banging on my door, vigorously to say the least.

Bam! Bam! Bam!

I grabbed my pistol and shouted, "Who is it?"

"It's the police."

So I promptly put my pistol away and opened the door, and the officer explained that he had arrested a gentleman who said he was staying in this room.

Turned out that when Renwick had turned from the road toward the parking lot he had pulled in front of the cop, the only other car on the road, who didn't need to be a rocket scientist to deduce that the driver was not exactly sober.

I looked out and saw my van by the side of the road, not more than 40 paces away, with Renwick passed out in the back seat. The officer said he could not move my vehicle but that if I wanted to drive it out of the way I was welcome. Otherwise, he would have to impound it.

The officer added that he was taking Renwick to a cell, and that I could collect him in an hour or so if I wanted.

I said Renwick could stay locked up all night as far as I was concerned, but I couldn't get to sleep because I was feeling guilty, so I eventually went and got him.

It was not the first time Renwick had been jailed.

This all happened on a Friday night.

A hungover Renwick duly caddied for Steve Elkington the next day and found himself with the 54-hole lead.

As coincidence would have it, meanwhile, the part-time weekend postman in town was a judge during the week, and the woman who owned the motel we were staying at was a friend of his. When he delivered the mail on Saturday, she asked him whether he could open the courthouse on Sunday morning to hear Renwick's case.

I represented Renwick as his "attorney" that day, and we pleaded guilty.

The judge said, "$500 and you're free to go," so I put five crisp $100 bills across the desk and out the door we went.

Renwick didn't know whether to tell Elkington or not. He was scared to death. He did not want to let his boss know that he had been thrown in jail for drinking and driving.

I kept saying, "Wait, wait, don't tell him until right up until you have to."

Elkington never found out as far as I know, and Renwick escaped with a victory when the final round was washed out and the 54-hole scores stood.

I mean, how lucky was Renwick? He got off with a $500 fine and collected $14,400 as his 10 percent cut for the victory.

Renwick had already enjoyed victory in Georgia that very same year when his man José María Olazábal won a little tournament called the Masters.

A year later, Elkington won a major of his own, the PGA Championship at Riviera. Elkington had told Renwick before the tournament that he could have 100 percent of the prize money if they ever won a major together.

So not long after Elkington lifted the Wanamaker Trophy and received his prize money of $360,000, Renwick asked for my advice. Several days had passed and he had not received any kind of payment. He was starting to get antsy and was thinking of having it out with Elkington in his blunt Scottish manner. He had previous form in this area, having quit Olazábal over a pay dispute.

But I suggested that this time he hold his proverbial horses.

"First man to speak loses," I said, advising Renwick to play it cool and say nothing.

Elkington ended up paying Renwick $100,000, which at the time was the biggest ever caddie payday, as far as I know.

Okay, it wasn't the promised 100 percent, but I told Renwick it was more than enough considering Elkington was prone to exaggeration and had probably made his promise off the cuff without really meaning it. I know a verbal contract can be legally binding, but 27 percent of the prize money was a darn sight better than the standard 10 percent usually paid to the winning caddie.

Renwick ended up making a not-so-small fortune over the next five years, winning three more majors with Vijay Singh and riding the Vijay gravy train during the Fijian's halcyon days. Renwick and I had long been best friends by then. I was the best man at his wedding in Glasgow and had worn a blue kilt in honor of his beloved Rangers soccer team.

But Renwick's life was not one long fairy tale. In 1989, he fell asleep at the wheel of his car near London en route from a tournament in Ireland to another in France. Two of his fellow caddies, Scotsman David Kirk and Englishman Bill Brown, were killed in the crash and Dave spent six months in prison for reckless driving.

Renwick died of cancer at the age of 62 in 2016. Though his life was cut short, he earned enough during his short time on this planet to leave a house to each of his three children. I never thought I'd live to see the day when caddies had that sort of money.

SMOOTH GREEN

One year in Atlanta, at the BellSouth Classic, I was rooming with a caddie by the name of Rick Motacki, better known as "Weed," and not because he was fond of gardening.

Late on Saturday night on the eve of the final round, he was arrested for simple assault after allegedly threatening the female front desk clerk at the Knights Inn where we were staying. For those readers not familiar with American chain motels, let's just say you can't get much more basic than a Knights Inn. We didn't tend to stay in posh places.

I don't know what Weed said or what he did—I was not there at the time of the incident—but he got thrown in a cell on a Saturday night in Atlanta at the DeKalb County Jail, and I didn't have a place to sleep, because we were ejected from our room.

It was getting late, so I went to the jail in the wee hours of the morning in the hope of bailing Weed out. I got a message sent down to him and received word back that he wanted to put his $1,500 bail on my credit card.

I told the police officer that under no circumstances was I paying, that if Weed wanted bail, he would have to pay for it himself, otherwise he could stay behind bars as far as I was concerned.

He reluctantly ponied up, but by this time it was so late that we debated whether it was even worth booking into a new hotel for just a few hours, especially as I had an early tee time.

Being the cheapskates that we were, we decided instead to head straight to Atlanta Country Club for the final round of the tournament.

It was a hot, humid night, and we decided to try and catch a few winks on the 18th green. So we lay down and had barely dozed off before the sun peeked over the trees and we were awoken by the grounds crew with their mowers, ready to cut the greens in preparation for the final round.

You can't make up a story like that.

Along similar lines, at the B.C. Open one year in Endicott in upstate New York, another caddie, Tim Thalmueller, was arrested after a fight with one of his peers.

Word on the street was that other caddies conspired to get Thalmueller, or "Smiley," as he was known, arrested on Saturday night in the hope that he would be stuck in a cell and miss his Sunday tee time.

Smiley was a friend, and still is as a matter of fact, and I figured it took two to tango, that both caddies had been drunk and behaved poorly, and that it was not fair that only one guy had been arrested. I wanted to help Smiley, who found an attorney at 11:00 PM and got arraigned and out of his jail cell at about 4:30 AM.

I was waiting there in my van to pick him up. It was a long night, and the thought I had when Smiley climbed into my vehicle was that being released from prison must be the greatest feeling in the world, whether you have been there for hours, days, months, or years.

Smiley and I went and had breakfast and he showed up on schedule for his tee time with Gene Sauers, and thus kept his job.

SIXTY-NINE

Lest one think only caddies behaved poorly, let me put you straight on that. Players were also known for some high jinks, if not on the same level as caddies.

David Berganio and another player, Jaime Gomez, had a joke at my expense after the Nike Tour Championship in Colorado in 1996.

I had worked the final few weeks of the season for Berganio as he attempted to seal his promotion from the secondary circuit to the PGA Tour. It was only a few months after I had caddied the weekend for him under unusual circumstances at the 1996 U.S. Open. (See Caddies Dumping Players chapter.) He was 42nd on the money list with six tournaments remaining when he called and asked me to come work for him. I told him I had just agreed to caddie for John Inman the next two weeks on the PGA Tour.

He made his pitch.

"John Inman! He's on the way out and I'm on the way in."

David was persuasive enough to lure me away from Inman. We had already had two runner-up finishes in five starts together by the time the Tour Championship rolled around and we had another second-placing at the season finale at Riverdale Dunes, where Berganio three years earlier had won the U.S. Public Links Championship.

We finished a shot behind Stewart Cink at the Tour Championship after David missed a 12-foot putt at the final hole.

David was upset, but his disappointment was tempered because he had achieved his primary goal of qualifying for the PGA Tour. I, on the other hand, was fuming, because the chance for a much bigger payday had evaporated.

Several drinks in the clubhouse did little to ameliorate my anger, and I was still so upset on the car ride back to our hotel that I punched the windshield in a fit of rage, putting a hole in it and leaving the rest of the window resembling a cobweb.

I was extremely drunk by the time we got back to our room. The three of us were sharing a room to cut costs—I was sleeping on the floor—and that is where I promptly passed out.

It was not until later after I had sobered up and was showering the next morning that I noticed someone had written with a Sharpie on my ass. On one cheek was a big 6, on the other an equally large 9.

I immediately phoned David, who had already checked out, and asked for an explanation of why I had "69" written on my ass. He said that I had been so comatose that he and Gomez had managed to pull down my pants, write on my cheeks, and then hitch my pants back up without me even stirring.

They got me good. I know it was rather juvenile humor, but I still had to acknowledge that it was a rather amusing prank. They were young at the time and were acting their age.

Berganio and I are still good friends and speak frequently by phone. He had a hardscrabble upbringing, born to a 15-year-old single mother and raised in a poor part of Los Angeles.

When I worked for him in 1996, I asked whether I could share a hotel room to cut costs, but did not request a bed, because if he was going to put up with me he at least deserved the comfort of a queen or king bed, rather than a double.

And anyway, I was used to traveling with my own blankets, so it was no problem to just set myself up on the floor.

ASBESTOS

But my choice for the top caddie behaving poorly story belongs to the late Steve Duplantis, a Canadian looper who became a legend in the mid- to late '90s working for Jim Furyk for more than four years.

Steve was one of those guys that everyone liked, because he was such a happy-go-lucky guy. He always had a smile on his face and was always in a good mood. And why not? He loved the ladies, and the ladies loved him. He also never met a bar or a strip club that he didn't like.

Furyk, at the time a rising star, liked him so much that Duplantis earned the nickname "Asbestos," because he was seemingly fireproof, no matter how many times he was late to report for work.

Though he eventually got canned by Furyk in 1999, the nickname stuck.

But while Duplantis often was late, there was only one time he arrived at the course naked.

It was at the PGA Tour's Tampa tournament around the turn of the century, early on a Friday morning of the second round, when a taxi pulled up at the caddie trailer carrying Duplantis, who disembarked wrapped in a towel and wearing no clothes, and I mean *none*. No underwear, no shoes, no nothing.

And of course he had no money. Plenty of caddies witnessed it. Without a wallet, he had no means to immediately pay his fare.

Which begs the question, why did the driver let Duplantis into his cab in that state of undress? I don't have the answer to that question.

What I can tell you is that Duplantis raced over to the caddie trailer, borrowed a pair of shoes from another caddie, along with a pair of shorts and a golf shirt, and borrowed the money to pay the cab driver.

He then bought a new yardage book, and even had time for breakfast before reporting on time for his then-boss Garrett Willis, just another day in the life of a larger-than-life character.

As for how Duplantis came to be without clothes is a mystery that went with him to his grave. As far as I know, he never told anyone on tour the full story. He probably did not even remember the full story.

It could well have been something along the lines I experienced one night in Denver early in my career when I met a woman at a bar. One thing led to another, and I thought I was quite the Casanova as she asked me to accompany her back to what she said was her house.

Next thing I knew I woke up and she had gone. Not only that, but she had found my keys to both my van as well as the safe I kept inside it. She cleaned out everything of value. Fortunately, there was not too much cash and nothing that could not be replaced.

I do not know whose house it was, and I should have reported the crime to the cops, but I just wanted to put the incident behind me and was also a little embarrassed.

I know of players who have had a Rolex watch stolen in similar circumstances and been too embarrassed to tell the authorities.

I learned my lesson never to leave a drink unattended when visiting the bathroom.

I am convinced she slipped me a mickey. Since then, I invariably force my bladder to wait until I have finished a drink.

In a sad postscript to the Duplantis story, he was killed in January 2008 while in Southern California to caddie at the tour's Torrey Pines stop.

After a night out drinking in nearby Del Mar, he was fatally struck by a car just before 2:00 AM on a Wednesday, the day of the tournament's pro-am. San Diego police reported that he had stepped from the median into the path of the vehicle.

Duplantis left behind a then-12-year-old daughter. He was only 35, his life cut way too short, as was the case with too many other caddies I had the pleasure of knowing.

So many of them lived hard and died young, but a smile invariably crosses my face whenever I think of Steve and others like him with whom I shared so much of my life.

Which is one of the reasons why I still love a job and a lifestyle I fell into only after failing at everything else in life.

It fills me with immense pride to have worked for long enough to see the reputation of caddies transformed from the sketchy figures of yesteryear into respectable cogs in the modern wheel of professional golf.

It has been a privilege to be part of the journey.

Final Word

Why Now?

*How a cancer diagnosis prompted me
to write this book*

In the mid-1990s a couple of journalists with whom I had become friends planted the seed in my head that I had enough interesting stories to fill a book. And while I agreed in theory, the idea remained on the back burner for the best part of three decades, during which time I compiled more and more good yarns, which I have finally shared in the preceding pages.

My life has been blessed with way more birdies than bogeys and until recently I had always been in excellent health. As the old saying goes, good health is something most everyone takes for granted until they no longer have it.

In the autumn of 2022, I started experiencing frequent and painful bowel movements. I did not worry at first, hoping they would go away, but they persisted relentlessly.

By the time I attended the 2023 Masters as a spectator, I could no longer deny reality. After six months of increasingly worse symptoms, I knew I was in serious trouble.

The following week I returned home to San Antonio and finally saw a doctor. A colonoscopy and biopsy revealed that I had Stage Four rectal cancer. I had a 31-millimeter tumor, and the prognosis was dire. I started chemotherapy almost immediately.

It was around the same time that my uncle Charlie, who I have mentioned several times in this book, suggested that if I was ever going to finally put my thoughts in print, perhaps it was now or never. There is nothing like the prospect of dying to focus the mind, so I decided to bite the bullet and put down these words for posterity.

Getting diagnosed with cancer has humbled me. I have not felt sorry for myself, but I can see why some people give up, because it is a daily struggle both mentally and physically. My nurse told me the battle is 50 percent mental. You have mountains to climb, and then more mountains to climb, and you just must keep plowing forward.

I certainly look at things differently now. I have a much greater appreciation of time and have learned to enjoy each day and each moment more than ever, because who knows how many more there will be?

Time is a commodity we are all running out of.

My doctor says my fitness level from a lifetime of caddying has helped my prognosis. I never took a long break from working on tour, which meant I always remained fit.

I walked about 18 miles a day during tournaments, according to my fitness tracker, and even after the diagnosis continued to walk three miles on most days.

My first round of chemotherapy was successful in shrinking the tumor to less than one millimeter, though at the time of writing this in mid-2024 I was undergoing a second round of treatment for a couple of lesions on my lungs.

All being well, I hope to return to caddying as soon as possible.

I wish now I had not waited so long to have my initial symptoms checked out by a doctor and would urge anyone in a similar boat not to dilly-dally.

I am thankful to my doctors for keeping me around long enough to complete this book and I hope you enjoyed reading it as much as I did writing it.